Editorial

I CERTAINLY NEVER GUESSED when we began five years ago that so much new and fascinating material would flow in to *Manchester Sounds*. In retrospect, though, it should have been obvious. Any comparable city in Germany has a large monograph series going back sixty years devoted to its musical history. In the later nineteenth century Manchester was one of Europe's major cities. (It is symptomatic that Hans Richter, after twenty-five years as head of the Vienna Opera, signed a ten-year contract with the Hallé Orchestra: we count ourselves very lucky to have Mark Elder, but we could hardly think of tempting Bernard Haitink or Claudio Abbado.)

Even so, we must be frankly jealous about the richness of operatic life here in the late nineteenth century. Mancunians heard Verdi's *Otello* and *Falstaff* within a year of their first performances; almost any season in the 1880s they could see *Lohengrin* and *Tannhäuser*, half a dozen Verdi operas, and much from elsewhere. True, they seem to have heard the *Magic Flute* in Italian and *Rigoletto* in Russian. But I would happily make that sacrifice for the chance of hearing *Rigoletto* in Manchester today.

For these and for the festivals that Lewis Foreman describes, some of the world's leading musicians were to be heard: Malibran of course, because she famously died here, but also the great Lablache, Dragonetti, Smart, and many others. It may be a slight disappointment that so many of the orchestra for the festivals came from London; but I'm pleased to see that this made it possible for the violins to include a Mr Fallows from Dublin. (No relation, so far as I know.)

But then it remains too easy to forget about Manchester's own musicians. Sally Drage's new material on Robert Wainwright clarifies the life of a man who was plainly among the most gifted English musicians of his time, though he died in his early thirties. Andrew Poulter has more to tell us about Henry Watson and his activities. Martin Thacker offers a tribute to a quiet man but a great librarian of the Henry Watson library, Leonard Duck. Ian Johnson's article about Alwyn accompanies the DVD of Paul Rotha's film *A City Speaks* that we are giving to subscribers through the generosity of the William Alwyn Foundation. Other Manchester composers are covered in John Turner's piece on Peter Hope, David Dubery's recollections of his first visit to the Aldeburgh Festival, Philip Barnes on how Sasha

Johnson Manning has a substantial career in America while remaining in Bowdon, and John Amis's marvellous account of his failed attempt at writing a biography of Rawsthorne. All this alongside an increased range of CD reviews and of course Geoffrey Kimpton's list of first performances in Manchester.

Many, though, will turn first to the reminiscences of Ida Carroll. Most of these appeared already in the programme for the concert to mark what would have been her hundredth year; but more have been added. Together they create a most vivid portrait of a remarkable musician, somebody who seems to have been loved and feared in equal portions. I met her only once; but the tributes assembled here stand as clear evidence of how much she did to change the face of musical life in Manchester. Let it not be forgotten, either, that the Ida Carroll Trust continues to support musical activity in the area; and indeed that without the support of the Ida Carroll Trust there would be no *Manchester Sounds*.

David Fallows
Old Trafford, April 2006

FREE DVD: *A CITY SPEAKS.* INSIDE BACK COVER

Manchester Sounds

Volume 6 ~ 2005–6

Editor: David Fallows
Reviews Editor: David Ellis

Editorial address: John Turner, 40 Parsonage Road, Heaton Moor, Stockport SK4 4JR.
Email: recorderist@zoom.co.uk

Reviews material and enquiries about advertisements should be addressed as above.

For current subscription rates please enquire to John Turner, address and email as above.

Manchester Sounds is published by The Manchester Musical Heritage Trust (Registered Charity
no. 1076473) in association with Forsyth Brothers Ltd.

ISSN 1471-3659

ISBN (Vol. 6, 2005 – 2006) 0-9539010-5-X

The publication of volume 6 of Manchester Sounds is made possible through the generous support
of the Ida Carroll Trust.

Manchester Sounds is designed and typeset by Martin Thacker using Serif PagePlus 11, and is
printed and bound by CPI Antony Rowe Ltd., Bumper's Farm, Chippenham, Wiltshire SN14
6LH. Tel: 01249 659705. Fax: 01249 443103

Single volumes are available from Forsyth Brothers Ltd., 126 Deansgate, Manchester M3 2GR,
price £10.00.

Cover: Sir John Barbirolli at Belle Vue, ca. 1946, from the film *A City Speaks*. (*North West Film
Archive at Manchester Metropolitan University*)

The logo of The Manchester Musical Heritage Trust is designed by Melanie Young.

In Search of Alan Rawsthorne

JOHN AMIS

THE RAWSTHORNE TRUST approached me in the early 1990s about writing a biography of Rawsthorne. 'What a good idea', I thought; there is one needed, I liked Alan and his music, knew people who knew him – and a sum of money was offered which seemed agreeable … in fact I thought of it in terms of one of Alan's favourite phrases which I'd heard so often from him: 'Time enough for that sort of thing.' I was to write about Alan's life, John McCabe would deal with the music – couldn't have anybody better, John knows the music backwards, more than anybody.

The Trust and I met, and a list of names and addresses was handed over. 'Here, they all knew Alan, you'll want to go and see them, won't you?' Yes indeed, and this article is an account of very pleasant times I had doing the rounds. Misgivings soon set in but I'll come to them by and by.

One of the first and most revealing encounters was with MARION LEIGH, widow of the composer Walter Leigh, whose talent was cut short when he was killed in the Second World War. After Alan left his first wife, the violinist Jessie Hinchliffe, he lived for several years with Marion, who worked as an executive in the National Film Board of Canada, a slim, attractive, vivacious lady; even in advanced years (she was born in 1912) she was bright and cheerful but suffering severely from loss of memory. After a few minutes she said, 'The great thing about Alan was, he was very secretive.' She kept returning to this observation. She spoke of her children, two of whom – Veronica and Julian – are good friends of mine: Veronica is a violist, living in New York with her psychiatrist husband, and Julian a composer who lives in Lancaster. There is also a second son, Andrew, manager of the Old Vic, but I don't know him so well. He is very nice now but wasn't so years earlier at one Christmas lunch I spent with the Leighs in Brewer Street, Soho, when he treated me to a whoopee cushion, put little round metal objects in my petits pois and perpetrated other delights until Marion remarked, 'My goodness, he *does* seem to have taken a dislike to you, doesn't he?' But by now Marion could not remember much about Alan except his secretiveness – leading me to believe that their parting was not such sweet sorrow. After I left her Soho flat I was walking down the street when I heard a summoning whistle; it was

Marion leaning out of her window shouting, 'John, come back, I've just remembered something important.' I climbed the stairs again only for her to tell me once more, 'The great thing about Alan was, he was very secretive.' This interview was revealing in that I realised that most of Alan's friends were now very old and likely to have infirm memories.

This proved to be the case with the composer ALAN BUSH, who could recall nothing of his early Berlin meetings with AR in their student days, nor any of their several visits together behind the Iron Curtain. AR admired AB greatly and, if he liked a student wanting tuition, would always advise him or her to go to AB. AB's memory, alas, was down practically to nil; rather pathetically, this communist through thick and thin was unaware even of the dismantling of the Iron Curtain and I thought it would be unkind to tell him. So the first two interviews were not an encouraging start – two down.

But meeting MOLLIE BARGER was quite different: positive, good memory, informative and utterly delightful. She had been a student in Bristol and became friends there with Jessie, Alan, Constant Lambert, the harpist Sidonie Goossens and Sidonie's first husband, the conductor Hyam 'Bumps' Greenbaum. In its infinite lack of wisdom the BBC had evacuated its Symphony Orchestra to Bristol. (Jessie graced the second desk of first fiddles, sharing it with Kathleen Washbourne, with whom she gave the premiere performance and recording of Alan's Theme and Variations for two violins. This was the piece that gave rise to Constant Lambert's review expressing astonishment that it contained so much double-stopping until he remembered that, before taking to composition, Rawsthorne had studied dentistry.) Until the bombing got disastrous many programmes, comic as well as orchestral, originated from Bristol. But when the bombing came, Jessie and Alan's place was destroyed, as were many precious and, it turned out, irreplaceable Rawsthorne manuscripts. Alan, Jessie and Bumps took over the old Clifton Arts Theatre, closed for the duration, and made it habitable; Bumps's bedroom was the stage, the Rawsthornes' had been the Green Room. Mollie described Alan as quite the dandy with his blond hair, cape and posh silver-topped walking stick, unable even to boil an egg and with drinking already quite a problem: the specialist Dr Sheila Sherlock commented, 'If I were served up your liver in a restaurant, I'd send it back.' Mollie recalls the bombings vividly and remembers Lambert quoting Gorky as he tried to put out a fire with a watering can. Mollie also gave me more information than the Army was prepared to vouchsafe to an enquirer like myself who was not a blood relative or 'next of skin'. Alan started in the Royal Artillery but fortunately never had to use any weapons for real. Somebody had him tagged in the files as a *compositor* and a handyman (which he eminently was not) capable of dealing with machinery. When they got nearer the truth they let him go to the Army Educational Corps and he was sent to Wembley to make a film with Peter Ustinov. He encountered Edmund Rubbra, who remembered AR telling him how he came across a cadet named Hastings; on investigation it was found that his rifle was numbered 1066. Another army story has our hero being ordered by his sergeant, 'Rawsthorne, band practice tomorrow morning – clarinet!' 'But sir, I don't *play* the clarinet; my instrument is the cello.' 'Rawsthorne, how many times do I have to tell you: there's a war on and we can't all do just what we please.' Mollie remained friends to the end with Alan, Jessie and, later, Isabel Lambert (née Nicholas). It seems that the crumbling of the first marriage was not bitter. Jessie tried her best to behave like a Bohemian but it wasn't really her character. She was a sensible, level-headed Yorkshire lass blessed with wonderful looks; three sensible meals a day at regular hours were not, it seems, the way to Alan's heart. Did Jessie have a miscarriage which somehow queered the marriage pitch? After leaving the BBC she ended up as a pillar of the Philharmonia Orchestra, and eventually died of cancer. Mollie's career and marriage took her all over the world – to the Middle East, Greece, China, Paris, the USA and India, mostly working for UNRRA – but she renewed her friendships when she came back to England and Soho. I never quite dared ask Mollie whether she and Alan ever… If Jessie had beauty, Isabel had beauty and intellect. My impression is that none of the women cared much for Marion Leigh (not surprising perhaps, given the circumstances).

I cannot remember when I first met AR; it must have been in the second half of the forties. We had various mutual friends and I would have 'seen him around'. I saw slightly more of him because of the Summer School of Music which I ran, first at Bryanston in Dorset from 1948 to 1952 and latterly at Dartington Hall (which of course Alan knew very well; more of that later). William Glock was the Director of Music and it was with his approval that I commissioned Alan to write a choral piece for the School. Our weeks used to run from Saturday to Saturday. On the Sunday of each week a choir was formed which rehearsed every morning and, on the Friday, performed the chosen work. At first Alan demurred about accepting the commission (for some ludicrous fee, probably £50, maybe a bit more): he said he wasn't keen on setting words, because he liked poetry too much and felt that music tended to destroy poetry. At length he agreed to compose a piece provided we could agree to ask his friend Randall Swingler to write some words specially. This was done and the piece, called *A Canticle of Man*, was duly performed in August 1952. It was a great month: Enesco was there playing the violin, teaching and conducting, Roger Désormière also conducted, Imogen Holst lectured, and so did Stanley Spencer; and Alan took a composition class and supervised the premiere of his piece for choir, flute, baritone and strings. The actual date was 22 August 1952 and the orchestra was the Boyd Neel, our chorus being conducted by Norman Del Mar. As always, Alan didn't raise his voice but quietly managed to get what he wanted. During the course of several visits he taught and gave seminars on works by two of his favourite composers, Haydn and Chopin.

Randall Swingler was a committed communist, a poet, teacher and amateur flautist, married to Geraldine Peppin who was half of a two-piano duo with her twin Mary. Gerry's daughter is married to the composer EDWARD WILLIAMS and it is probable that the couple's move to Essex prompted AR and Isabel to follow suit. The Williamses live now in Bristol and I had a splendid lunch at their house before and after which they both talked, often at the same time, into my mike. When Edward first met AR (with Muir Mathieson),[1] his impression was of a dapper, genial, well-educated, civilised man. Alan was soon sharing the Brewer Street flat with Marion Leigh, having moved in when her son Julian and his friend Richard Rodney Bennett left (don't jump to conclusions: they were just good friends). AR at that time was writing a lot of film music. Soho was his bailiwick: he and his friends drank either at the French Club, run by Olwen Vaughan, or the Colony Club, presided over by the foul-mouthed but fascinating Muriel Belcher. Elisabeth Lutyens and her husband Edward Clark, the pioneering BBC music administrator, later would-be conductor, were part

---

[1] Mathieson, musical director of over 500 films and chief conductor of film music in this country, worked for Korda and later the Rank organisation, and was responsible for getting Bliss, Alwyn, Rawsthorne, Walton, Richard Rodney Bennett – then only 19 – and many others to write for films; he was king of the biz at Pinewood and Denham in the forties and later, at a time when every film had a hundred-piece orchestra playing away in the background. (Strangely, the rival firm, Ealing, had Muir's brother, known as Doc, as big a cheese in their music department as Muir in his, although at Ealing Ernest Irving was the supremo with Doc as his assistant.)

of the scene, prodigious drinkers both. Liz Lut used to say that AR had only one tune (the *Street Corner* one, itself derived probably from Hindemith's *Mathis der Maler*); Isabel used to upbraid AR with that one, too. Edward Williams said 'We rather took Alan for granted', and so did many other folks I interviewed. 'He was rather a randy chap' was another oft-heard remark. At one party AR told Edward that he had slept with every woman present but one (can't help wondering how big the party was). EW remembers AR falling over once in the Brewer Street flat, but he also said (as did many others) that Alan was almost never actually drunk despite being fairly well plastered. After doctors had at one time ordered him successfully right off booze, some fool of a new medico told him that an occasional glass of red wine wouldn't do him any harm, which, alas, started the (terminal) rot; at one stage, towards the end, AR was on two bottles a day of vermouth, one dry, one sweet, which he would mix (what a way to go!).

Edward recalled Alan saying that the worst thing in the world was to see (sometimes bad) publicity advertising the premiere of a work not yet started. He went on several 'official' visits abroad with Alan, one with the Composers' Guild in 1963 to Bulgaria, an international festival which included a trip to the cave where Orpheus was said to have gone to retrieve Eurydice. In 1964 there was a Christmas gathering at the Williamses' house in Piddletrenthide in Dorset with Alan, the pianist James Gibb, Randall and Geraldine Swingler, and their son. As I was to find frequently during my researches, people didn't seem to have a lot to say about Alan; he was a wonderful chap, never nasty, never loud or disagreeable, funny but no examples forthcoming, pity he drank such a lot... but then so did most of us. Oh yes, an exception in the sharp line department was when AR said 'I hear that Edmund Rubbra has written a new tedium'. If people didn't have anything illuminating to say about Alan, I am sure it wasn't so much that they were failing to remember or holding back as that there was nothing particularly memorable about Alan except his lovable self and his music (and he didn't like talking about that).

Another hindrance to the research was that, Alan having been born in 1905 (the same year as Tippett and Lambert), most of his pals were either dead or getting on in years. Two 'golden oldies' I enjoyed going to see were ANNE MACNAGHTEN (1908–2000) in Hitchin and IRIS LEMARE (1902–97) near York; their joint concerts in London in the thirties had helped to set AR on the musical scene. Anne led a string quartet bearing her name and Iris was a conductor with an orchestra bearing hers. Anne gave the first performance of AR's 1932 String Quartet, for example, and Iris in 1936 conducted Alan's first orchestral work, an Overture for chamber orchestra. They were now approaching four score and ten years. Anne was still beautiful despite her face being craggy in the Auden style, with skin like mud flats dried in the sun. Iris was skiing in her seventies but had an accident which crippled her. I had great talks with them both but I cannot pretend that they brought me much nearer to AR.

Next I went down to Sussex to see the composer DENIS APIVOR (1916–2004) who had been a composition pupil of Alan's but said that his turning to serialism seemed to put a barrier between them. He thought that AR didn't find him very sympathetic; it is true that Liz Lutyens's serialism didn't impair her friendship with AR, but then of course she was a friend, not a pupil. Denis also complained that he could never have a serious conversation with Alan (I had the same experience). He told me that the only time he ever saw AR express emotion was when he burst into tears on the way to Constant Lambert's funeral. Denis put forward the notion that, sexually, AR found the grass was greener in other people's marriages, which was perhaps part of Isabel's attraction for him. But only part, I think: Alan was clearly utterly devoted to Isabel – and she to him. What I do find mighty curious is that, after her various amours and marriage, after the high life of Paris and London, Isabel settled down apparently happily in rural East Anglia with Alan.

Isabel Nicholas changed her name three times before finally becoming Mrs Rawsthorne. Before that she was Epstein, later Delmer, then Lambert. Her biography would be a far meatier one than Alan's. She first changed her name by deed poll to that of Jacob Epstein, the great sculptor; she initially knocked on the door of his house to see if there was any modelling work going. Epstein's bust of Isabel shows a ravishingly beautiful young girl. Like some of his other models she became pregnant. Although in her sixties at the time Mrs Epstein touchingly sought to minimise any new scandal by shopping locally with a cushion stuffed in her clothes. Isabel's first marriage was to Sefton Delmer; she lived in Paris with him when he was the *Daily Express* correspondent there. During the Second World War Delmer directed the so-called Black Radio as a vital Allied propaganda instrument; he later wrote a fascinating book about it. In Paris Isabel enjoyed contact, to put it mildly, with many artists, including Derain, Picasso and Giacometti. She lived with Giacometti for a long period, but recent biographers seem to suggest that his capacity for sex was limited to the point of nullity. Isabel once left a party of his hand in hand with the conductor and serialist expert René Leibowitz and was from that moment out of the sculptor's life, although many years (and a couple of husbands) later Giacometti took a taxi one evening from London to visit the Rawsthornes at Little Sampford, had a lot to drink and returned by taxi to London in the small hours. Isabel was also a great friend of Francis Bacon. Perhaps the only thing about her that was not beautiful was her corncrake voice, but towards the end of her life it was her eyes that gave out: she was nearly blind in her old age. She had her own studio at Sampford to which she could retire to work or escape unwelcome visitors. All the local inhabitants adored her and would do anything for her.

The pianist JAMES GIBB, now in his eighties, was a good friend of practically everybody I have written about. As with many of them, the comradeship with AR had begun and been cemented, as it were, in the pub, in this case the Washington in England's Lane, Hampstead. Jimmy's initial impressions were of a mild-mannered, dignified, fastidious, almost Edwardian gentleman. They took to each other straight away – indeed, quite soon Alan entrusted Jimmy with the premiere of his piano Sonatina, which was typical of Alan's faith in certain performers. Jimmy found it difficult to get Alan to comment on or criticise his playing of his music, although when he could be prevailed on, his views were always understanding and instructive. Even when Jimmy did something not quite as written, Alan would be prepared to consider or even accept the new interpretation. Although Alan professed not to like Brahms, Gordon Green told Jimmy that Alan's own performance of the old Hamburger's Handel Variations was excellent; Alan never referred to his own playing and Jimmy, like most people, scarcely ever heard the composer play a note. AR was always reasonable, too, to opponents or with those whose views he did not share. The only occasion on which he did round on someone was when Peter Heyworth, who had criticised a piece of Alan's in the *Observer*, started to apologise when offered a lift in Alan's taxi. (It is also on record somewhere that Alan once almost came to blows with an anti-Semitic bigmouth in a pub.) To revert to Brahms, it was noticed that AR often advised young composers to study his works if they wanted to improve their craftsmanship.

If they needed a teacher he would recommend that they study with his friend Alan Bush. AR himself said that he learned most about his own craft not from a teacher of 'compo' but from Frank Merrick, his piano teacher at the Royal Manchester College of Music. Jimmy got on equally with both of Alan's wives. He agreed that it was a strange measure of Alan and Isabel's mutual devotion that Isabel settled down happily in the Essex countryside, which she walked vigorously, map in hand, whereas Alan never walked anywhere if he could help it, possibly because of the rheumatism he suffered from as a child and later. James Gibb played most of AR's piano music, the concertos many times, including the first concerto at Tonypandy where there was an Army symphony orchestra (Rubbra was stationed there for a time too).

BIDDY NOAKES lived with her husband ROY in fairly remote Yorkshire. Roy was a sculptor whose death mask of Alan will be known to readers of *The Creel*, the annual newsletter of the Friends of Alan Rawsthorne. Biddy, a daughter of the actor Bernard Miles, was for a long time the guardian of Isabel's personal effects including a bundle of her passports. It was Biddy who told me about a correspondence between Alan and Isabel during Isabel's travels in Africa. Letters from Alan? Wow! Letters, according to Biddy, that would grace, if not the *News of the World*, perhaps the *Sunday Times*. Where were they? Not with the trunkful of effects that had been in Biddy's possession but were later transferred, I gather, to Isabel's trustees at Tate Britain. The letters, Biddy told me, were with Isabel's brother Warwick Nicholas, who lived in Canberra. I wrote asking for sight of them, but in his reply Mr Nicholas informed me that there was no corrrespondence relating to the African visit, only some poems which, from the handwriting, could be from Alan to Isabel.[2]

I was interested to see that a detailed biography of Louis MacNeice had been published but disappointed that it contained only a couple of references of the 'and Alan Rawsthorne' kind, frustrating considering that they were supposed to have been great friends. I was similarly disappointed when Humphrey Searle's widow granted me access to his autobiography, *Quadrille with a Raven*.[3] His slight acquaintance with Alan in London grew when they were both in Bristol in wartime. Humphrey speaks well of Alan's *Kubla Khan*, performed there and

---

[2] The letters eventually found their way to the Archive of the Royal Northern College of Music, and extracts were printed in John McCabe's *Alan Rawsthorne: Portrait of a Composer*, published in 1999.

[3] Though unpublished in book form, the memoirs are available online at <http://www.musicweb-international.com/searle>.

lost shortly afterwards in the bombing. He tried to persuade Alan to reconstruct the work but it never happened.[4] Humphrey found AR's company congenial and his humour 'pawky'.

Encouraged by the two John members of the Rawsthorne Trust, Belcher and Turner, I went to the States in 1995, going first to Los Angeles to garner further information from Alan's friend and protégé, the composer Gerry Schurmann. Gerry also took me to see the actor and mime Basil Langton, who was at Dartington Hall whcn Alan was resident pianist to the mime and dance class. Basil has written a fascinating memoir of his friendship with Alan, so I do not need to rehearse it again here. But he did put me on the trail of Paula Morel (1905–96), then still at Dartington.[5] She started off in the Dance School, fell in love with Alan, and was with him in a nasty car crash in Devon in 1934; Paula married and later became librarian and wardrobe mistress at Dartington, where she and I often had contact during the time I was organising the Summer School of Music be-tween 1953 and 1981. Latterly Paula did marvellous flower arrange-ments at the Hall. Gerry enjoyed a unique relationship with Alan and I need not say more about that because Gerry has written extensively about it in *The Creel*; Alan was as much mentor as friend to him, though Alan would never lay down the law to the younger man.

Down in Dorset I saw JULIAN BREAM who told me about Alan's last composition, not quite finished at the time of its composer's death but, as Julian explained, it was clearly in ABA form and all that was required was to represent the A2 section maybe with some slight variation and invent a final chord. Julian was present at the funeral and says he will never forget the scene when those present filed past the grave and each threw in a flower. When Isabel's turn came she hurled her flower with all her force. Rage, frustration or grief? Or maybe she had tanked up before the service.

ALUN HODDINOTT adored AR's music and the man likewise, but apart from some gobbets about AR the trencherman and AR the bibber there was not much fodder for the biography, except that he confirmed AR's inability to boil an egg. The violinist and conductor HARRY BLECH said similar things about AR's lack of domesticity but since

---

[4] *Kubla Khan* has been reconstructed from the vocal score by Edward Harper (commissioned by the Ida Carroll Trust), and it is proposed that the work in its new form will have its premiere at the Royal Albert Hall, London, on 30 March 2008.

[5] Some letters from Alan survive in the Paula Morel papers at Dartington <http://www.dartingtonarchive.org.uk/pages/morel.html>.

Harry's domestic competence was roughly on a par with AR's I wonder how he would ever have noticed it. Harry knew AR from their student days in Manchester and they shared a flat in London when AR came back from his studies in Berlin and Poland with Egon Petri. AR's letters to Harry are printed in the biographical section of Alan Poulton's three-volume study published in 1984–6.

It was Poulton's work, along with Barbara Rawsthorne's *Diary of an Edwardian Childhood* (issued posthumously in 1995) plus my interview with her cousin Elizabeth Bridge, that enabled me to finish the first three chapters of the biography commissioned from me by the Rawsthorne Trust. These were not too difficult to put together, leaning heavily on these three sources. After that there is practically nothing for a biographer to work on. There are no diaries, a handful (*one* hand) of letters, an article or two – beyond that, not a thing to go on. Which is why, after two years of interviewing, writing letters, visiting the archive at the Royal Northern College of Music in Manchester and the archive at AR's publisher, the Oxford University Press, I threw in the sponge. Sir John Manduell at the College had nowt, the late Alan Frank, AR's OUP minder, the same. The pity of it is all the more considering the few excellent letters that AR did pen, chock-full of vivid descriptions and witty accounts of people met and places visited. He was always saying to me, 'Time enough for that sort of thing, young man'; he might have had his would-be biographers in mind.

But let me continue my odyssey. ELIZABETH BRIDGE, who shared a flat with Alan's sister Barbara, was most helpful. My notes after our first meeting begin: 'Hale (where she lives in Cheshire) but not hearty.' Fortunately our second meeting a year later in Dunster near Minehead found her in much better health. She had known Alan since their childhood and confirmed the universally held impression of Barbara's great qualities. Incidentally, Liz Lutyens once composed a piece for unaccompanied violin (which my late wife Olive Zorian broadcast) called *Aptote*, a series of portraits of her friends. They are rather spiky (more enigmatic than 'Enigma') and it is not easy to recognise in them much likeness to anyone, though their verbal designations are, well, apt. Her husband comes out as a snail, Humphrey Searle a cat, Constant Lambert a bat, Alan Rawsthorne a moth and Barbara as a glow-worm. Liz's autobiography contains some eighteen references to Alan, mostly of the 'and Alan Rawsthorne' variety, which seems to be the case in any books that do mention AR. Typically frustrating for a biographer – Alan was 'there' but is all but invisible, like a well-behaved moth.

Six
Sonatas

— for the —

HARPSICHORD or PIANO FORTE,

With an Accompaniment for a

VIOLIN

Composed, Dedicated by Permission to the

Hon.ble LADY EGERTON, By

Dr. Mainwright,

ORGANIST OF THE

Collegiate Church Manchester.

— Opera I —

LONDON:

Printed for the AUTHOR; and sold by C.&S. THOMPSON N? 75 S! Paul's Church
Yard, and M! CAHUSAC N? 203 opposite S! Clement's Church, STRAND.

The Wainwright Family: A Reappraisal – Part 2: Robert Wainwright

SALLY DRAGE

THE WAINWRIGHTS of Manchester, like the Broderips of Bristol, and the Valentines of Leicester, were an important eighteenth-century family of musicians. John Wainwright, whose fame rests on a single composition, the tune to 'Christians awake', was discussed in a previous article in *Manchester Sounds*,[1] but the contribution of other family members to the thriving musical scene of provincial Georgian England also needs re-evaluation. The subject of this article, Robert Wainwright, was an accomplished composer and a leading figure in the musical life of both Manchester and Liverpool.

Most earlier biographers, such as Henry Heginbotham,[2] who were chiefly interested in John Wainwright and in the family's Stockport connections, rarely included references, and so it is hard to check whether their facts are correct: as the local historian T. Merion Griffith discovered in 1972 when he wrote a paper to be read before the Lancashire and Cheshire Antiquarian Society, most included the same material, 'duplicated, repeated and re-quoted endlessly'.[3] Griffith's valiant attempt to untangle the existing evidence was hampered, as he wrote his paper on board ship, sailing to and from South Africa, and so had to rely exclusively on printed books and articles. The most authoritative modern secondary source, Watkins Shaw's *The Succession of Organists*,[4] provides well-referenced if brief biographies of John, Robert and Richard Wainwright but, as one would expect, it is concerned almost exclusively with the organist posts they held in Manchester and Liverpool.

Basic details of the Wainwrights' births, marriages and deaths are be found in church records. Some remain elusive, but further snippets of evidence can be found in trade directories, subscription lists, title pages of music, and in personal memoirs of the period. The major primary source of information about the Wainwright family's musical activities, however, is the advertisement columns of local newspapers,

---

[1] Sally Drage, 'The Wainwright Family: A Reappraisal – Part 1', *Manchester Sounds*, 3 (2002), 91–106.

[2] Henry Heginbotham, *Stockport Ancient and Modern* (London, 1892).

[3] Manchester Central Library Archives: GB127.C26/1/1.

[4] Watkins Shaw, *The Succession of Organists of the Chapel Royal and the Cathedrals of England and Wales from c.1538* (Oxford, 1991), 186–7.

although even these should be used with caution. As Stainton de B. Taylor (who, as music critic for the *Liverpool Daily Post and Echo*, had first-hand knowledge of the perils of newspaper reporting) warned in the preface to his *Two Centuries of Music in Liverpool*:

A preliminary advertisement gives no guarantee that the event publicised actually took place – or that if it did so, programme performers remained exactly as advertised: even the printed programme used on the occasion may contain erroneous information because circumstances now long forgotten dictated last minute changes.[5]

Manchester

Robert, the eldest child of John and Anne Wainwright, was baptised at Manchester Collegiate Church on 17 September 1748. As some children were not baptised immediately after birth, and his parents were married on 30 December 1746,[6] he could have been born earlier. We know nothing of his general education, but he probably received his early musical training from his father, whose occupation is given as 'Musick Master' in the baptismal register. From 25 June 1759, when he was elected as a chorister at the Collegiate Church,[7] he would have been taught by Edward Betts, the organist and instructor of choristers. He remained in the choir until 30 October 1764, perhaps leaving when his voice broke. Under a new foundation charter granted to the Collegiate Church by Charles I in 1635, the choir at Manchester consisted of four boys skilled in music and four singing men.[8] The singers' appointments, together with the names of those whom they replaced, are included in the Chapter Registers, but it is hard to be sure exactly how many there were in the choir at any one time: in the mid-1700s there would seem to have been only two singing men; but it may well be that not all names were properly recorded.

We still need to discover what Robert Wainwright did after leaving the Collegiate Church choir in 1764 until he returned there at the age of 19. Some biographers state that he was organist at St Ann's, Manchester, but this cannot be proved, as the church records for this

[5] Stainton de B. Taylor, *Two Centuries of Music in Liverpool* (Liverpool, 1976), p. vii.
[6] St Peter, Blackley, parish records.
[7] Manchester Cathedral Archives: Chapter Registers, vol. 2, 9 December 1714 – 21 December 1870.
[8] Samuel Lewis, *A Topographical Dictionary of England* (London, 1831), vol. 3, pp. 242–6. Quoted in the Lancashire Online Parish Clerks project: <http://www.lan-opc.org.uk/Manchester/Cathedral/home.html>

period no longer exist. Alternatively, he could have played the organ at another church, for instance, St Mary's Parsonage, where he was living in 1767, though again, documents, such as churchwardens' accounts or vestry minutes, have not survived. According to an anecdote first told by the Doncaster organist and composer Dr Edward Miller, Robert applied unsuccessfully for the position of organist at Halifax Parish Church.

Mr Herschel and six others were candidates for the organist's place. They drew lots how they were to perform in rotation. My friend Herschel drew the third lot – the second performer was Mr Wainwright, afterwards Dr. Wainwright, of Manchester, whose finger was so rapid, that old Snetzler, the organ-builder, ran about the church exclaiming, 'te tevil, te tevil, he run over te key like one cat; he vil not give my piphes room for to shpeak.' During Mr Wainwright's performance, I was standing in the middle with Herschel. What chance have you, said I, to follow this man? He replied, 'I don't know; I am sure fingers will not do.' On which, he ascended the organ loft, and produced from the organ so uncommon a fulness – such a volume of slow harmony, that I could by no means account for its effect. After this short extempore effusion, he finished with the old hundreth psalm tune, which he played better than his opponent. Aye, aye, cried old Snetzler, 'tish is very goot, very goot indeed, I vil luf this man, for he gives my piphes room to shpeak.' Having, afterwards, asked Mr Herschel by what means, in the beginning of his performance, he had produced so uncommon effect? He replied, 'I told you fingers would not do,' and produced two pieces of lead from his waistcoat pocket. One of these, said he, I placed on the lowest key of the organ, and the other upon the octave above: thus, by accommodating the harmony, I produced the effect of four hands instead of two. However as my leading the concert on the violin, is their principal object, they will give me the place in preference to better performer on the organ; but I shall not stay long here, for I have the offer of a superior situation in Bath, which offer I shall accept.[9]

The Snetzler organ at St John the Baptist, Halifax, had three manuals and twenty-five stops.[10] As English organs at this period did not include pedals, the addition of a low, held bass note would have been quite effective. Mr Herschel, later better known as the astronomer Sir William Herschel, got the job but stayed for only a few months before moving to Bath to become organist at the Octagon Chapel. Miller does not record the date of the organ auditions, but the latest *Oxford*

---

[9] Edward Miller, *The History and Antiquities of Doncaster and its Vicinity* (Doncaster, 1804), 162, n.1.
[10] Stephen Bicknell, *The History of the English Organ* (Cambridge, 1996), 176.

Dictionary of National Biography gives 1766,[11] which is concordant with the date when Snetzler finished building the organ.

There was usually at least one Wainwright listed among the participants in oratorio performances and concerts given throughout the north-west in the mid-eighteenth century but, as they are often referred to as just 'Mr Wainwright', exactly which one is open to conjecture. However, in March 1767, the *Manchester Mercury* included the following advertisement:

For the Benefit of Mr R. Wainwright At the Theatre, in Manchester, On Thursday the second of April 1767, will be perform'd A Concert of Vocal & Instrumental Music By the best Hands in these Parts. The Vocal Parts by Miss Ratcliff and Miss Wood.

Act First	Act Second
An Overture with Trumpets and Kettle Drums, by Handell	An Overture with French Horns, by Abel
A Song in the Oratorio of Samson	A Song
A Concerto by Stanley	A French Horn Concerto
A Duet in the Oratorio of Samson	A Song
A Concerto by Avison	A Song and Duet
	The Overture in the Fairies[12]

Tickets cost two shillings each and could be obtained from local coffee houses, inns, booksellers, and from 'Mr Wainwright at the Parsonage' – presumably St Mary's Parsonage, which runs parallel to Deansgate. As Richard Wainwright was aged only nine at this date, it seems likely that Robert was the beneficiary. During the late eighteenth century and the first half of the nineteenth most musicians gave an annual benefit concert. Other performers also took part, and their aid would be reciprocated when they, in turn, held their own concert. According to another concert advertisement noted by Giles Shaw in his *Annals of Oldham and District*, Molly Ratcliffe and Joanna Wood were treble singers from Hey Chapel, near Oldham.[13] The women singers from Oldham and the nearby Hey and Shaw chapels were nationally famous and sang at most oratorio performances in the midlands and in the north of England during the later eighteenth century. As can be seen, the programme of a benefit concert was usually made up of short, popular works, and the inclusion of brass

---

[11] Michael Hoskin, 'Hershel, William (1738–1822)', *Oxford Dictionary of National Biography* (Oxford, 2004): <http://www.oxforddnb.com/view/article/13102>
[12] *The Manchester Mercury and Harrop's General Advertiser*, 24 March 1767.
[13] Giles Shaw, *Annals of Oldham and District* (Oldham, 1904), vol. 2, p. 152.

and timpani was always an added attraction. Individual items cannot be identified apart from *The Fairies* overture, which is probably from John Christopher Smith's 1755 comic opera of that name, based on Shakespeare's *A Midsummer Night's Dream*.

Perhaps surprisingly, notice of another concert given by a Mr Cleavin, with a very similar programme and to be held only nineteen days later, appeared in the same column just below R. Wainwright's on both occasions when the advertisement was printed.[14] One might suspect competition, except that the harpsichord was to be played by Mr Wainwright – presumably either John or Robert. According to the subscription list of Robert's *Six Sonatas*, Mr Cleavin was organist of St Ann's, Manchester, in 1774–5.

On 18 February 1768, Robert Wainwright was 'elected singing man and appointed Organist and Instructor of the Choristers in the Room of John Wainwright deceased',[15] and on 19 April, two months after his appointment, he received a whole year's salary of five pounds, as John Wainwright had held the post for only eight months and had died before he could be paid.[16] Why he was elected 'singing man' as well as organist is as yet unclear: presumably he could have sung only if a deputy played the organ, or if, as is less likely, the choir performed unaccompanied.

An annual salary of five pounds and the proceeds of a benefit concert would not have provided much financial security. The first Manchester trade directory of 1772 gives Robert's occupation as 'Musick-master', rather than as an organist, so it is likely that he augmented his income by teaching. His address was 'St Mary's Churchyard',[17] so he was still living in the Parsonage, perhaps in Seven-houses, which was also part of St Mary's and was given as his address in 1773, when he was also listed as 'Musick-master'.[18]

After John's death, we can be more positive about identifying Robert as the 'Mr Wainwright' mentioned in newspaper advertisements. For instance, on Easter Monday, 4 April 1768, he conducted *Messiah*, at Hey Chapel, near Oldham, for the benefit of the singers

---

[14] *The Manchester Mercury and Harrop's General Advertiser*, 24 and 31 March 1767.

[15] Chapter Registers, 1714–1870.

[16] Henry A. Hudson, 'Organs and Organists of the Cathedral and Parish Church of Manchester', *Lancashire and Cheshire Antiquarian Society*, 24 (1916), 131.

[17] Elizabeth Raffald, *The Manchester Directory for the year 1772* (Manchester, 1772), 42.

[18] Elizabeth Raffald, *The Manchester Directory for the year 1773* (Manchester, 1773), 49.

there,[19] and the next day he conducted *Judas Maccabaeus*, for the benefit of Mrs Tarvin and Miss Radcliffe, at the Theatre, Manchester.[20] At both concerts, it was proudly announced that the 'Grand Chorus's will be as full as possible with Kettle Drums, Trumpets, &c. &c.'. Miss Radcliffe was presumably the same as Miss Ratcliffe who sang at Robert's benefit concert noted above. According to another advertisement, Mrs Tarvin was probably Sally Tarvin of Manchester, 'late of Shaw Chapel'.[21]

One other concert that Robert Wainwright conducted while still in Manchester is worth mentioning because of its novelty value. On 15 May 1770 the *Mercury* included the following notice:

At the Opening of the Organo Chord (being an Instrument of an entire new Construction, and is the nighest in Sound to an Organ of any Instrument of the Stringed Sort extant), For the Benefit of Edward Hardy and Aaron Ogden (Inventors and Makers of the above Instrument), And James Nield, Singer will be performed at Mossley Chapel, on Monday the 21st of this Instant, the Sacred Oratorio of The Messiah. By the best Hands from Manchester, Halifax, Hey, Oldham & Shaw. Between each Part a Concerto upon the Organo-Chord. The Whole to be conducted by Mr Wainwright. The Doors to be opened at One, and begin precisely at Two o'Clock. The Chorus's will be as full as possible, with Kettle-Drums, Trumpets, &c. Gallery 2s, Bottom 1s.
N.B. Nothing under full Price during the whole Performance.

The 'N.B.' suggests that at other concerts latecomers were allowed pay less, but that on this occasion the promoters wanted to guard against loss of revenue, as some members of the audience might prefer to save money and attend only the last part of the concert out of curiosity. The Organo Chord was presumably an 'organochord', rather than a harpsichord, but as no instrument of this name is known to have survived, its mechanical construction must remain a mystery.

Although Robert Wainwright's *Six Sonatas* are described as his 'Opera I' on the title page, his first published work may have been, *The Lord is risen. A Favourite Anthem, or Hymn, for Easter Day, in Score*, 'The Words by Dr. Byrom, set to Music by Mr. Wainwright. London: printed for C. & S. Thompson, No. 75 St. Paul's Church Yard.' The British Library online catalogue gives an approximate date

---

[19] *The Manchester Mercury and Harrop's General Advertiser*, 15 March 1768.
[20] *The Manchester Mercury and Harrop's General Advertiser*, 29 March 1768.
[21] Shaw, *Annals*, vol. 2, p. 157.

of '1770?' and attributes it to 'John or Robert Wainwright',[22] but if John were the composer, one would expect him to be described as the 'late' Mr Wainwright. I have not examined the British Library copy, but that at the Bodleian Library, unless it is a later edition, can be dated to 1771 at the earliest:[23] there is a list of six other publications on the title page including John Alcock's *Six and Twenty Select Anthems*, the preface of which contains a complaint that no engraving proofs were received until April 1771. Musically, *The Lord is risen* is an English Baroque-Classical hybrid: it opens with a Purcellian orchestral sinfonia for strings, two trumpets, timpani and organ, then a short treble recitative precedes a *galant* 3/4 duet for treble and bass, marked 'Air', which, although unfigured, was probably accompanied by the organ, and which alternates for six verses with a fully scored chorus.

Doctorate

The first definite reference to Robert Wainwright as a composer is in an advertisement in the *Manchester Mercury* for a performance at the Collegiate Church on 31 October 1773 of a 'Grand Te Deum, Jubilate, and Magnificat' by R. Wainwright, for which the 'best Vocal and Instrumental Performers will be selected'.[24] This may have been a practice outing for the Te Deum, which Robert submitted as his degree exercise. On 29 April 1774 he matriculated from Magdalen College, Oxford, with the accumulated degrees of both B.Mus. and D.Mus. His success merited a notice in the *Mercury*:

On Tuesday last, Mr Robert Wainwright, Organist of the Collegiate Church in this Town, returned from Oxford, where he received the Degrees of Bachelor and Doctor in Music. Previous to his admission a Grand Te Deum, composed by him for Voices and Instruments, was performed at the School for Musical Exhibitions.[25]

But, as Hudson noted ruefully, when a year later Robert was termed 'Dr' in the Collegiate Church accounts, there was no increase in his salary.[26]

---

[22] London, British Library: <http://www.catalogue.bl.uk>. All further approximate dates are taken from this source.
[23] Oxford, Bodleian Library: Tenbury Mus.c.97.
[24] *The Manchester Mercury and Harrop's General Advertiser*, 19 October 1773.
[25] *The Manchester Mercury and Harrop's General Advertiser*, 17 May 1774.
[26] 18 April 1775. Hudson, 'Organs and Organists', 132.

At this period, supplicants for Oxford degrees could not read music at the university as it was not a taught subject; but they did have to provide evidence of seven years of study for a B.Mus. and a further five for a D.Mus. To obtain a B.Mus., a candidate had to submit a song of five parts, while a D.Mus. required one in six or eight parts, and both had to be performed publicly in the Music School. By achieving a D.Mus., Robert Wainwright joined an elite group of musicians including William Croft, John Stanley and Charles Burney. The manuscripts of most degree exercises were systematically deposited at the Music School during the second half of the eighteenth century and are now held at the Bodleian Library. There are only seventeen for B.Mus. and eight for D.Mus., of which only four are joint degrees.[27] Although we know of at least two others whose D.Mus. exercises are not included in the collection, namely John Alcock senior and Samuel Arnold, the number of successful candidates is still small.

Robert Wainwright's D.Mus. exercise, an extended setting of the Te Deum, 'We praise thee, O God',[28] is scored for 'canto', 'counter', tenor and bass soloists and choir, accompanied by strings, two flutes, two oboes, two horns, timpani and organ. It is composed in twenty-one sections, with choruses, solos, a trio and a duet, using varied instrumentation, tempi and keys to show versatility. Fuguing passages and echoes of Handel are particularly apparent, perhaps because, as Susan Wollenberg has suggested, there seems to have been a general unwritten rule that candidates should demonstrate evidence of contrapuntal technique, and they may have paid tribute to Handel because his music was championed by both William and Philip Hayes, who between them held the Heather Chair of Music from 1749 to 1797.[29] Robert's exercise includes extra pencilled comments: 'a fine chorus indeed' at the end of a Moderato fugue, 'Thine honourable, true and only Son'; 'bravo' at the foot of the first page of a Largo e Staccato chorus, 'When thou hadst overcome the sharpness of death'; 'beautiful movement' after an Adagio chorus, 'We believe that thou shalt come to be our judge'; and 'too much like Handel to the same words in his Utrecht' above an Allegro con spirito chorus, 'Day by day we magnify thee'. One would presume these comments to have been made by an examiner, were it not for a peculiar discrepancy in

---

[27] Susan Wollenberg, 'Music in 18th-Century Oxford', *Proceedings of the Royal Musical Association*, 108 (1981–2), 69–99, at 97–9.
[28] Bodleian Library: Ms Mus. Sch. Ex. d. 142.
[29] Wollenberg, 'Music in 18th-Century Oxford', 72–3.

dates. Susan Wollenberg gives the date of the performance of Robert Wainwright's Te Deum at the Music School as 29 April 1774, and this is corroborated by the newspaper article and the entry in the Collegiate Church accounts for 1775 quoted above. Yet his obituary says that he had intended to apply only for a B.Mus. and gives the date of his doctorate as 1776; and the Te Deum manuscript includes the inscriptions 'D.Mus. 1777', 'Dr Wainwright's Exercise Organist of Liverpool' and, at the end, 'Alexr Reed Script Octr 6th 1777'. At present this remains a puzzle and further investigation is needed: either the date when Robert was thought to have received his D.Mus. is wrong; or whoever wrote his obituary was mistaken; or, as is perhaps most likely, his Te Deum could have been re-copied. According to *Gore's Liverpool Directory for the Year 1777*, Alexander Reed was organist at St Catherine's,[30] and also seems to have worked as a music copyist.

Although Robert Wainwright was a professional organist, we know of no printed church music by him, except for several hymn tunes and, possibly, *The Lord is risen*, mentioned previously. Two of his tunes were published in 1774 in *Divine Harmony ... by the most eminent Masters, Antient and Modern* 'selected and carefully revised by Richard Langdon, Batchelor in Music Subchanter & Organist of the Cathedral Church of Exeter'.[31] Other 'eminent masters' represented in the collection include Tallis, Tomkins, Carissimi, Croft and Handel, so Robert was in exalted company, and, as both tunes are ascribed to 'Dr Wainwright', this is another piece of evidence that proves he did receive his degree in 1774. However, only the second tune, to Psalm 103, now called 'Manchester', is still sung today.

Perhaps secular music, composed for personal domestic use rather than for public display, provided better financial rewards than church music. Robert Wainwright's next published compositions were *Six Sonatas for the Harpsichord or Piano Forte, With an Accompaniment for the Violin* 'Composed, & Dedicated by Permission to the Hon[oura]ble Lady Egerton, By Dr Wainwright, Organist of the Collegiate Church, Manchester. Opera I. London: Printed for the Author; and sold by C. & S. Thompson, No. 75 St. Paul's Church Yard, and Mr. Cahusac No. 203 opposite St Clement's Church, Strand'. They are elegant and extremely competent works for an Opus 1. Like all his compositions they are undated, but they must have been

---

[30] John Gore, *Gore's Liverpool Directory for the Year 1777* (Liverpool, 1777), 104.
[31] London: Printed for the Editor by Messrs Longman, Lukey, & Comp[an]y No. 26, Cheapside.

published either in 1774 after he received his doctorate, or in 1775 before he left Manchester. Keyboard sonatas with an instrumental accompaniment, usually for the violin, were popular in England during the later eighteenth century, and were often published in sets of two, three or six. In many, the accompanying instrument did little more than double the keyboard, often in thirds or sixths, and fill in the harmony with long notes. Some of Robert Wainwright's violin parts follow the same pattern, but at times the instruments are more equal, and occasionally the violin predominates: in the second and third sonatas there are a few passages where the keyboard part is reduced to just a figured bass line, and a continuo realisation would have been required. Although it made financial sense to designate the sonatas for harpsichord or pianoforte, the dynamic requirements, from *pianissimo* to *fortissimo* with a number of *crescendo*s (but no *diminuendo*s), suggest that Robert was writing for the more modern instrument. Stanley Sadie described the first movements as of 'modest interest', but thought that the 'minuets and the Rondeau of the final sonata have real charm, and there are lively finales to nos. 4 and 5'.[32] The dedicatee was Lady Egerton, probably the heiress Eleanor Assheton, wife of Sir Thomas Egerton, who began the building of Heaton Hall, Prestwich, in 1772. It is possible that a search through the Egerton family papers, held at Greater Manchester Record Office, may reveal further links between Robert Wainwright and the family, although the Samuel Green organ at the Hall today was not built until 1790. 'Printed for the Author' was an early form of vanity publishing, by which a new or little-known author or composer paid for his or her own work to be published, often by raising subscriptions. The 93 subscribers to Robert Wainwright's *Six Sonatas* included Dr [William] Hayes, Professor of Music, Oxford, who may have examined Robert's doctoral exercise; two Musical Societies, from Manchester and Liverpool; and 23 organists, including Mr Williams from St Peter's, Liverpool. The Liverpool contacts may be an indication that Robert was already planning to relocate.

Liverpool
On 12 January 1775, Robert Wainwright married Mary Woodworth at Manchester Collegiate Church, and on 1 March in the same year he

---

[32] Stanley Sadie, 'Music in the Home II', *The Blackwell History of Music in Britain*, vol. 4: *The Eighteenth Century*, ed. H. Diack Johnstone and Roger Fiske (Oxford, 1990), 340.

was elected organist at St Peter's, Liverpool, by the Common Council of Liverpool.[33] By the late eighteenth century Liverpool had become more cosmopolitan than Manchester and had overtaken it in size. St Peter's, the most fashionable church in the town, was built in 1704 and became the pro-cathedral in 1880. It was described by Richard Brooke, as 'of the nondescript style' and the 'reverse of handsome',[34] and was demolished in 1922. The specification of the organ in 1775 is unknown. In the first extant Liverpool directory published after his move, Robert's occupation is given as 'Doctor in Music', and his address as 1 College Lane, which is only two streets away from where St Peter's stood in Church Street.[35] Robert and Mary's only child, Mary, was born on 10 May 1776 and baptised on 21 May 1776, at St James, Toxteth Park, Liverpool, but less than two years later, Robert's wife died, and was buried at Manchester Collegiate Church on 18 March 1778.

In the baptismal register, Robert is described as 'Professor of Musick', so here as in Manchester, he must have supplemented his income by teaching. The composer and diarist John Marsh wrote in 1777 how 'we all went to a concert at Mr Burgat's where my sister played a favorite concerto of Dr Wainwrights of Liverpool (w'ch she had learned of him there) with the "Air of the Widow Brady" introduced in it'. As noted by Brian Robins, the editor of Marsh's journals, it is unclear whether Mary Marsh studied formally with Robert Wainwright or just learned this one concerto from him.[36] No concertos by Robert exist today, so if they were published, all copies must now be lost – unless Marsh was referring to one of the quintets, which do contain some concerto-like elements. The 'Air of the Widow Brady' may be from *The Irish Widow*, a farce by David Garrick, which included a character called Widow Brady who sang the epilogue, and which was first performed at Drury Lane in 1772.[37] It may also be the same as an Irish tune known as 'Widow Brady's Jig'.

---

[33] Liverpool Record Office: Liverpool Town Books, vol. 11, p. 696. Quoted in Shaw, *The Succession of Organists*, 187.

[34] Richard Brooke, *Liverpool as it Was during the Last Quarter of the Eighteenth Century* (Liverpool, 1853), 47.

[35] Gore, *Liverpool Directory for 1777*, 82.

[36] Brian Robins, ed., *The John Marsh Journals: The Life and Times of a Gentleman Composer (1752–1828)* (New York, 1998), 169.

[37] Anon., *The Dramatic Souvenir: Being Literary and Graphical Illustrations of Shakespeare and other celebrated English Dramatists* (London, 1833), 162.

Within two months of his appointment at St Peter's, Robert Wainwright was involved in a four-day music festival. An advertisement in the *General Advertiser* announced the performances of three oratorios: on Tuesday, 25 April 1775, *Messiah*; on Wednesday *Samson*; and on Thursday, *Jephtha*, 'never performed before in this country'. On Friday there was to be a Miscellaneous Concert, including Dryden's Ode (probably that to St Cecilia) 'set to music by Dr Wainwright, in which will be introduced several select pieces of vocal and instrumental music'. The whole was to be conducted by Dr Wainwright, and the soloists included celebrated London performers: the soprano Frederika Weichsell, the violinist Thomas Pinto and the oboist Johann Fischer, as well as the Edinburgh cellist Johann Schetky.[38] In a later advertisement, there was an apology that Fischer would not be available as he had a benefit concert in London, and that he would be replaced by John Parke.[39] Also, according to Brian Pritchard, there was a further change to the programme and *Jephtha* was replaced with *Judas Maccabaeus*.[40] Robert's music to Dryden's Ode was apparently not published and no printed or manuscript copy is known today.

Robert Wainwright's Opera II, *Six Duetts for a Violin and Violoncello*,[41] are dated c.1775. As they are 'humbly dedicated to Henry Rawlinson Esq.', who was MP for Liverpool for four years from 1780, they were presumably published after he moved to Liverpool. There is no subscription list, and they were not 'printed for the author', so perhaps Robert was now well enough known for the publisher, William Napier, to sell them without any additional financial inducement. Stanley Sadie again approved, describing Robert as a 'talented' man, and his duets as 'skilfully written, with a variety of pace that mitigates the thinness of texture … the first of the set, consisting of an Adagio followed by a spirited Allegro and a graceful minuet, or the last, in G minor, with a fiery central movement, could well stand revival'.[42]

The only other known chamber music by Robert, *Six Quintettos for the Harpsichord or Piano Forte two Violins a Violoncello and Bass*,

---

[38] *The General Advertiser*, 10 March 1775.

[39] *The General Advertiser*, 28 April 1775.

[40] Brian Pritchard, 'The Music Festival and the Choral Society in England in the Eighteenth and Nineteenth Centuries: A Social History' (Ph.D. dissertation, University of Birmingham, 1968), vol. 1, p. 71.

[41] London. Printed for Willm. Napier, No. 474 Strand.

[42] Sadie, 'Music in the Home', p. 332.

were published, again by Napier, probably in 1778.[43] By now his works must have been selling well, as there was no need to 'humbly' dedicate them to anyone. A catalogue of William Napier's publications, dated c.1781, includes Robert's duets for sale at 7s 6d, and his quintets at 10s 6d.[44]

The piano quintet of the late eighteenth century was derived from the accompanied keyboard sonata and also shared some similarities with the keyboard concerto. Such quintets were often written for amateur performance, and could include wind as well as string instruments. Robert Wainwright's quintets are scored for keyboard, two violins, cello and bass or, possibly, a second cello. As I was able to take only a brief look at them in the British Library, I quote Stanley Sadie once more:

Robert Wainwright used the same instrumentation as Giardani in his quintets of 1778, but here each opening tutti closes on the tonic, giving an even more concerto-like structure; in some finales (the pieces are mostly in two movements) the opening theme is, again, concerto-like, stated by the keyboard and repeated by the strings. As in most English concerto publications, the harpsichord shows a reduction in the tuttis (generally melody and bass); this is presumably what the harpsichordist was expected to play. His solo music is fairly elaborate, and there is also a high, often melodic part for the first cello. These works show polished craftsmanship and a style influenced by J.C. Bach, for example the leisurely gait of the first movement of no. 2, the minuet finales of nos. 1 and 4 and the 3/8 finale of no. 6. The other finales – a gavotte in no. 2 and 'Vauxhall rondos' in nos. 3 and 5 – are more characteristically English. These elegant, attractive quintets stand high among English music of the *galant* era.[45]

The population of Liverpool grew rapidly during the eighteenth century because of its increasing involvement with the slave trade. Alongside its more dubious commercial enterprise there was a developing interest in the arts and, perhaps as a salve to its conscience, in charitable institutions. Ranelagh Gardens opened in 1759, the Theatre Royal in 1772, and the Music-Hall in 1786. In 1778 the Liverpool Dispensary opened to supply free medicines and to give medical and surgical care to the poor. A list of 102 'principal and most respectable merchants and individuals of Liverpool', most of whom contributed one

---

[43] London. Printed by Willm. Napier, No. 474 Strand.
[44] British Library: RB.23.a.6754.(11*).
[45] Sadie, 'Music in the Home', p. 349.

guinea to its establishment, included a 'Dr Wainwright', who, as he was not one of the physicians or surgeons connected with the Dispensary, may well have been Robert Wainwright.[46] If so, by then he must have been financially secure and must have gained a reputable place in Liverpool society. He was also becoming a musical entrepreneur.

In 1778, and probably in earlier years as well, the 'Gentlemen of the Musical Society' held a series of subscription concerts,[47] but the following season, in November 1779, it was announced that subscriptions were inadequate, so the concerts would be discontinued.[48] Within a few weeks, another advertisement appeared: 'Dr Wainwright Respectfully acquaints the Ladies and Gentlemen of Liverpool That he intends opening a Subscription Concert, at Forshaw's Great Room'.[49] There were to be four concerts, at three-week intervals, and Robert's intentions seem to have been successfully realised, although in March 1780 there was a slight setback: 'We hear that Dr Wainwright's Public Concert, which should have been on Tuesday next, is obliged to be postpon'd till the week following'.[50] In October 1780, Robert was confident enough to promote a further series of eight concerts, again at Forshaw's Great Room,[51] which was probably quite small by today's standards, and which was part of the Golden Lion, a coaching inn in Dale Street.[52] He may also have organised concerts in the autumn of 1781, but there are no available microfilms of the *Liverpool General Advertiser* for this period.

Liverpool's Ranelagh Gardens were pleasure gardens, designed to imitate their namesake and the more famous Vauxhall Gardens in London. The attractions included secluded walks and bowers, as well as spaces for small chamber music ensembles and for an orchestra, and musical entertainments often ended with firework displays. The most popular soloist at Vauxhall Gardens was Frederika Weichsell, who sang there for twenty-two seasons. Composers including J. C. Bach, Hook, Shield, Giordani and also Robert Wainwright wrote sets of songs for her to perform at Vauxhall. Robert would have met her in 1775 when she sang at the Liverpool festival. His last-known printed compositions, *The Favorite Songs and Cantata Sung by Mrs Weich-*

---

[46] Brooke, *Liverpool as it Was*, pp. 360–3.
[47] *The General Advertiser*, 18 September 1778.
[48] *The General Advertiser*, 5 November 1779.
[49] *The General Advertiser*, 10 December 1779.
[50] *The General Advertiser*, 24 March 1780.
[51] *The General Advertiser*, 13 October 1780.
[52] Brooke, *Liverpool as it Was*, p. 288.

sell at Vaux-Hall-Gardens, were published in about 1780.[53] Most
demand considerable vocal agility, but they are delightful, engaging
pieces, ideally suited to performance on a balmy summer's evening.
There are eight songs and a cantata, which would be classed as another
'song' were it not for an opening recitative. Five songs are accompanied by two violins and 'cembalo' (i.e. harpsichord), which would
have had greater carrying power when played in the open air than a
fortepiano. A Trumpet Song, 'Adieu ye scenes of soft repose', is
scored for trumpet, two oboes, two violins, harpsichord and cello: its
text, with a comment, 'Set to Music by Dr Wainwright', is included in
a collection of poems by a near contemporary of Robert's, William
Roscoe, a Liverpool historian, patron of the arts, and anti-slavery
campaigner.[54] 'When Damon languish'd at my feet' includes parts for
two clarinets as well as two violins and harpsichord, and 'Ye virgin
powers defend my heart' and the cantata, 'See Mira see the lilly [sic]
fair', add a flute to the basic scoring. A Favorite Scotch Song, 'All on
the pleasant banks of Tweed', includes the inevitable Scotch snaps,
but another Scotch Song, 'Beneath this grove' has a gentler, more
flowing melody, and this – together with the first song, 'Gentle air
thou breath of lovers', and the sixth, 'Leave me Damon cease to woo
me' – particularly deserves a modern performance. The Trumpet Song
could also be effective.

As organist of the most fashionable church in Liverpool, Robert
Wainwright continued to be in demand as both a conductor and a
performer, and his reputation as a composer was increasing. In May
1779, both acts of a benefit concert for Mrs Vincent opened with an
overture by him,[55] and in September 1779, another festival of music
held in Liverpool over three days included *Messiah*, *Judas Maccabaeus*, a Grand Miscellaneous Concert, and a 'New Oratorio, called
The Fall of Egypt, by Dr. Wainwright', who also conducted the whole
festival.[56] Unfortunately, neither the overtures nor *The Fall of Egypt*
have survived. *Manchester Faces and Places* noted that Robert sold
the copyright of *The Fall of Egypt* for a thousand guineas,[57] but while
copyright could be sold, this price seems excessive and one wonders

---

[53] London: Printed by Longman and Broderip No. 26 Cheapside.
[54] George Chandler, *William Roscoe of Liverpool* (London, 1953), 322.
[55] *The General Advertiser*, 14 May 1779.
[56] *The General Advertiser*, 30 July 1779.
[57] Anon., 'Mr John Wainwright', *Manchester Faces and Places*, vol. 15, no. 2 (1904),
44.

if it may have been inflated by an over-enthusiastic local historian. According to *The New Grove Dictionary of Music*,[58] a copy of *The Fall of Egypt* was included in a sale catalogue in the British Library of a 'professor of music' in 1813. The shelfmark is not given and I have not yet been able to check it personally; but there is one item in the online catalogue which seems to match this description: '<u>A catalogue of a most complete, scarce and valuable collection of music, being the duplicates of the library of a professor of music ... which will be sold by auction, by Mr. White ... on Tuesday, April the 27th, 1813</u>'. [59]

Although it is probable that Robert Wainwright usually conducted from the harpsichord, or organ, on at least one occasion, when *Judas Maccabaeus* was performed at St Helen's, Prescot, he apparently directed from and played first violin. Perhaps he changed his instrument in order to provide work for his younger brother, Richard, who played the harpsichord: the concert seems to have been a family affair, as his uncle, William Wainwright, played the double bass.[60]

In 1782, the Preston Guild, which is held every twenty years, arranged a festival virtually identical with that held in Liverpool in 1779, except that it was to last for five days, and there were to be two Grand Miscellaneous Concerts instead of one. *The Fall of Egypt* was still billed as a 'new' oratorio, and as before the whole proceedings were to be conducted by Dr Wainwright.[61] But there was a change to the advertisement in the *Liverpool General Advertiser* for 25 July 1782: the conductor was not mentioned, and the composer of *The Fall of Egypt* was given as 'the late Dr Wainwright'. Robert Wainwright had died on 16 July, aged only 33, or possibly 34, years. His obituary expressed genuine regret:

On Tuesday died, universally lamented, Doctor Robert Wainwright, Professor of Music. He was honoured with his degree by the University of Oxford in the year 1776, at a time when he only applied for that of Batchelor, his great abilities entitling him to a first rank in the profession, which he has since supported by some of the most elegant compositions that have appeared for many years. His extraordinary talent, added to liberality of sentiment, an unreserved openness of heart, a generosity and benevolence, and many other

---

[58] Ronald Kidd, 'Wainwright', *The New Grove Dictionary of Music and Musicians*, ed. Stanley Sadie and John Tyrrell (London, 2001), vol. 27, p. 2.
[59] British Library: S.C.1076.(3.)
[60] *The General Advertiser*, 31 May 1781.
[61] *The Liverpool General Advertiser*, 27 June 1782. (*The General Advertiser* changed its name on 13 June 1781.)

excellent qualities which he was possessed of, justly procured him the regard of a numerous train of friends, who now deplore his loss with real grief, and in whose remembrance he will long live with respect and esteem.

Robert Wainwright was remembered for at least a few more years in Liverpool: *The Fall of Egypt* was apparently revived there in 1801,[63] and some of his songs remained popular after his death. *The New Liverpool Songster; or, Musical Companion* contains songs performed at the Liverpool Music Hall since its opening in 1786, including two by Robert: Miss Harwood sang 'All on the pleasant banks of Tweed', from his *Favorite Songs and Cantata*; and Mr Harwood sang 'Thou child of summer, blushing rose'.[64] The Harwoods originally came from Darwen. Mary was a celebrated soprano; Burney states that she was a principal singer at the Handel Commemoration in Westminster Abbey in 1784.[65] Her brother Edward Harwood might have gained wider fame as a vocalist had he not also died prematurely, aged 31 years. He is better known as the composer of the most popular funeral piece of the late eighteenth century, and most of the nineteenth, 'Vital spark of heav'nly flame'.

Conclusion

Had Robert Wainwright not died prematurely, and had he continued to develop as a composer, he might well have become much better known. His present reputation rests on only a few compositions, and would surely be enhanced if we could find copies of his works which are now lost: the Jubilate and Magnificat; the keyboard concerto containing the 'Air of the Widow Brady'; the setting of Dryden's Ode; the two overtures; *The Fall of Egypt*; and the song 'Thou child of summer'. There may well be others, but in the meantime we must cherish the music we do have. The Henry Watson Music Library holds copies of Robert Wainwright's *Sonatas*, *Duetts*, and *Favorite Songs*, as well as many other book rarities, especially from the eighteenth century. The music of our unsung and unplayed local heroes still needs to be researched and performed. Perhaps we need a Henry Watson concert series, or even a Wainwrightfest?

---

[62] *Liverpool General Advertiser*, 18 July 1782.
[63] Kidd, 'Wainwright'.
[64] *The New Liverpool Songster; or, Musical Companion* (Liverpool 1789), 42–3.
[65] Charles Burney, *An Account of the Musical Performances in Westminster Abbey* (London, 1785), 19.

Plate 1: The Collegiate Church, Manchester (the engraving to face the inserted 'Chronological Account of Madame de Beriot' [ie Malibran] as frontispiece to *The Musical World* Vol III (Sept-Dec 1836), where it has the caption 'The scene of Malibran's last greatest triumphs, and where for a time her remains were deposited.' (*Author's collection*)

The Twilight of an Age: The Manchester Grand Musical Festivals of 1828 and 1836, the Development of the Railway, and the English Choral Festival in the Nineteenth Century

LEWIS FOREMAN[1]

WE TEND TO THINK of the British Choral Festival movement as a phenomenon of the second half of the nineteenth century, perhaps starting with the first performance of Mendelssohn's *Elijah* at Birmingham in 1846. Yet in the first three decades of the century there had been a tremendous growth in music festivals, followed by a retrenchment before the pattern of the later festivals emerged. Although there had been such festivals at the Three Choirs (in rotation at Worcester, Hereford and Gloucester) since the early eighteenth century, the growth in such activities between 1810 and 1836, featuring large-scale performances and the leading singers of the day, came about as the result of enthusiasts in one musical centre or another trying to emulate the great Handel Commemorations in London at Westminster Abbey in 1784 and on five further occasions: for the next three successive years 1785, 1786 and 1787; and in 1790 and 1791.

Two sources have been used to make a very brief survey of the growth of choral festivals outside London over the first two decades of the nineteenth century, first John Crosse's *Account of the Grand Musical Festival held in … York* published in 1825,[2] and then by a search of COPAC[3] using just the phrase 'Musical Festival' in the title field and the inclusive dates 1800–40 in the date field. This finds holdings of programmes, prospectuses, local histories and collections of concert ephemera. From these two sources, and programmes in the author's collection, we deduce the following list of festivals.

---

[1] Paper given at the 'Music in 19th-Century Britain, Fourth Biennial Conference', University of Leeds, 24–27 July 2003.
[2] John Crosse, *An Account of the Grand Musical Festival held in September, 1823, in the Cathedral Church of York* (York: Printed and sold by John Wolstenholme, Minster-Gates, 1825).
[3] <http://www.copac.ac.uk>

Table 1: Some choral festivals in the early nineteenth century excluding the Three Choirs Festivals)

Bath and Somerset: 1824
Birmingham: 1802, 1805, 1814, 1817, 1820, 1823, 1829, 1834. 1837, 1846
        etc.
Bordesley Musical Festival: 1824
Bristol: 1814
Bury St Edmunds: 1828
Cambridge: 1831, 1833, 1835
Chester: 1814, 1821, 1829
Derby: 1895, 1810, 1816, 1819, 1822, 1831
Doncaster: 1809?
Dublin: 1831
Edinburgh: 1815, 1819, 1824, 1843
Exeter: 1814, 1820
Glasgow: 1821
Halifax: 1830
Hull (Kingston-upon-Hull): 1807, 1834, 1840
Isle of Man: 1825
Kidderminster: 1832
Liverpool: 1805, 1813, 1817, 1823, 1827, 1833, 1836
Manchester: 1828, 1836
Newcastle (also known as Northumberland, Durham and Newcastle upon
        Tyne): 1814, 1824, 1842
Norwich: 1811, 1813, 1817, 1822, 1824, 1827, 1830, 1836, 1837
Oxford: 1827, 1834
Reading (Berkshire Grand Musical Festival): 1819, 1822, 1831
Reading: 1822
Salisbury: 1821
Sheffield: 1800, 1806
Stoke-on-Trent: 1833
Wakefield:1824
Westminster Abbey: 1834
Winchester: 1814
Wrexham: 1827
York: 1823, 1825, 1828, 1835

John Crosse in 1825 summarised the position as far as the rise of large-scale musical meetings in support of local charities, usually hospitals, in the eighteenth century.[4] It was, he reported

first suggested by the members of the Three Choirs of Gloucester, Worcester, and Hereford, in 1724. We have not met with any such meetings; at least in the North, for, as to the Southern and Western counties, we are not competent to speak positively: until 1769 when the Leeds Infirmary was benefited by an oratorio. A similar performance took place at Norwich in 1772; but it does not appear that those at Halifax and Liverpool in 1766, unquestionably the earliest in the North of England, or at Beverley in 1769, and at Liverpool in 1770 and 1778, were held for any charitable purpose: they were all of them; however, previous to the first oratorio at Birmingham, also in the latter year, at which place the meetings were made triennial in 1787, and first began to lay claim to superior excellence in 1799. The Sheffield and Hull Infirmaries were assisted in 1786 and 1792, by musical performances on a scale of some extent, and the adoption of the plan of management by a Committee, under the sanction of patrons of rank – at Chester, Liverpool, Derby; and Edinburgh, for the benefit of the local charities, has been related above.

He might have added that in September 1785 Manchester had mounted a festival emulating Westminster the previous year and featuring the double drums from Westminster Abbey (see Plate 2).

Michael Kennedy has reminded us of the active musical life in nineteenth-century Manchester before Hallé formed his orchestra.[5] In July 1824, for example, Liszt's father was able to accept a last-minute engagement for the twelve-year-old to play two concerts at the Theatre-Royal at the beginning of August for a fee of 100 guineas,[6] though he may not have been so pleased when he found his son on a programme which also featured a four-year-old harpist who received most of the press coverage.

Brian Pritchard has noted a festival at Liverpool as early as 1740, and gatherings which celebrated the 'openings of organs in St Peter's Church, Liverpool on 30 April, 1 and 2 May 1766, in St Thomas's, Liverpool on 7–10 August, 1770, and in St John's, Manchester on 29–31 August 1770'.[7] Manchester did not develop a continuing music festival tradition, yet there were festivals in 1777 and 1792, the early

---

[4] Crosse, *op. cit.*, p. 128.

[5] Michael Kennedy, *The Hallé 1858-1983: A History of the Orchestra* (Manchester: Manchester University Press, 1982), 1–4.

[6] Alan Walker, *Franz Liszt*, vol. 1: *The Virtuoso Years, 1811–1847* (Ithaca, NY: Cornell University Press, rev. edn, 1983, 1988), 106–9.

FESTIVAL of MUSIC
At MANCHESTER.

Rt Hon. Lord GREY DE WILTON,
Sir WATTS HORTON, Bart.
Sir JOHN PARKER MOSLEY, Bart.
JOHN BLACKBURNE, Efq.
} Stewards.

On WEDNESDAY MORNING, the 21ft of Sept. 1785,
will be performed, in the

CONCERT ROOM,
The ORATORIO of
SAMPSON,
And, in the EVENING, a
MISCELLANEOUS CONCERT;
In which will be introduced,
L'ALLEGRO IL PENSOROSO.

On THURSDAY MORNING the 22d, a
SELECTION
From the different Performances in Weftminfter-Abbey.

On FRIDAY MORNING the 23d,
The Sacred ORATORIO of
The MESSIAH;
And, in the EVENING, a
GRAND MISCELLANEOUS CONCERT.
The Orcheftra will confift of a very numerous and felect
BAND, with the Addition of the
DOUBLE DRUMS
From WESTMINSTER-ABBEY.
Principal Vocal Performers.

Madame Mara	Mrs. Shepley
Mifs Harwood	Mr. Saville
Mrs. Crouch	Mr. Meredith

Amongft the Inftrumental Performers, are

Mr. Cramer	Mr. Alcock
Mr. Crofdill	Mr. Haigh
Mr. Parke	Mr. Beilby
Mr. Burchell	Mr. Crawthorne
Mr Sharpe	Mr. Mafters
Mr. Shield	Mr. Wainwright
Mr. Gariboldi	Mr. Atherton
Mr. Parkinfon	Mr. Larber
Mr. Serjant	Mr. Surr
Mr. Jones	Mr. Nicholfon
Mr. Afbridge	Two Mafter Haighs
Mr. Lawton	And
Mr. Carke	Mr. Buckley.
Mr. Mountain	

Books opened for Subfcription (at ONE GUINEA
and a HALF for the Five Performances) at J. HARROP'S
Printer.

Plate 2: Announcement of the Manchester Festival 1785.
(*Manchester Libraries and Information, Henry Watson Music Library*)

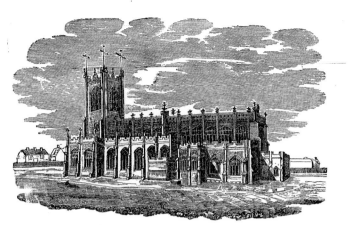

Plate 3: The Collegiate Church from the History of the 1828 Festival. (*Manchester Libraries and Information, Henry Watson Music Library*)

meetings at Manchester and Liverpool being among the first provincial festivals of their kind outside the Three Choirs. Pritchard suggests that they 'may well be placed among the cultural first-fruits of the Industrial Revolution and they almost certainly represent attempts to satisfy a growing desire for cultural standing and prestige among the rising generation of northern manufacturers'.[8]

The week-long festival of 1828, according to a correspondent to the *Manchester Guardian* sixty-two years after the event, 'partook far more of a carnival character than any of its predecessors' with a 'grand dress ball on the Wednesday in the Assembly Rooms on the Wednesday evening; and on the Friday evening a Fancy Dress ball', which attracted some four thousand people 'in all sorts of fancy costumes'.[9]

It is worth remembering that the growth in population in Manchester in the early nineteenth century was enormous. Pigot's directory[10] published in the year of the 1836 festival cited the population in 1801 as 70,409 and by 1831 as 142,026. The 1838 charter which encompassed Manchester, Hulme, Ardwick, Chorlton on Medlock and Beswick gave a joint population of 242,000.[11]

It has become a cliché to suggest that the growth of music in Manchester at the end of the nineteenth century owed much to German

---

[7] Brian Pritchard, 'Some Festival Programmes of the Eighteenth and Nineteenth Centuries: 3. Liverpool and Manchester', *RMA Research Chronicle* no. 7 (1969), 1–27.

[8] Ibid., p. 1.

[9] 'Some Manchester Festivals', *Manchester Guardian*, 5 August 1890.

[10] *Pigot and Sons General and Classified Directory of Manchester and Salford* (Manchester: J. Pigot, 1836).

[11] G. S. Messinger, *Manchester in the Victorian Age* (Manchester: Manchester University Press, 1985), 32.

immigration and German immigrant middle-class business families, all part of the cotton trade. From a similar background in Bradford came the composer Frederick Delius, whose father was in the wool trade. Certainly there were German businessmen entering the country as a consequence of the Napoleonic wars. The number of Merchant Houses in Manchester reached 28 by 1820 and, Panikos Panayi tells us, the migration of German merchants began to develop on a large scale from about this time.[12] This immigration was certainly felt to be a contributory factor to the success of the festival under discussion. 'The people of Lancashire', noted the *Manchester Examiner* in September 1836, 'are musical, especially those of Manchester, where Germans and other foreigners have naturalised a taste for the science.'[13] Yet apart from the many well-paid musicians visiting from London for the occasion, it is notable on looking at the published lists of choir members and those attending the fancy dress ball (see Tables 2 and 3) how few non-English names appear.

Another reminiscence of the festival published by the *Manchester Guardian* fifty years later reminded us that:[14]

The town put on its gala attire, and, as many of the old black and white timbered houses still remained, the general effect was very much more picturesque than would be possible now. … Flags made the streets gay, and every window which commanded a view of the approaches to the church entrance was crowded with eager spectators. And in some respects the display in the streets was such as could not be possible were such a festival to be held in Manchester in our time. The county people came in their carriages and four, and the streets along which they drove were lined with holiday makers. All round the churchyard, too, the available space was fully occupied, and many were satisfied with hearing the choruses from outside.

One of the features of the decoration was the draping of buildings with advertising playbills measuring 11 ft by 3 ft, printed in black and red. The example in Plate 4 is from 1828.[15]

These early festivals attract our attention, not only for the large audiences they received, but for the practical logistics in attracting

---

[12] Panikos Panayi, *German Immigrants in Britain During the Nineteenth Century 1815–1914* (Oxford: Berg Publishers, 1995), 23.

[13] *An Historical Account of the Grand Musical Festival Held in Manchester the Second Week in September 1836: taken from the Manchester and Salford Advertiser of September 17* (Manchester: Printed at the Advertiser Office, No. 78 Market Street, 1836).

[14] 'The Last Manchester Musical Festival – II', *Manchester Guardian*, 23 March 1889.

[15] Photograph of the example in the author's collection. The poster is linen mounted and rolled on a dowel.

Plate 4: The playbill for 1828. Over 11 feet long, the surviving copy is on a roll and backed with linen. One assumes these would have been widely seen on buildings at the time of the Festival. (*Author's collection*)

Plate 4a: upper portion of the 1828 playbill

A BALL,

On THURSDAY MORNING, Handel's Sacred Oratorio,

MESSIAH,

On THURSDAY EVENING, at the Theatre.
A Grand Miscellaneous

CONCERT.

ON FRIDAY MORNING A GRAND SELECTION OF

SACRED MUSIC,

From the Works of HANDEL, HAYDN, MOZART, MARCELLO, Attwood, Beethoven &c.

AND ON FRIDAY EVENING,

At the THEATRE and ASSEMBLY ROOMS, which will be connected for this occasion

A GRAND FANCY DRESS BALL,

For which the celebrated New French Quadrille Band at Almacks is engaged.

PRINCIPAL VOCAL PERFORMERS,

Madame Catalani,

Madame STOCKHAUSEN, Madame PUZZI,
AND
Madame CARADORI ALLAN,
Miss PATON,
Miss LOVE, Mrs. WM. KNYVETT, Miss GODFREY,
AND
Miss STEPHENS

Mr. BRAHAM,
Mr. VAUGHAN, Mr. Wm. KNYVETT,
Mr. E. TAYLOR, Mr. ISHERWOOD,
AND
Mr. PHILLIPS,
Signor CURIONI & Signor PELEGRINI.

INSTRUMENTAL.

Leader of the Morning Performances - MR. F. CRAMER.
Leader of the Evening Performances - MR. MORI

SOLO PERFORMERS.

Viola, Mr. MORI.   Flute, Mr. NICHOLSON.   Clarinet, Mr. WILLMAN,   Violoncello, Mr. LINDLEY and
Mr. W. LINDLEY   Horn, Signor PUZZI

Principal Instrumental Performers,

Violins, Mr. Morah & Mr. Watkins   Oboes, Mr. Witton and Mr. Hughes   Trombones, Mr. Marriott and Mr. Smithies
Tenors, Mr. F. Ware & Mr. Calkin   Clarinets, Mr. Willman and Mr. Powell   Serpent, Mr. Freke
Violoncellos, Mr. Lindley & Mr. W. Lindley   Bassoons, Mr. Mackintosh and Mr. Tully   Bass Horn, Mr. Mecutcheon
Double Basses, Mr. Dragonetti & Mr. Taylor   Horns, Signor Puzzi and Mr. Tully   Double Drums, Mr. Chipp & Mr. Wilkinson
Flute, Mr. Nicholson & Mr. T. Hughes   Trumpets, Mr. Harper and Mr. Hyde   Harps, Mr. Stockhausen & Mr. Challoner

Conductor, Mr. GREATOREX.
Who will preside at the ORGAN and Grand PIANO FORTE.

THE BAND AND CHORUS,
WHICH WILL CONSIST OF NEARLY

400 PERFORMERS!
Will be complete in every department, the Committee having engaged additional performers of eminence, from some other large
towns in the Kingdom, to complete the strength of the Orchestra.

THE PRICES OF ADMISSION

TO EACH PERFORMANCE WILL BE AS FOLLOWS:
ON TUESDAY MORNING, AT THE COLLEGIATE CHURCH,
Patrons' Gallery, 5s.   Rest of the Church, 2s. 6d.
AFTER THIS SERVICE A COLLECTION WILL BE MADE FOR THE BENEFIT OF THE CHARITIES

Oratorios on Wednesday, Thursday and Friday Mornings,
Patrons' Gallery (all reserved Seats) 21s. | Galleries and Seats under them 10s.
Body of the Church (not under the Galleries) 15s. | Choir 5s.

TO THE CONCERTS AT THE THEATRE,
Patrons' Seats (all reserved) - 21s. | Upper Boxes 10s.
Rest of the Pit and Lower Boxes - 15s. | Gallery 5s.

BALL AT THE ASSEMBLY ROOMS ON WEDNESDAY EVENING,
Gentlemen, Ladies, 10s. including Refreshments.

GRAND FANCY DRESS BALL
ON FRIDAY EVENING,
(including Refreshments) - 21s.

Plate 4b: lower portion of the 1828 playbill

some of the biggest musical names of the day before the arrival of the railway, and for the fact that it became the norm for a festival to include a ball often in fancy dress. In the case of Manchester there were both, at which enormous numbers of people attended. From our point of view they are of most interest because full attendance lists were published in the local newspapers. We are focusing on the Manchester Festival of 1836, the festival immediately preceding the Liverpool Festival of the same year, now celebrated for the first British performance of Mendelssohn's *St Paul*. In order to explore it we also need to take note of the 1828 festival and the earlier triennial festivals at Liverpool at this time. These are significant not only for musical reasons, but because they come just as the railway was beginning to be a significant factor. By 1835 there was a well-established train to Liverpool, but not yet to London – that came the following year,[16] and before Manchester Town Hall was built.[17] There is also the curious factor that the Manchester Festival of 1836 was in fact the last one in Manchester, then a recognised music centre where, within twenty years, Charles Hallé would found his concerts.

In fact the first festival to find the railway a notable determinant as far as both audience and performers were concerned had been the festival at Liverpool, held on 4–8 October 1830. In the history of that Liverpool Festival published locally soon afterwards it was noted that

the influx of strangers has not been so great as it was at the last triennial festival in 1827 … and perhaps the injury afflicted in other quarters, if there be any, has been counterbalanced by the expeditious, cheap, and pleasant conveyance of the musical public of Manchester by the railway. During the week the principal streets have presented a very animated appearance, being filled by crowds of persons well and fashionable dressed, and we believe the proprietors of the various hotels and inns … have very little reason to complain.[18]

The Liverpool festival tradition was a more established one, the festival having met regularly since 1813, and triennially since 1823. It was sufficiently near Manchester to attract Manchester music lovers, and must have been one of the models that would inform the way Manchester's two festivals would be structured when the decision was made to go ahead in 1828 and 1836.[19]

---

[16] Liverpool Road Station, Manchester, was opened on 15 September 1830.

[17] Alfred Waterhouse's Town Hall was built 1868–77.

[18] *A History of the Liverpool Musical Festival, 1830, with engravings* (Liverpool: Printed by E. Smith and Co., Mercury Office, Lord Street, [1830]).

[19] In fact Manchester had to move its preferred date in 1836, when it was found it clashed with the date already set for Liverpool.

Table 2: Soprano and alto choir members at Manchester, 1836

CANTOS

Acton Miss, Manchester
Amphlett Miss, ditto
Andrew Mrs Henry, ditto
Barry Miss, Liverpool
Bickerdyke Miss, Duckinfield
Birch Mrs, Manchester
Brand Mrs, Liverpool
Carrington Mrs, Stockport
Chadwick Miss, Oldham
Clough Miss, ditto
Cordwell Miss, Pendlebury
Davies Miss, Liverpool
Duckworth Miss E., Whitefield
Duckworth Miss R., ditto
Dutton Mrs, Liverpool
Eckersley Miss, Chowbent
Edwards Miss, Liverpool
Entwisle Miss, ditto
Greener Miss, Manchester
Hallwood Miss, Liverpool
Henshaw Mrs, Manchester
Heywood Miss, Heywood
Hiles Mrs, Liverpool
Hughes Miss, ditto
Hulme Mrs, Manchester
Hulton Mrs, Failsworth
Isherwood Mrs T., Manchester
Jackson Mrs, Oldham
Jackson Miss, Liverpool
Jones Miss, Pendlebury
Kay Miss, Bury
Kelly Miss, Liverpool

Leach Miss, ditto
Leeming Mrs, Bury
Linacre Mrs, Liverpool
Lord Miss, Rochdale
Maddocks Mrs, Liverpool
Marsden Miss, Manchester
Morrow Mrs, Liverpool
Openshaw Miss, Bury
Peace Mrs, Huddersfield
Pemberton Mrs, Liverpool
Ripley Master, 'Collegiate' Church, Manchester
Rudd Mrs, Stockport
Schofield Miss, Rochdale
Sewells Miss, Oldham
Shepley Mrs, Newton Heath
Sutcliffe Miss, Disley
Swain Miss, Liverpool
Taylor Miss, Oldham
Thorley Miss M. A., Manchester
Thorley Miss Z., Eccles
Travis Miss S., Shaw
Turner Mrs, Manchester
Walton Miss H., Bury
Walton Miss S., ditto
Wild Mrs, Shaw
Winterbottom Mrs, Oldham
Wright Miss, Manchester
Wrigley Miss, Shaw

ALTOS

Arnold R., Manchester
Ashworth G., Bury
Ball H., Liverpool
Barlow W., Swinton
Barlow J., Bury
Barratt S., Stockport
Boothby T., Liverpool
Bradbury B., Ashton

Buck T., Manchester
Butterworth A., Shaw
Clegg James, Rochdale
Collins J., Blackley
Cordwell D., Pendlebury
Cordwell J., ditto
Cordwell J., Manchester
Dutton W., Liverpool
Fletcher J., Unsworth
Fletcher R., Manchester
Fletcher W., Prestwich
Gaskell S., Didsbury
Gleave J., Liverpool
Gledhill J., Manchester
Hampson James, ditto
Hartley J., Liverpool
Henshaw W., Manchester
Hilton J., Oldham
Jones D., Pendlebury
Jones H., Liverpool
Malone P., Manchester
Malone T., ditto
Marsden J., Liverpool
Mills E., Rochdale
Ogden J., Stockport
Oliver J., Duckinfield
Peace J., Huddersfield
Penny J., Manchester
Platt S., Ashton
Richards S., Manchester
Stott J., Liverpool
Swift N., Sheffield
Turner W., Manchester
Waddington J., ditto
Walker J. S., Bury
Walsh D. T., ditto
Walton E., ditto
Weston R., Manchester
Weston R., Stockport
Wilkinson J., Chester
Willis T., Manchester
Winterbottom S., Oldham
Woodward C., Liverpool
Wright W. C., Manchester
Wroe T., Bury

The resumption of a Handel Festival at Westminster Abbey in 1834[20] must also have been a stimulus for Manchester to resume its festival after eight years. Ignaz Moscheles was at Westminster Abbey and wrote to his relatives:

2700 persons found accommodation; the best seats cost two; and the others one guinea each. … In front were the solo singers, then the small chorus, 40 strong; close to this chorus, at a piano, sat Sir George Smart, the director of the music; behind him, the band, ranged in tiers; the cellos on either side, the violins in the centre, then the wind-instruments; above all, the magnificent organ, built by Gray for the occasion … The solo singers were … the admirable Phillips; the tenors were represented by Hobbs and the inimitable Braham; Miss Stevens and Madame Caradori Allan, both excellent, sang the soprano parts … with Lindley's violoncello, and Braham, with Harper's trumpet-obligato. Phillips had a song with a bassoon accompaniment, Miss Stevens and Grisi also had parts assigned them in this selection.[21]

As well as the artists who seem to have been working a circuit at the various festivals, the key link in organising the artists and the repertoire was the conductor Sir George Smart. Smart did not appear as a virtuoso conductor of today would: he did not direct with a baton; yet he was equally important in the practical detail of putting over the music.

He directed music by presiding at the piano or organ, not by wielding a baton; and the qualities that made him efficient in this office were his social position, administrative ability, punctilious accuracy and thorough knowledge of performing traditions. He was also an excellent keyboard player. For several decades he was much in demand as director of musical festivals and other performances on a large scale. He conducted festivals at Liverpool in 1823, 1827, 1830, 1833 and 1836; Norwich, 1824, 1827, 1830 and 1833; Bath, 1824; Newcastle upon Tyne, 1824 and 1842; Edinburgh, 1824; Bury St Edmunds, 1828; Dublin, 1831; Derby, 1831; Cambridge, 1831 and 1835; London (Handel Festival, Westminster Abbey), 1834; Hull, 1834 and 1840; and Manchester, 1836.[22]

---

[20] William Henry Husk in his Introduction to the programme for the bicentenary Handel Festival at Crystal Palace in June 1885, p. 4, estimated the total number of performers at Westminster Abbey in 1834 as 600.

[21] Charlotte Moscheles, *Recent Music and Musicians as described in the diaries and correspondence of Ignatz Moscheles* (New York: Henry Holt, 1875), 203–5.

[22] 'Smart, (1) Sir George (Thomas) Smart', *The New Grove Dictionary of Music and Musicians*, ed. Stanley Sadie [and John Tyrrell]. 2nd edn (London: Macmillan, 2001), vol. 23, p. 533. The article is Nicholas Temperley's revision of the original one by W. H. Husk.

Table 3: Some attendees at the Fancy Dress Ball, Manchester, 1836

Appleton Miss, Colly-hurst, in a fancy dress

Appleton Miss E., Colly-hurst, in a Swiss dress

Averduck Mr Frederick, Heathfield, as a Polish officer

Appleton Miss, Smedley, as a Venetian lady

Appleton Miss Ann, Sm-edley, as a peasant of the south of France

Appleton Mr, Everton, as a Highland chieftain

Appleton Miss, Egerton, in a fancy dress

Appleton Miss E., Coop-er-street, in a fancy dress

Appleton Rev. Richard, Liverpool

Appleton Miss, Liverpool, as a peasant of Berne

Appleton Mr William, jun, Smedley, as a Neapolitan

Appleton Mr P. F., Falkn-er-street, as a red-cross knight

Appleton Mrs P. F., Falkner-street, in a fancy dress

Arnold Mr, Salford, as a Highland chief

Arnold Mrs, Salford, in a fancy dress

Armstrong Mr Thomas, Broughton, in a court dress

Armstrong Mrs, Broughton, in a fancy dress

Armstrong Mr Joseph, jun, Bedford Square, as Earl of Leicester

Armstrong Mr William, in an old court dress

Armstrong Mrs William, in a fancy dress

Armstrong Mr E., Broughton, in an old court dress

Armstrong Mr J. A., Broughton, in a naval uniform

Armstrong Miss, Broughton, as a Mexican lady

Armstrong Mr James, Dublin, as a Greek Cor-sair

Armstrong Mr H., Preston, as a collegian

Armstrong Miss, Oxford-place, in a fancy dress

Armitage, Miss, Rastrick, as Amy Robsart in *Kenil-worth*

Ashton Mr, jun, St George's Road, in a splendid Turkish dress

Ashton, Mr Thomas, in a fancy dress

Ashton Mrs Sam, Flowery field, as a Polish lady

Ashton Mr Samuel, jun, Flowery field, as a Cir-cassian

Ashton Miss, Flowery field, as a Catalonian

Ashton Miss Sarah, Flow-ery field, as a Catalonian

Ashton Mr Thos, Flowery field, in a fancy dress

Ashton Mr Thomas, jun, Flowery field, in a Polish dress

Ashton Mrs Elizabeth, in a fancy dress

Ashton Mr Richard, in a Swedish dress

Ashton Dr, Mosley-street, in a Spanish dress

Ashton Mr John as a Turk

Ashurst Mr John, in a Highland costume

Aspinwall Mr T. H., Hulme, as a Greek sailor

Aspinwall Mr, Cornbrook, as a 10th hussar

Aspinwall Miss, Corn-brook, in a fancy dress

Aspinall Mr John, Standen Hall, as a Spanish noble

Aspinall Mr Lawrence, Blackburn, as Robin Hood

Astley Mr W. R., Strange-ways, as Figaro

Aspell Mr J., Radcliffe, as a captain in the navy

Atherton Miss, New Brighton, as Edith of Lorn

Atherton Mr James, Pend-leton, in the uniform of the 2nd Royal Lancashire Militia

Atherton Mrs, Pendleton, as Catherine Seyton

Atherton, Mr Thomas, Cheetham, as a Knight of Malta

Atherton Captain, 6th Foot, Alkincoates, in his uniform

Atherton Mrs, Holting-worth, in a fancy dress

Atkinson Mr Charles, Huddersfield, as a Greek sailor

Atkinson Mr Charles, Manchester, as a Spanish nobleman

Atkinson Miss M., Bamp-ton, Westmoreland, as a flower girl

Atkinson Mr jun, in a court dress

Atkinson Miss, London, as a Swiss peasant

Atkinson Mr H., Liver-pool, in a masonic dress

Atkinson Mr M., Gartside-street, in the costume of Upper Austria

Atkins Mr J., Blackburn, as Montrose

Ayre Mr W. S., Vine Grove, in a Spanish cos-tume

Correspondents of the time[23] also mention the Derby[24] Festival of 1831 and the York Great Festival (Yorkshire Grand Musical Festival) of 1835. From these, models for the numbers of concerts, the repertoire, the artists to be engaged and their cost would also have been taken, doubtless with considerable input from George Smart, the music director. These were all festivals focused on religious repertoire performed in churches or cathedrals, and given on an increasingly massive scale, but with a similar number of miscellaneous concerts consisting of concert encores and opera arias, where the leading singers of the day did their stuff. It seems likely that the singers were at least as important in attracting an audience as the oratorios, and they commanded very high fees.[25]

The soloists at the 1836 festival were: the soprano Maria Caradori-Allan (1800–65); Mme Assandri; Maria-Felicia Malibran (1808–36); the Russian tenor Nicola Ivanoff (1810–80); Luigi Lablache (1794–1858); Anna Bishop (1810–84); Mrs W. M. Knyvett (Deborah Travis) (1795–1876); soprano Clara Novello (1818–1908); contralto Mrs Alfred Shaw (1814–76); veteran tenor John Braham (1774–1856) returning as a baritone; Mr Bennett; bass Mr William Machin (1799–1870); baritone Henry Phillips (1801–76); Mr Terrail.

Not unexpectedly, contemporary engravings of such festivals tend to have recurring features, yet they make one wonder how far these impressions of such matters of the platform settings, orchestra and audience on such occasions were stereotyped images introduced by the artists, probably working against the clock, and how accurate the detail of such illustrations were of what actually took place. Nevertheless they can be enormously vivid and we have to rely on them.

Until the Town Hall was built, Manchester did not have so large a space for its festival as many other cities. The festivals took place in the Collegiate Church, now Manchester Cathedral, and the Theatre Royal. The rather crude contemporary images published in the *Man-*

---

[23] Cuttings and letters from the Manchester Music Festival collection in Henry Watson Music Library.

[24] Interesting though that Moscheles (*op. cit.*, p. 173) notes: 'Derby – The committee is hardly satisfied the pecuniary results of the festival, two hundred tickets at a guinea each, two hundred at twelve shillings, and two hundred at seven shillings, being all that were sold'.

[25] For example, the papers for the 1828 Festival include receipts from the soprano Catalani for 300 guineas; from Braham for 200 gns, from Phillips for 75 gns, while the cellist Robert Lindley received 50 gns and the timpanist Chipp only 20 gns.

Plate 5: Manchester Festival: the platform in the Collegiate Church (from 1836 History). (*Manchester Libraries and Information, Henry Watson Music Library*)

chester Examiner and its histories of the events do not give us a good idea of what it must have been like, and particularly the scale when populated.

Before the days of easy travel or widely available regular concert series, and long before there was any concept of sound recording, an event such as this festival would have been something very special for most people. The existence of the Liverpool Festival would have provided a magnet for the musical better off with the leisure to spend several days in Liverpool, and doubtless many who would support a Manchester Festival would have been to Liverpool on those occasions. There they would have previously heard Maria-Felicia Malibran (Madame Malibran de Bériot) in 1836 at the age of 28, at the peak of her powers as the Callas of her day. Her death during the 1836 Festival has tended to be the reason for its securing a footnote in history.

The Manchester Festival represented a wide-spanning economic activity which had positive financial impact far outside the actual audiences for the music. As in the case of all these early nineteenth-century festivals they were underwritten by a guarantee fund, the guarantors a mixture of aristocratic, well-off local figures and musical entrepreneurs. The 1828 guarantee fund[26] was around £20,000 (nearly double the actual final outgoings), the total receipts amounted to over £15,000, and the profit of about £5,000 was divided among Manchester charities. There was no call on the guarantors. The 1836 festival started with a guarantee fund of £11,000 which rose to £30,000 within a month of the first announcements. Receipts were announced on the Wednesday night during the festival as being £12,500. In fact the profit was less than the 1824 festival, because artists' fees were more, but a substantial sum was still distributed.[27]

Interest extended far beyond the aristocratic and leading business people who formed the patrons and guarantors. A contemporary account of the 1828 festival reported that

The clerks, salesmen, and other principal servants of the merchants and tradesmen, held meetings to consult together on the propriety of requesting their employers to give them leave of absence during some portion of the week. In this they perfectly succeeded. It was even suggested that factories should be closed; but the loss which the masters, as well as the families of the workmen

---

[26] All figures are taken from the reports in the *Manchester Examiner* and its histories of the festivals for 1828 and 1836, cited at notes 13 and 28.
[27] *An Historical Account of the Grand Musical Festival ... 1836.*

Plate 6: Manchester Festival: the Patrons' Gallery in the Collegiate Church (from 1836 History). (*Manchester Libraries and Information, Henry Watson Music Library*)

might sustain, together with the additional bustle which such a step would occasion in the already overcrowded streets, at once pointed to the impolicy of such a measure. The hackney coaches were soon found to be insufficient; and an additional number (some from other towns) were promptly licensed by the Commissioners of Police, and authorised to charge double fares for the twelve days.[28]

This economic fallout was widely felt, for example in providing lodgings for the many visitors attracted from a wide catchment area. This is from the 1828 festival again:

Those who had 'Lodgings for the Festival' to let, *very modestly*, considering *great folks* were coming, demanded from *two* to *twenty* pounds, in streets which before the Festival were considered perfectly obscure. These, however, as the time approached, grew into importance, and tenants, who but a few days before, were at their wits end for their rents, suddenly discovered they might as well make ten or twenty pounds as not.[29]

The Musical Director of the 1828 festival was the 69-year-old Thomas Greatorex, conductor of the Birmingham Festival, who died in 1831. We have his extensive correspondence,[30] which makes clear that not only did he direct the concerts on behalf of the organising committee, but he was also the fixer for all the performers, negotiating terms and issuing contracts, an enormous load. For the 1836 festival, as we have seen, they turned to Sir George Smart, then the pre-eminent festival musical director of the day.

   The concerts were extensively reported in the local papers and, in the case of Manchester and Liverpool and elsewhere, these reports were later published as pamphlets together with contemporary ac-counts of the genesis of the festival, the finances, and a list of all attending the ball. Presumably printing all these names was intended to ensure sales at least to those who had been present.

   It is also worth noting another brief press report reminding us of the practical realities, then as now: 'Four "gentlemen" from London,

---

[28]*An Account of the Manchester Festival, 1828, containing the names of the Patrons Committee; A Report of the Oratorios and Concerts, and a list of the principal vocal and instrumental performers; with a description of the characters who attended the Grand Fancy Dress Ball* (Manchester: Printed by T. Sowler, St Ann's Square, 1828).

[29] Bound volume: *Material in Connection with the Manchester Festival, 1828* ('Found at Queen's Park Art Gallery and transferred by Art Galleries Committee to Libraries Committee'). Henry Watson Music Library Rf 780.64 Me645.

[30] Ibid.

Table 4: home towns of members of the orchestra in 1836
(* Return engagement: appeared in 1828)

Leader of the Band:
Mr. F. CRAMER*
Principal Second Violin:
Mr. WAGSTAFF.
Organist:
Mr. W. WILKINSON.

FOR THE EVENING CONCERTS

Solo-Violin:
Monsieur DE BERIOT.
Leader of the Band:
Mr. MORL

VIOLINS
Anderson, London*
Banks, Manchester
Barnes, Oldham
Barton, Dublin
Blagrove, London
Brand, Liverpool
Bywater, Leeds
Clough, Manchester
Cramer, W., London
Cudmore, Manchester
Ella, Manchester*
Eyton, Liverpool
Fallows, Dublin
Frobisher, Halifax
Gregory, Manchester
Hacking, Bury
Hampson, Manchester
Herrman, Liverpool
Jackson, Oldham
Johnson, Stockport
Kearns, London
Levey, Dublin
Litolfe, London
Mori, N., London*
Patey, London
Piggott, London*
Reeve, London
Rudersdorff, Hull
Seal, Sheffield
Seymour, London
Thomas, Liverpool*
Tolbecque, London
Ward, Manchester
Wilde, Ashton

TENORS (i.e. VIOLAS)
Mr Moralt, London

Sherrington, London
Abbott, London
Andrews, Manchester
Calkin, London*
Challoner, London *
Cummings, Leeds
Dando, London
Daniels, London*
Hime, Liverpool
Mountain, London
Napier, Edinburgh
Smith, Manchester
Sudlow, E., Manchester
Taylor, Oldham
Waddington, jnr, Manchester

VIOLONCELLOS
Mr. Lindley, London*
Crouch, London*
Hatton, London
Jackson, Liverpool
Lindley, W, Worcester*
Lucas, London
Piggott, Dublin
Scruton, Liverpool
Stewartson, York
Sudlow, Manchester

DOUBLE BASSES
Signor Dragonetti, London*
Mr. Howell, London
Mr. Beeley, Stockport
Flower, London*
Hardman, York
Hill, London
Hill, I., Manchester
Smart, C., London
Taylelire, Liverpool
Taylor, London*

FLUTES
Mr. Nicholson, London*
Card, London*
Brown, Liverpool

PICCOLO FLUTE
Card, London

OBOES
Mr G. Cooke, London
Keating, London

Hughes, Manchester
Scruton, Liverpool

CLARINETS
Mr. Willman, London*
Powell, London*
Blomiley, Manchester
Glover, Manchester

BASSOONS
Mr. Baumann, London
Tully, London*
Boardman, Middleton
Molineux, Manchester

HORNS
Mr. Platt, 1st, London*
Rae, 2nd, London
Arnull, 3rd, Hull
Gaggs, 4th, Manchester
Bean, York
Thompson, Liverpool

TRUMPETS
Mr Harper, London*
Irwin, London
Clegg, C, junr Sheffield

TROMBONES
Mr. Smithies, jun., *(alto)* London
Bean, *(tenor)* London
Robinson, *(bass)* Manchester
Smithies, *(bass)* London

OPHICLEIDE
Mr Ponder, London

DRUMS
Mr Chipp, London*

HARP
Mr. Challoner, London

visitors to the ball on Monday, were taken up for picking pockets, and remanded till Saturday.'[31]

All the festivals attracted their patrons at comparatively high prices by offering them not only the leading singers of the day, but also the leading instrumentalists in the front-desk positions in the orchestra. This meant the players included many London players, and during the 1820s and 30s they, and the singers, tended to appear on a festival circuit of similar events. Some of the artists at Manchester came on from the Three Choirs at Worcester; and in 1836 many of them would go on to Norwich for the Norwich Festival the following week before going to Liverpool for the Liverpool Festival, which followed three weeks after Manchester.

The tradition, dating from the Westminster Handel Festivals, was already well established for the forces used in these festivals to be massive. In the case of Manchester, in fact, the make-up of the orchestra had to take account of the available venues. Although announced as '400 performers', according to the lists of names in the programme there was an orchestra of 101: 70 strings and 31 other instruments. It is worth noting that the contingent of players from London, while substantial, was not completely overwhelming. Of 34 violins, 11 were from London; of 16 violas half were from London, and so on. Many of the leading names of the day can be seen there on front desks: for example Lindley in the cellos, Dragonetti on double bass. Of the orchestra of 101, in fact 48 came from London. An orchestra on this scale would have been outside the regular experience of most members of that audience: it was something special.

Looking at the names of the choir is also interesting, not only for the breakdown of singers which, while impressive, was not particu-larly massive compared with what was to come, at a little over 200 – 60 sopranos, 53 altos, 53 tenors and 58 basses – but for the fact that all the altos were men. This is something that has received very little attention from period performers – what sort of noise did they make? We do not know; I cannot trace an account describing what distinctive noise they made, nor what effect having a male alto section had on the total sound. The tradition of male altos in festival choirs gradually declined over the nineteenth century, and certainly by the early twen-tieth century they were pretty well gone. A brief glance at Birming-ham Festival programmes for the later nineteenth century shows the

---

[31] Ibid.

" LET THE BRIGHT SERAPHIM."

Plate 7: the trumpeter Thomas Harper and Clara Novello (frontispiece to Volume II of *The Musical World*, June – September 1836) (*Author's collection*)

CORELLI'S SONATA, OP. 9.

Plate 8: Domenico Dragonetti and Robert Lindley (frontispiece to Volume I of *The Musical World*, March – June 1836). (*Author's collection*)

tradition dying out; at Birmingham in 1855 there were 71 men and 10 women altos; in 1867 there were still more men than women altos – 54 to 37 – but by 1897 there were only nine male altos and by 1903 the men were gone.[32]

The home town of each singer is given in the Manchester programme. From this we can see that 48 came from Liverpool and 117 from towns around Manchester. Indeed the Liverpool contingent held local rehearsals, and several of the works performed, including *Messiah*, were for them in effect a dry run for their own festival three weeks later. Only just over a quarter came from Manchester itself.

The repertoire was centred on *Messiah* and *The Creation*. Manchester had missed the boat in that Mendelssohn had promised his new oratorio, *St Paul*, to Liverpool. The miscellaneous nature of the programmes represents a by then only gradually changing tradition, and their considerable length would be characteristic of the whole nineteenth century. A few years ago the present writer was fortunate to acquire a set of programmes of the three 'Grand Miscellaneous Concerts' for this festival, which had been carefully interleaved and annotated by a now anonymous contemporary member of the audience.[33] We will refer to some of these annotations below.

The festival consisted of seven concerts preceded by a service and a ball, and ending with a fancy dress ball. This is *The Examiner*'s account of the sale of tickets:

The sale of tickets for all the performances, both at the church and theatre, and for the fancy dress ball, commenced at nine o'clock, on Friday, Sept. 9, in the spacious room of the new Grammar School, Long Millgate. The arrangements were admirable, there being a separate stall for tickets for each performance, and one or more gentlemen appointed for the sale of each priced ticket separately, thus avoiding all the pressure and difficulty which attended the procuring of tickets at the last Festival. Parties buying tickets for reserved seats drew a check or ballot-ticket with a progressive number, determining the order in which the places were to be chosen. The sale of tickets for reserved seats proceeded so rapidly, especially for favourite performances, that it was found necessary to reserve a certain number of tickets of each day and each price, for sale on Saturday and Monday. Of course for the tickets to seats which were not

---

[32] Bound programmes of the Birmingham Triennial Festival; copies in the author's collection.

[33] The concerts on the evenings of 13, 14 and 15 September 1836. It has not been possible to determine the provenance of these, and the dealer concerned could say only that he bought them some years ago at an auction in California.

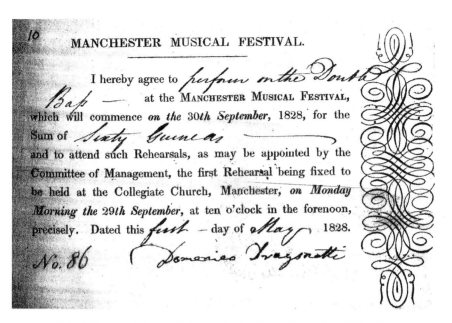

Plate 9: Dragonetti accepts terms at 60 guineas for the 1828 Manchester Festival. (*Manchester Libraries and Information, Henry Watson Music Library*)

reserved there was comparatively little demand, as there would be no advantage in purchasing them so early. On Saturday and Monday the demand for the remaining tickets was equally great; and the whole, with the exception of a very small number reserved for Tuesday, were quickly sold off. On Monday the sales were only held in the morning till ten o'clock, and for another short period in the interval between the times appointed for the choice of reserved seats. Those for the various morning performances were chosen at ten o'clock in the morning, and those for the evening performances at half-past two in the afternoon. At these periods the grammar school was much thronged; but owing to the excellent arrangements there was nothing like the confusion and pressure which are remembered to have been experienced on the like occasion in 1828. On Tuesday and Wednesday morning, and again in the afternoon, at four o'clock, sales took place at the town hall, of tickets for the various performances, and for the fancy dress ball, which had been withheld, in order to accommodate strangers and others not able previously to secure any.[34]

The organisers were thus in the very satisfactory position of knowing in advance of the performances that, not only did they not have to call on the guarantors, but that they had covered all their costs and made a

---

[34] *An Historical Account of the Grand Musical Festival ... 1836*, p. 10.

profit of up to £5,000 to benefit the charities which were the ostensible reason for the festival.

The festival required substantial temporary and permanent building in order to accommodate so large an assembly. The quantities of food consumed at the ball are a useful indicator of the scale of the exercise:[35]

Table 5: Food served at the Fancy Dress Ball in 1836

2,000 veal pieces
2,200 sandwiches
500lbs grapes
65 pineapples
25 pecks[36] of plums, apples and pears
73 pieces montes[37]
250 quarts jellies and creams
220 quarts of ices
137 dishes of pastry
72 dishes of savoy cakes
2 hogsheads of sherry and 2 of port made into negus[38]
10 bris lemon and orangeade

A substantial catering operation, but in reality one might wonder if it was not fairly inadequate for the numbers there.

As has already been suggested, the festival was a community event, and those who could not afford the ticket prices still wanted to know about it, to see who had come to town for it and even to hear a distant echo of the music from the performances: 'On Sunday the Collegiate Church was crowded in every part, by persons, many of whom there is little doubt, were attracted … more from curiosity to see the preparations that had been made, than from any feeling of devotion.'[39] As was general practice for much of the nineteenth century, there was a paying audience at the rehearsals, doubtless including many of those who could not afford the actual performances.

---

[35] 'The Fancy Dress Ball: Friday Evening.' *An Historical Account of the Grand Musical Festival ... 1836*, p. 22.

[36] A peck = 2 gallons or a quarter of a bushel; a hogshead = 1½ barrels or 52½ Imperial gallons.

[37] *Pièce montée*: a pyramid-shaped cake made of choux pastry.

[38] Negus: wine and hot water, sweetened and flavoured with lemon and spice.

[39] *An Historical Account of the Grand Musical Festival ... 1836*.

Monday morning was ushered in by the ringing of bells; and the weather being fine, the town assumed a gay and animated appearance. The first general rehearsal of the festival music was fixed for Monday morning to commence at nine o'clock. The majority of the performers engaged, both vocal and instrumental, had arrived on the Saturday and Sunday, and a strong muster took place in the Collegiate Church soon after the time appointed. Sir George Smart, who bad been in town about a week, superintending the necessary arrangements, was early at his post. His professional brethren, well aware of his punctuality on such occasions, were no loiterers, and before ten o'clock the rehearsal commenced. … The rehearsal did not terminate till nearly five o'clock, and at its conclusion the conductor addressed the band, chorus, and solo singers, in a complimentary strain. … There was also a general rehearsal the same evening, *at* the theatre, of many of the pieces to be played at the concerts. At this rehearsal, also, the same assiduity and attention were evinced. This rehearsal was not over till eleven o'clock at night.[40]

The difficulties of travelling before the railway are illustrated by two news stories in *The Musical World* concerning coach accidents.[41]

We regret to learn that the Peveril of the Peak, London and Manchester coach, was upset on Saturday night, near Bedford; when a gentleman of the name of O'Brien was killed on the spot, and Mr Pigott, (not the violinist, but his brother, who resides in Dublin) and Mr Ponder, the performer on the ophicleide, were much injured in their arms. The Committee at Manchester have behaved in a manner that does them credit, by ordering every attention to be paid to the sufferers. The absence of Mr Ponder, with his ponderous instrument, must be particularly felt; but we hope that he will be soon enabled to resume his professional duties.

Quoting the *Morning Post* they also reported an accident which had befallen the leading soloists including the Italian bass Luigi Lablache, who were travelling together.

A carriage, which was conveying Mori, Lablache, and Co. to Leicester, broke down close by the inn. The first who made his *debut* out … of the broken vehicle was Ivanoff; then followed Madame Assandri and her daughter; and last, though not the *least*, out crept Lablache. On seeing his mighty bulk, the crowd laughed right out; in which the basso buffo joined, with his accustomed good-humour. The Duke of Brunswick was passing through Leicester, on his

---

[40] Ibid.
[41] *Musical World*, vol. 3 no. 27, 16 September 1836, p. 12.

way to the Manchester Festival; and offered Lablache a seat in his carriage, which he accepted. When they arrived at Derby, a crowd gathered around, to have a peep at the Duke; when an old dame exclaimed, after eying Lablache, and taking him, as a matter of course, for the great man, 'Aye, aye, no wonder the balloon broke down with such a tremendous bulky piece of *goods.*'

There were seven concerts: four morning concerts of sacred music in the church, and three Grand Miscellaneous evening concerts of other music, in the Theatre. As far as the music was concerned, the first major attraction was a complete performance of *The Creation*, which opened the festival. This was an enormously long concert, for the complete oratorio was given as the first half, the second half consisting of extracts from Mozart's Requiem and the first performance of Bishop's cantata *The Seventh Way*, separated by four solo vocal numbers by Handel, Neukomm, Haydn and Cimarosa. From the report in *The Musical World* we learn that at the request of Lord Wilton the Benedictus of the Mozart Requiem was encored and – herald of what would happen the next day – that Malibran had fainted in the ante-room during the morning, but nevertheless she

came forward to sing the 'Holy, Holy Lord' of Handel. At the commencement of her singing, a tremulousness of voice was very perceptible, which, perhaps, did not detract from the sentiment of the words. … But, shortly after, in the 'Deh parlate' of Cimarosa, she summoned up all her energy of character, and produced one of the most perfect specimens of sublime pathos in singing we ever heard.[42]

The account of Lablache's powerful singing reports how he 'almost shook the roof off the church in the "Pro peccatis" of Haydn's *Stabat Mater*'. In the evening the same critic, while being duly appreciative of the performances, and especially 'Monsieur de Beriot's solo on the violin, which was brilliant, and exquisitely delicate', noted that 'the evening concert was not remarkable for novelty in the selection'.[43] The first part consisted of a Haydn symphony, eight vocal numbers (arias and ensembles), and a virtuosic flute and clarinet duet. Thus we had Haydn's Symphony No. 8 (i.e. No. 103, 'The Drumroll'); the Recitative and Romanza 'Cara suono lusinghier' from *Teobaldo ed Isolina* (with harp and flute obbligato) by Morlacchi (Assandri); the duet 'Non fuggir' (Ivanoff and Lablache) from Rossini's opera *Wil-*

---

[42] *Musical World*, vol. 3 no. 27, 16 September 1836, p. 6.
[43] Ibid., p. 8.

Plate 10: Luigi Lablache (from *The Illustrated London News*, 22 April 1843, p. 275). (*Author's collection*)

liam Tell; a song by Sir John Stevenson, 'Give that wreath to me' (Knyvett); a *Dialogo Brillante* for flute and clarinet by Nicholas Charles Bochsa; the scena 'Laws are mine' from Hérold's opera *Zampa* (Braham); a female trio (Bishop, Novello and Shaw) 'Night's lingering shades' from Spohr's *Azor and Zemira*; the recitative and aria 'Non più di fiori' from Mozart's *La Clemenza di Tito* (Malibran with *corno di bassetto* obbligato by 'Mr Willman'); the duet 'Deh con te' from Bellini's *Norma* (Caradori Allan and Assandri) and the sextet 'Sola, sola' from Mozart's *Don Giovanni* (Malibran, Assandri, Novello, Ivanoff, Phillips and Lablache). The second part was equally miscellaneous, starting with the overture to Beethoven's *Fidelio*, followed by another eight vocal numbers, and a violin concerto by Bériot,[44] the whole rounded off by Weber's overture to his opera *Oberon*. The vocal numbers were: the recit and aria 'Io l'udia' from Donizetti's *Torquato Tasso* (Caradori Allan); the recit and aria 'The light of other days' from Balfe's opera *The Maid of Artois* (Phillips) with harp and *cornet à piston* obbligato; the duet 'Oh! guardate che

---

[44] The celebrated violinist and composer Charles-Auguste de Bériot had married Malibran only the previous March.

figura' by Guglielmi (Malibran and Lablache); the song 'Come, summer come' by Henry Bishop (Mrs Bishop); the barcarolle 'Or che in cielo' from Donizetti's opera *Marino Faliero* (Ivanoff); Beethoven's terzetto 'Tremate! Empi tremate' (Novello, Bishop and Lablache); the song 'A Lonely Arab Maid' from Weber's *Oberon* (Shaw); and 'Largo al factotum' from *The Barber of Seville* (Lablache).[45]

The second sacred concert, given on the next day, was very much in the tradition of miscellaneous concerts, broken into three parts. The second part included the first British performance of Spohr's *The Christian's Prayer* (A. Mahlman's *Vater unser* set for four soloists, chorus and orchestra, first performed in Berlin in 1831). Malibran was again the highlight of the evening concert:

Marcello's duet 'Qual anelante cervo', was sung by Mme. De Beriot [Malibran] and Miss Clara Novello. For exquisite quality of tone in the two singers, correctness of style, and accuracy of execution, this performance was pronounced on all hands to be one of the gems of the day; while the effect that it produced upon the audience was so simultaneous and unequivocal, that many, forgetting the place where they were assembled, applauded openly. The piece was encored, and some time after it was repeated; for Mme. De Beriot was too ill and exhausted to go through the task immediately. In the descending passage in the bass, at the close of the quick movement, we were delighted with the crisp and beautiful playing of Lindley and Dragonetti.[46]

The Thursday morning concert consisted of *Messiah* and on Friday the musical performances ended with another enormous programme, which included Beethoven's *Christ on the Mount of Olives*. Barabara Mohn, in her pioneering paper on 'Personifying the Saviour',[47] has drawn attention to the religious objections to treating Christ as a person with a singing role in this work, but although she does not mention this Manchester performance, in fact it was sung in English, and it had a remarkable acceptance by the press. The concluding chorus, to the English words 'Hallelujah, This is the Kingdom', was encored. Subsequently it engendered a critical sermon and press comment.

---

[45] [Programme of the] *Manchester Grand Musical Festival 1836. On Tuesday Evening, September the 13th. A Grand Miscellaneous Concert at the Theatre-Royal* (Manchester: Printed by Henry Smith, 20 St Ann's-Square). Author's collection.

[46] *Musical World*, vol. 3 no. 28, 23 September 1836, p. 24.

[47] Barbara Mohn, 'Personifying the Saviour: English Oratorio and the Representation of the Words of Christ', *Nineteenth-Century British Music Studies*, vol. 1, ed. Bennett Zon (Aldershot: Ashgate, 1999), 227–41.

It is worth noting the practical logistics of these concerts. We are told of the first concert, for example, that the doors were open at 9.30 a.m.; the performance began at 11.00 and did not end before 3.15 p.m. A notable and possibly surprising feature of oratorio performances at early provincial music festivals is the proportion of women to men in the audience. From the view of the audience at York in 1823 in the engraving that prefaces Crosse's account of the York festival of 1823,[48] we can see that women outnumber men by perhaps five times. It was similar at Manchester. This is before the inception of public conveniences and I have not explored how the demands of personal comfort and hygiene were taken care of within such large and lengthy gatherings at that time.

The press was nothing if not thorough. We even have reports of the number and classification of carriages delivering members of audience to the halls, from which we may deduce that most people walked.[49]

The Musical World found that on the first day the town was

brim full, resembling more a clan-gathering than an emporium of mercantile occupation. On Tuesday the Collegiate Church presented a very imposing sight. The Patron's gallery, calculated to hold 764 persons (appointed to the 1 guinea subscribers) was full. The body of the church, that will contain 1013 (the fifteen shilling subscribers), was also full. The galleries, for the unreserved tickets, that will hold 952 persons, at half a guinea each, was only partially filled.

The last fact was explained by its being market day. 'At the theatre, in the evening, the boxes and pit, capable of containing about 1060 persons, were full. The gallery was not full.[50] *The Musical World* continued to report in a similar vein:

On the second day the whole of the reserved places were occupied; the unreserved ones (those in the gallery) not fully though more so than on the first day. … The Second Evening Concert was very crowded … The Third Day was

---

[48] Drawn by John Browne of York and engraved by Edward Finden, it was published by John Wolstenholme of York on 1 October 1824 and forms the frontispiece of Crosse's *An Account of the Grand Musical Festival.*

[49] 'The following is an account of the number of carriages that took up company at the Patron's Gate this afternoon: Noblemen's Carriages 3 (containing 13); Gentleman's Carriages 56 (200); Open Carriages 6 (16); Hackney Coaches and other hired vehicles 13 (50); Total Carriages 78 containing 279 occupants.' For the Wednesday morning concert the totals were 106 and 368 (*An Historical Account of the Grand Musical Festival … 1836*, p. 10).

[50] *Musical World*, vol. 3 no. 27, 16 September 1836, p. 6.

Collegiate Church
Thursday 1st October 1858.
MESSIAH.

By Ghost & Co. 12 Henrietta Street, Covent Garden.

MANCHESTER MUSICAL FESTIVAL.

BALL

MONDAY 12TH SEPR 1836.

Plate 11: Engraved tickets for the Festivals. Clockwise from top left: *Messiah* (1828); *The Creation* (1836); the Tuesday Concert (1836); the opening Ball (1836). (*Manchester Libraries and Information, Henry Watson Music Library*)

devoted to the *Messiah* … the church was crowded … The Third Evening Concert – By the hour of commencement, not a seat in the theatre was unoccupied; and even the standing room was almost equally full … The Fourth and Last Day, saw the church crowded to excess. [51]

Perhaps of greater interest, from the point of view of the celebrated singers taking part and for the nature of the programmes, were the miscellaneous concerts which very much continued the existing tradition of concert-giving. A large number of mainly vocal miscellaneous items, sung by the biggest names of the day, was the attraction. Inevitably we focus on the second miscellaneous concert, held on Wednesday evening, because that is the one event usually remembered from this festival, when Malibran collapsed, subsequently dying nine days later.

The first half of this concert started with Mozart's 'Sinfonia in D', though it is difficult to tell if it was the 'Prague' or the 'Haffner', and then continued with a succession of vocal numbers. Malibran appeared in a duet with her rival Caradori Allan. This was the last piece that Malibran ever sang, and during the duet 'Che diel? – In petto, si di solni' from Mercadante's opera *Andronico*, a vocal duel developed between these two leading prima donnas of the day. *The Musical World* gives us the basic facts: 'A composition of the most florid character. It was received with immense applause, and the last movement encored. She did repeat it; and then even her great energy gave way.' We learn rather more from the Manchester paper:

The duet from Andronico would have been charming, but for a trick of unlovely rivalry in Malibran, who, being second, took it upon herself to oversing the principal in the graces and shakes of Caradori's own choosing. This may have been a joke. It looked very like earnest. Malibran's eyes, let us hope, do not always shoot those fires to her friends.[52]

Clearly determined not to be outdone, in the encore Malibran redoubled her efforts:

In this last piece her exertions were prodigious, taking a fearful shake at the top of her voice with her customary daring enthusiasm. The storm of cheering which followed the stupendous essay was still unabated, when the unfortunate

---

[51] *Musical World*, vol. 3 no. 28, 23 September 1836, pp. 22–8.
[52] Reprinted in *An Historical Account of the Grand Musical Festival … 1836*, p. 18.

MARIE-FÉLICITÉ MALIBRAN.
BORN, MARCH, 24 1808.
DIED SEPT. 23. 1836.

WILLIAM BALLY, SCULP

Plate 12: Malibran by William Bally. According to a note left by Henry Watson after Malibran died, the Manchester sculptor William Bally was able to model this bust in wax, despite instructions left by Malibran's husband that there should be no death mask. The medallion was presented to the Henry Watson Music Library by John Towers in 1908. Owing to shrinkage of the wax, the medallion has cracked, fortunately without affecting the image of the singer's head. (*Manchester Libraries and Information, Henry Watson Music Library; photograph by Lewis Foreman*)

idol of an enraptured audience, who but a moment before was lighted up with fire and animation, sank in an exhausted state under the effect of her excitement.

The annotated programmes have the following first-hand comment, presumably made long before it was known that Malibran would not survive: 'This duet excited an extraordinary sensation and was encored. Never were the full rich tones of Malibran's voice heard to more advantage – Splendid Felicia.' It was well into the second half before it was announced that Malibran would be unable to sing again,[53] and she was replaced by Caradori Allan in 'Sento, o Dio' from *Così fan tutte*. Malibran's husband Bériot later substituted a violin concerto for a duet they were to have performed in the second half. Malibran did not recover, and died in Manchester nine days later on 23 September at the age of 28.

The Manchester Festival was soon followed by the Liverpool Festival of 1836, now remembered for the first English performance of Mendelssohn's *St Paul*, and which consequently upstaged Manchester artistically. Yet in 1836 Liverpool seems to have been a financial disaster, solely because of the absence of its star turn, Malibran. It proved to be the last Liverpool Festival, and the opening of the Philharmonic Hall in 1849 underlined that it continued to be a leading musical centre.

Neither Liverpool nor Manchester became part of the festival circuit of the later nineteenth century; and with the arrival of the railways, Birmingham and later Leeds became the festival centres, while the Hallé concerts in Manchester and the Liverpool Philharmonic Society in Liverpool would be among the country's first regular concert series from the mid-1850s.

To us the Manchester Festival of 1836 may well seem backward looking, with its miscellaneous and overlong programmes and its arrangements made via stagecoach links, but it also looked forward with its religious independence in presenting Beethoven's *Christ on the Mount of Olives*, with its forces roughly the same size as at most later nineteenth-century festivals (other than the Crystal Palace), and with a wide audience taking an interest, even if the cost of admission put it out of the reach of most working people. Perhaps over all the

---

[53] In the interleaved set of programmes, the contemporary commentator has written before Malibran was due to sing in the quintet 'Sento, o Dio' from *Così fan tutte*: 'Here it was announced that Madame Malibran was much indisposed, and their indulgence was solicited to a change rendered imperative by her absence. Alas poor Maria!!'

advent of the railway to Liverpool signalled how things would soon be, a reality once the rail link to Birmingham and London was complete less than two years later. This wonder of the age is vividly evoked in Moscheles's account of going by train from Manchester to Liverpool in February 1832 for the first time:

On the 18th I went by rail from Manchester to Liverpool; the fare was five shillings. At 1.30 I mounted one of the omnibuses, which carried all passengers gratis to the great building called the 'station'. Eight to ten carriages, each about as long as an omnibus, are joined closely to one another; each carriage contains twelve places with seats like comfortable arm-chairs; at a given signal every traveller takes his place, which is marked with the number of his ticket, and the railway guards lock the carriages. Then, and not before, the engine is attached to the foremost carriage; the motion, although one seems to fly, is hardly perceptible, and the traveller is amazed when he looks out of the window and observes at what incredible speed the train approaches the distant object and suddenly whirls by it. Words cannot describe the impression made on me by this steam excursion on the first railway made in England, and the transports I felt with an invention that seemed to me little short of magic.[54]

---

[54] Moscheles, *Recent Music and Musicians*, pp. 166–7.

Opera in Manchester, 1848–1899

ROBERT BEALE

A MANCHESTER OPERA ANNIVERSARY passed almost unnoticed[1] on 14 August 2005: 150 years since the first performance of *Raymond and Agnes* by Edward Loder, at the Theatre Royal, Peter Street. That the title and the name of the composer probably mean little to most readers is itself an indication of the extent to which the city has lost touch with its operatic history – and indeed our general ignorance of the Victorian flowering of original English vernacular opera before Gilbert and Sullivan. And yet this work is described in the *New Grove Dictionary of Opera* as its composer's 'masterpiece' in which 'the sense of drama and depth of musical characterization is close to Verdi'. Nigel Burton's article continues by referring to Loder's 'spiritual kinship with Schubert' and concludes: 'It is not exaggerated to regard Loder as the foremost composer of serious British opera in the early Victorian period.'[2]

Nicholas Temperley staged a revived version of *Raymond and Agnes* at Cambridge in 1966. He wrote then that: 'Loder's musical and dramatic gifts were far more impressive than those of his contemporaries, Balfe[3] and Wallace.[4] But he never achieved their degree of popular success because he aimed at a far higher level of sophistication – a level which was, on the whole, too high for the early Victorian public'. Of the confrontation scene between the hero Raymond and the evil Baron, which ends in a knife fight, he said: 'Loder piles one

---

[1] My article in the *Manchester Evening News* of 26 April 2005, headlined 'British opera that time forgot', is the only exception of which I am aware.

[2] Nigel Burton, 'Loder, Edward (James)', *The New Grove Dictionary of Opera*, ed. Stanley Sadie (London, 1992), vol. 2, pp. 1302–3.

[3] Michael Balfe (1808–70) was an Irish violinist, basso cantante, conductor and composer, studying in Rome, Milan and Paris. His career as a composer of English opera spans from 1835 to the end of his life: among his greatest successes were *The Siege of Rochelle*, *Keolanthe*, *The Bohemian Girl*, *The Rose of Castille* and *Satanella*, and his last work was the through-sung Italian opera, *Il Talismano*.

[4] Vincent Wallace (1812–65) was an Irish violinist, pianist and composer, friend of Berlioz, and chiefly known for *Maritana*, *Lurline* and *The Amber Witch* (premiered by Hallé at Her Majesty's Theatre, London, in 1861).

musical climax upon another with a dramatic intensity that I can only compare with Verdi.'[5]

Excerpts from the opera were included in the BBC's *Fairest Isle* series in 1994, with Judith Howarth, Justin Lavender and Gidon Saks in the principal roles. But apart from that the opera has lain unsung. The full score is in the Library of Congress in the USA (as is that of another Loder opera, *The Night Dancers*[6] – a version of the Giselle story. When Temperley restaged and republished it in 1966, the original spoken text was thought lost, and a reconstruction, with new dialogue by Max Miradin, was made from contemporary reports and summaries: it involved some plot adjustments and character name-changes, mainly for practical production reasons. Professor Temperley tells me[7] the original full libretto is now available. Perhaps one day it will live again.

Why *Raymond and Agnes* has never had a higher profile is illustrative of the outrageous fortunes that beset English opera and its composers in the nineteenth century. Loder (1813–65), whose father was musical director of the Theatre Royal, Bath, and a professor at the Royal Academy of Music, was a pupil in Frankfurt of Ferdinand Ries, the Beethoven acolyte and composer who later settled in London. His 1834 opera *Nourjahad* (libretto by S. J. Arnold, the playwright and manager who had first staged *Der Freischütz* in London, ten years earlier) was described by Sir George Macfarren,[8] no less, as 'the inaugural work of the institution of modern English opera'.[9]

Loder became musical director of the Princess's Theatre in London in 1846 and wrote *The Night Dancers* there (it was staged in New York and Sydney in 1847 and revived at Covent Garden in 1860). But

---

[5] *Musical Times*, 107 (1966), 307–10. This scene, 'strongly dramatical in expression', was encored on the first night, despite its strain upon the singers, according to the *Manchester Guardian* (15 August 1854). The overture, Act III quintet and Act IV quartet were also much admired.

[6] Princess's Theatre, London, 1846. It was revived at Manchester Theatre Royal under Loder in 1851 and at Covent Garden in 1860. Materials including a vocal score are in the Carl Rosa Archive in Liverpool Libraries. Perhaps not surprisingly, it is a hybrid opera-ballet, with the second half mainly terpsichorean.

[7] Personal communication, 2005.

[8] 1813–87: Principal of the Royal Academy of Music, Professor of Music at Cambridge, friend and biographer of Mendelssohn, he edited Chappell's *Popular Music of the Olden Time* and his English operas included *Robin Hood* (premiered by Hallé at Her Majesty's in 1860), *She Stoops to Conquer* (probably the only opera to include a staged presentation of a cricket match) and *Helvellyn* (set in the Lake District at the time of the Industrial Revolution).

[9] Quoted by Henry C. Banister in his *George Alexander Macfarren* (London, 1891).

financial success for an opera composer in England was elusive: keeping the wolf from the door depended far more on a regular output of music-shop ballads, on which he laboured constantly – in fact he was for some years under contract to a publisher to produce one a week. *The Old House at Home* is his, originally included in his opera *Francis the First* (Drury Lane, 1838).

The Manchester Theatre Royal, opened in Peter Street in 1845,[10] attracted him to its musical directorship in 1850. Charles Hallé, who had arrived two years before, was not the only musician to see opportunities in the burgeoning industrial city, but Loder's duties included the production of music for pantomimes, farces and plays, seemingly leaving little time for serious composition. However, the operatic content of the theatre's schedule increased dramatically in 1851, and Loder was able to engage the star performers Clara Novello[11] and Sims Reeves[12] for a season from 20 October to 13 December, almost nightly, which offered his own *The Night Dancers* along with thirteen other works, including *Don Giovanni*. Almost certainly this lost money, but Loder had an ally in the theatre's owner-manager John Knowles, and in 1853 they returned to the fray, with Italian, German and English opera from 17 October to 10 December, from a variety of performers, both touring[13] and locally based (Loder came up with his own version of Scribe's *Marco Spada*, entitled *Marco Tempesta*, which used his own music plus Auber's

---

[10] The third theatre of that name built in Manchester.

[11] Soprano (1818–1908), the fourth daughter of Vincent Novello, the organist, conductor, composer and publisher. She made her debut at Windsor in 1833, married and temporarily withdrew from public life in 1843, returning in 1850 and becoming the favourite of the Crystal Palace Handel festivals.

[12] John Sims Reeves (1818–1900), the favourite tenor of the Victorian public and known for his singing of *Tom Bowling* and *Come into the Garden, Maud*, made his debut in 1839 in Newcastle upon Tyne, and at La Scala, Milan, in 1846. He sang at Drury Lane in 1847 under Berlioz's baton and subsequently on practically every English stage.

[13] They included the famous bass Carl Formes (1815–89 – a particular favourite in London for his Caspar in *Der Freischütz*) and the conductor 'Herr Anschuetz', presumably Carl Anschütz, the German who by 1860 was enjoying a successful career at the Metropolitan Opera, New York. Anschütz had conducted in a German opera series at Drury Lane shortly before (*Musical World*, 10 September 1853). Formes's debut was as Sarastro in Cologne in 1842, and in 1849 in London. He was evidently a character. Santley, *Student and Singer: The Reminiscences of Charles Santley* (London, 1893, 289–91) describes him as a tall man with something of Baron Munchausen about him. He claimed, *inter alia*, once to have killed a grizzly bear with his hunting knife alone, to have played a key role in a victory in the American Civil War, and to have saved a ship in a storm on the Atlantic by taking the wheel when a wave dislodged its regular

overture, and ran for thirteen performances).[14] Emboldened, the two attempted an even longer autumn season in 1854, from 2 October to 16 December (preceded by a week's visit from the Covent Garden company), with the best names in the business – and in this season Charles Hallé's services as conductor were called upon.[15] It was announced as the 'annual operatic season', and the company included Hermine Rudersdorff[16] (her Manchester debut), Maria Caradori,[17] Alexander Reichardt[18] and Carl Formes.

Oddly, Hallé's account in his memoirs, written about forty years later, does not even mention Loder, only Knowles.[19] But Hallé's first biographer, E. J. Broadfield, writing in 1890, acknowledges the joint nature of the project,[20] as well as retailing some of Hallé's anecdotes about it. It is clear enough (despite the rose-tinted spectacles through which Hallé was determined to view things in later life) that the burden of a large repertoire and nightly changes resulted in increasing chaos and confusion as the season progressed,[21] in performances

---

occupant. He was also, Santley says (citing the evidence of Madame Rudersdorff – see note 16 below), a genuine crack shot. The Manchester English season featured Louisa Pyne and William Harrison, later the leaders and managers of the New English National Opera Company (see note 29 below).

[14] With a ballet in the second act and a tarantella in the third, it put over a hundred on stage in its crowd scenes. The *Manchester Guardian* admired an 'energetic and wild' brigands' chorus (22 and 26 October 1853). It included a Mr A. Harris and Mrs J. Wood among the performers.

[15] Described as 'the Royal Opera', the company had a chorus of thirty based on Drury Lane and Covent Garden singers, and a ballet. Smaller groups also performed in Liverpool (*Musical World*, 9 and 23 September 1854).

[16] 1822–82: Ukrainian-born German soprano, she made her debut at Karlsruhe in 1841 and Drury Lane in 1854, after which she appeared frequently at Covent Garden and other UK theatres and concert halls.

[17] Soprano (1800–65). She sang in the Philharmonic Society premiere of Beethoven's ninth symphony in 1825, and in the premiere of *Elijah* in 1846. It was in competition with her, in Manchester, that Maria Malibran Garcia so over-exerted herself that she died shortly afterwards, in 1836 – or so the story goes. For more on this, see Lewis Foreman's article in this issue of *Manchester Sounds*.

[18] Tenor (1825–85). Born in Hungary, he made his English debut in 1851.

[19] *The Life and Letters of Sir Charles Hallé: Being an Autobiography (1819-1860) with Correspondence and Diaries*, ed. C. E. Hallé and Marie Hallé (London, 1896), 120–2.

[20] E. J. Broadfield, *Sir Charles Hallé: A Sketch of his Career as a Musician* (Manchester, 1890), 44–7.

[21] The high (or low) point seems to have been on 4 December, when the originally advertised *Zauberflöte* was changed on the morning to *Robert le Diable*, and then at the time of performance to *Lucrezia Borgia*: it did not start until 8.30 pm, and everyone present was given a ticket for another night by way of compensation. Clearly there were plenty of spare tickets to go round (*Manchester Guardian*, 6 December 1854).

conducted by both Hallé and Loder (they seem to have shared the burden roughly equally) – quite apart from the meagreness of some attendances.

Hallé later blamed it all on the Crimean War, though there is little evidence of that having played a significant part in their failure. More to the point perhaps was the fact that the 'Philharmonic Hall' in Fountain Street, Manchester (an opportunist scheme designed to fill the gap between the two Free Trade Halls),[22] opened in late October with a series of concerts featuring London musicians conducted by Alfred Mellon, and singers including Clara Novello and Sims Reeves. Attendances were reported to have exceeded 4,000, and Louis Jullien and his orchestra were announced as a forthcoming attraction.[23] It is noteworthy that only a year later, Hallé was complaining to his private diary about the 'hocus-pocus' of another Jullien visit, spoiling attendances at one of his chamber concerts.[24]

Two things are certain, however. First, the experiment of establishing a long season of Manchester-produced opera was never attempted again. Second, that Loder was inspired at the time to write a new 'grand opera' of his own. Announcements in the press in autumn 1854 said that *Raymond and Agnes* was 'in rehearsal' and would be included by the end of the year.[25]

It did not appear. The annual pantomime superseded the opera season in December 1854, and that was the end of the Loder-Hallé venture.[26] But Loder was not done for yet: his programmes the following summer (1 July – 17 August and 27–31 August) included not only the new comic operas *Leonie* (by Joseph F. Duggan) and *Mephistofeles* (Meyer Lutz), but also, at last, *Raymond and Agnes*. Its conception during the glorious debacle of 1854 was undoubtedly the reason for its ambitious nature, a point not lost on the *Manchester Guardian*

---

[22] Possibly using the 1807 building which had previously been the second Theatre Royal and for a time the Queen's Theatre.

[23] *Manchester Guardian*, 25 October, 8 and 18 November.

[24] *Life and Letters of Sir Charles Hallé*, 354; *The Autobiography of Charles Hallé, with Correspondence and Diaries*, ed. Michael Kennedy (London, 1972), 151–2.

[25] *Musical World*, 23 September; *Manchester Courier*, 11 November.

[26] Hallé mistakenly says the season was 'in the winter of 1855' and this has usually been corrected to read '1854–5', but in fact it was all over on 16 December 1854. Compare *Life and Letters of Sir Charles Hallé*, 120–2; *The Autobiography of Charles Hallé*, 130; Broadfield and Fuller-Maitland in *Grove*, 2nd edn (1906); Michael Kennedy, *The Hallé Tradition*, (Manchester, 1960), 28; Ann Kersting, *Carl Halle – Sir Charles Hallé: Ein europäischer Musiker* (Hagen, 1986), 30.

reviewer, who observed that it had been designed to be sung by performers of the stature of Reichardt and Formes, engaged for the previous autumn's season.

As it was, the tenor, George Perren,[27] 'did his best'[28] and the cast included the debutante Miss Johnson along with Miss Sophie Lowe and the comic baritone Henry Drayton in the villainous role of the Baron. The opera ran for a week, plus two days more (after a visit from the Royal Italian Opera of Covent Garden). It was produced again in 1859 in London (modified to three acts instead of four) with Susan Pyne[29] and Madame Rudersdorff, where it ran for a week again. But the conductor was now George Loder (probably the composer's uncle), as Edward was seriously ill. He had resigned his Manchester position in 1855, and soon after the London performances of *Raymond and Agnes* lapsed into a coma from which he never recovered. Few were aware of his illness or his passing, but one who did not forget him was Hallé: in April 1862 he wrote to the *Manchester Guardian* appealing for donations to help Loder, now suffering paralysis and 'in a state of such destitution as to call for immediate assistance'.[30]

To modern tastes Loder's opera is a strange thing, with a plot based on an episode from the 'gothic horror' novel of 1796, *The Monk*, by Matthew 'Monk' Lewis, in which two young lovers seek to escape from the cursed Baron by staging an appearance of the bloodstained ghost of St Agnes, reputed to walk on a certain night – and then the real ghost appears.[31] But the elements of an orgy, a ghost, a trance, an escape, a robbers' gambling chorus and a wedding are not unfamiliar in other operatic stories, and the librettist, Edward Fitzball,[32] added a

---

[27] Later to be associated with the Crystal Palace opera company and to help save the fledgling Carl Rosa company at its birth in Manchester in 1873 – see John Ward, 'Carl Rosa Comes to Town', *Manchester Sounds*, 5 (2004–5), 5–27, at 17–18.

[28] *Manchester Guardian* review, 15 August 1855.

[29] The sister of Louisa Pyne (1832–1904), a celebrated soprano. Louisa and Susan were the elder siblings, by about twenty years, of J. Kendrick Pyne, the organist of Manchester Cathedral and Town Hall, who died in 1938.

[30] *Manchester Guardian*, 12 April 1862.

[31] The episode also formed the basis for *La Nonne sanglante*, the opera written by Scribe, begun by Berlioz and finished by Gounod, which had considerable success in its day.

[32] 1792–1873: Dramatist and reader at Covent Garden and Drury Lane, he also authored Balfe's *The Siege of Rochelle*, *Keolanthe* and *The Maid of Honour*, Wallace's *Lurline* and Macfarren's *She Stoops to Conquer*, and co authored Wallace's *Maritana*.

classic villain in the Baron (bringing its references, to our ears, uncomfortably close to Gilbert and Sullivan's *Ruddigore*).

The exceptional qualities brought by Loder, however, were the minimal use of 'ballads' (reflective songs often included in English operas, with the front-parlour sheet music trade in mind), a Germanic influence amid the cantabile-cabaletta arias of the familiar Italian style (the opera includes melodrama and narrative ballad, as used by Weber, and echoes of *Fidelio* and *The Marriage of Figaro* have been discerned, to Loder's credit),[33] and the 'Verdian' quality of some of the writing – the duets and ensembles in particular. And hereby hangs a minor mystery. Could Loder, labouring away in the Manchester of the 1850s, have actually encountered the mature style of the Italian genius? *Il Trovatore* and *La Traviata* are contemporary with *Raymond and Agnes*, but had not been heard in England when Loder was writing (*Il Trovatore*, however, came to Manchester in the Italian season just after Loder's premiere: *La Traviata* and *Rigoletto* followed in 1857, and *Luisa Miller* in 1858).[34] *Nabucco* had been heard in London in 1850, and *Rigoletto* in 1853, so perhaps Loder picked up some ideas on a visit there. One Verdi opera, however, not only had been heard in London as long before as 1845 but was performed in Manchester, at Edward Loder's own theatre, in the summer of 1854, brought by the visiting Royal Italian Opera (conducted by Julius Benedict) shortly before the lengthy Loder-Hallé season began, and that was *Ernani*. Could this have been the spark that fired the English composer to produce his Verdian 'masterpiece'?

The list
The story of opera in Manchester in the second half of the nineteenth century, except for *Raymond and Agnes* (which I shall stick my neck out to claim as the only serious opera of any stature to be composed, rehearsed and premiered in the city), is not notable for great historic landmarks. But there have been minor ones – and the compilation which ends this article, though highly provisional and more a sketch

---

[33] George Biddlecombe, *English Opera from 1834 to 1864* (New York, 1994), 93–8.
[34] In a season given by the 'New National English Opera Company' (led by J. H. Tully), which also included Bishop's *Guy Mannering*.

of territory to be surveyed than an accurate chart, demonstrates one thing with particular clarity: there was, certainly after the 'Cotton Famine' of the early 1860s, no lack of appetite for musical theatre in the city, and after the inauguration of the Carl Rosa Opera Company in the city in 1873 it seems to have been almost insatiable.

This approximate summary of performances and the repertoire on offer each year also puts into perspective the supposition, sometimes made, that the Manchester of the past lacked real interest in opera.[35] In fact, its later nineteenth-century inhabitants enjoyed a far greater number of opera performances than we are accustomed to now. It is true that from the 1870s the market was dominated by comic opera (particularly French light opera, which was never displaced by the success of Gilbert and Sullivan – the genre that they did pretty well see off, with the exception of the three pieces rather comically known as 'the English Ring',[36] was that of English 'ballad' opera). Such material overlapped in kind with what we would now call 'musicals', and so comparisons with the present should not be unrealistic (and drawing the line as to what should count as opera, even if called 'comic opera', is always a problem). But it is also true that the Manchester population, if offered it in accessible terms – i.e. in translation rather than a foreign language – would often flock to 'grand opera', too, and that the range of fare they were given puts today's attempts at operatic enterprise into the shade.

The Theatre Royal was joined in musical presentation by the Prince's Theatre (near the corner of Oxford Street and Mosley Street)[37] in 1867, the Queen's Theatre[38] (Bridge Street – site of the present Masonic Hall) in 1872, the Comedy Theatre (Peter Street, opposite the YMCA)[39] and the St James's Theatre (Oxford Street)

---

[35] Cf. Kennedy, *The Hallé Tradition*, 194: 'Since the days when Hallé conducted opera in 1850s [until 1915], it had enjoyed only fitful popularity.' And Kersting, *Carl Halle*, 188–9, suggests that the number of operatic excerpts in Hallé's concert programmes was attributable to the fact that neither Manchester nor Liverpool had a dedicated opera house or resident operatic ensemble.

[36] *The Bohemian Girl* by Balfe, *Maritana* by Wallace and *The Lily of Killarney* by Benedict. These three remained in popular repertoire well into the twentieth century – indeed, the first was revived by Beecham in Liverpool and London for the Festival of Britain in 1951.

[37] Built in 1864, it became a regular receiving house for musical theatre of various forms, and in 1875 temporarily renamed itself the Prince's Opera House.

[38] Built in 1862, and reopened in 1870. When it closed in 1911, a new theatre built on Quay Street was at first called the New Theatre, then the New Queen's Theatre. Designed primarily for non-musical performances, it is today, somewhat ironically,

both in 1884, and in 1892 by the new Palace Theatre (though its main purpose was variety). Alfred Cellier's[40] time as musical director of the Prince's Theatre (1872/3–1877) was exceptionally fruitful.

The companies that visited the city included both the major London troupes: the long-established Italian Opera, based at Her Majesty's Theatre (usually conducted by Luigi Arditi[41] and his colleague Auguste Vianesi)[42] and for many years managed by 'Colonel' James Henry Mapleson;[43] and the Royal Italian Opera, which was established at Covent Garden in 1845, when Sir Michael Costa led a secession from Her Majesty's. The company formed by Louisa Pyne and William Harrison in 1857 became known as the Royal English Opera and was also briefly based at Covent Garden: it visited Manchester in 1865 (the later Royal English Opera Company was a D'Oyly Carte creation: the house he built for it, opened in 1891 and closed in 1892,[44] is now London's Palace Theatre).

But it was the formation of Carl Rosa's[45] English Opera Company in 1873 – inaugurated in Manchester – which transformed the situation for the city's opera-lovers and led the flood of touring opera

named the Manchester Opera House in recognition of Beecham's First World War seasons there.

[39] Later renamed the Gaiety, it became the base for Miss Horniman's exploits in repertory theatre.

[40] Alfred Cellier, like his brother François, was closely associated with Sullivan. Like Sullivan, he was a boy chorister at the Chapel Royal, and after his time in Manchester was the first permanent conductor of D'Oyly Carte's company, at the Opera Comique in London. François Cellier shared the role with him and was chiefly associated with the Savoy Theatre, while Alfred later pioneered the D'Oyly Carte operation in the USA and Australia. His story is told in Raymond J. Walker, 'A Manchester Connection: Alfred Cellier (1844–1891), Composer and Conductor', *Manchester Sounds*, 5 (2004–5), 89–104.

[41] Luigi Arditi (1822–1903), who settled in London in 1858, was a leading conductor of Italian opera of his generation, appearing at Vienna, St Petersburg, and in the USA. He premiered *Cavalleria Rusticana* in the UK in 1891 and *Hansel and Gretel* in 1894. He was also the composer of the once very popular *Il Bacio* (*The Kiss*).

[42] Auguste Vianesi (1837–1908), opera conductor in London, Paris, St Petersburg and New York.

[43] 1830–1901: Manager at Drury Lane 1858, Her Majesty's 1860 and 1862-67, Lyceum 1861, Drury Lane 1868 and 1871–6, Her Majesty's 1877–81, 1887 and 1889, he was also active in the USA and operatic touring in Britain.

[44] This was the second doomed attempt to establish an English National Opera House in the later part of the century. Mapleson proposed something similar in 1875; his chosen site is now New Scotland Yard.

[45] Carl Rose (later Rosa), 1842–89, was born in Hamburg and made his official English debut at the Crystal Palace in 1866. However, a 'young German' violinist named as 'Carl Rossi' appeared in Manchester early in 1859, so Manchester may have heard him first (see *Musical World*, 19 February 1859). He met the amply proportioned soprano

enterprises that lasted to the end of the century. Its beginnings have already been vividly described in this journal.[46]

One observation on the repertoire performed is that some works which we would consider among the most popular of classic operas today enjoyed only relatively modest success in the nineteenth century – mainly, one suspects, on moral grounds, in a city where many of the middle class were devout and some suspected the theatre generally of being evil. *La Traviata*, which made its first appearance in the city in 1857 (the year of the great Art Treasures Exhibition which brought Hallé's own orchestra to birth), was at first roundly condemned by the *Manchester Guardian* as 'a compound of vice and sickly sentiment'.[47] Later in the century, *Carmen* also progressed in people's affections slowly, and probably for similar reasons.

Gounod's *Faust*, however, first seen in 1863, was a constant favourite, particularly in the English version, also entitled *Faust and Marguerite*. Other Gounod operas such as *Mirella*, *The Mock Doctor* and, in 1880, *La Reine de Saba* (under the English title, *Irene*), were presented in the light of *Faust*'s popularity, but never emulated it. *Romeo and Juliet* (1890) made more impression: *Philémon et Baucis* (1893) less. Manchester's first taste of Offenbach was in 1868, with *The Grand Duchess of Gerolstein*; Burnand and Sullivan's *Cox and Box* made its debut the following year (*The Contrabandista* came in 1874). Both were to be enduring favourites. *Orphée aux Enfers* came in 1870, followed by a string of French novelties over the years including Offenbach's *The Princess of Trebizonde*, *La Belle Hélène*, *Barbe-Bleue*, *Geneviève de Brabant*, *La Périchole*, Hervé's *Chilperic*, Lecocq's *La Fille de Madame Angot*, *Giroflé-Girofla* and *Pepita*, and Planquette's *Les Cloches de Corneville*, *Rip van Winkle* and *Paul Jones*.

In 1871 there was a season of German operetta, which oddly does not seem to have caught on, despite Manchester's large German

Euphrosyne Parepa, one of Hallé's associates in his London opera season of 1860–1, while on tour in the USA in 1867 and married her, forming the Parepa-Rosa Opera Company there in 1869. The venture was revived in the UK in 1873 (using Carl Rosa's name only). Parepa died in 1874 – see following note.

[46] Ward, 'Carl Rosa Comes to Town'.
[47] 29 August 1857.
[48] Sullivan's Manchester connections were comprehensively explored in Martin Thacker, 'Sullivan: The Manchester Connection', *Manchester Sounds*, 2 (2001), 89–112.

community: perhaps at the time they were too respectable and committed to Hallé's music to indulge in such levity.

The new English operetta phenomenon of Gilbert and Sullivan[48]
did, however, decidedly catch on. After *Trial by Jury* in 1876, then
The Sorcerer and *H.M.S. Pinafore* in 1878 (and *The Children's
H.M.S. Pinafore* in 1880 – children's versions of the most popular hits
were a recurrent attraction), new titles came almost every year with
great success: *The Pirates of Penzance* in 1881, *Patience* in 1882,
Iolanthe in 1883, *Princess Ida* in 1884, *The Mikado* in 1885, *Ruddigore* in 1887, *The Yeomen of the Guard* in 1888, *The Gondoliers* in
1890. The D'Oyly Carte company had by then already evolved into
the touring repertory troupe of recent memory, though new Sullivan
pieces came to Manchester as they appeared, too: *Haddon Hall* in
1893, *Utopia Ltd* in 1894, *Ivanhoe* and *The Chieftain* in 1895, *The
Grand Duke* in 1896.

Serious opera was chiefly served by the Carl Rosa company. In its
heyday a remarkable mobile production factory, it served not only to
preserve some of the earlier tradition of native English opera but also
to bring new work from abroad to British, and particularly northern,
ears. Works such as Balfe's *Satanella*, *The Siege of Rochelle* and *Il
Talismano*, Wallace's Lorelei-story *Lurline*, Macfarren's *Robin
Hood*[49] and Wallace's *The Amber Witch*[50] were occasionally revived,
and novelties such as Stanford's *The Canterbury Pilgrims*, Boito's
Mefistofele, Verdi's *Aida*, Halévy's *La Juive*, even Frederick Cowen's
Thorgrim and Hamish MacCunn's *Diarmid*, and a range of repertory
from Gluck to Wagner were offered to the Manchester public. In the
1890s came the new hit by Mascagni, *Rustic Chivalry*, Bizet's
Djamileh, Verdi's *Otello*, Leoncavallo's *Pagliacci*, and
Humperdinck's *Hansel and Gretel*. Rosa's policy – at least as seen
with hindsight after his death[51] – was to bring a new addition to his
company's repertory to open in Manchester each season, and even at
the end of the century this continued, with Victor Holländer's[52]
operetta, *San-Lin*, the last example in the century (11 May 1899).

---

[49] Originally premiered by Hallé in London in 1860, with Sims Reeves, and then brought
to Manchester Free Trade Hall in 1861, but not conducted by Hallé, who was busy at Her
Majesty's with *The Amber Witch* by Wallace.

[50] Originally premiered by Hallé in London in 1861.

[51] According to the *Manchester Guardian,* 12 May 1899.

[52] It had premiered the year before in Breslau and been taken to Berlin. Victor Holländer
was the father of Friedrich, who was to write *Falling in Love Again* for Marlene Dietrich.

The summer of 1888 was notable for a visit from the Russian National Opera Company, appearing at the Comedy Theatre from 9 to 20 July, and again from 20 August to 1 September. They presented Glinka's *A Life for the Czar*, ten performances of Anton Rubinstein's *The Demon*, *Rigoletto* in Russian, and four showings of a new work from the pen of Peter Tchaikovsky: *Mazeppa*. The *Manchester Courier* identified the first night of *The Demon* as its first performance in England:[53] this was not, however, stated of *Mazeppa*, although it might nearly have been – it was announced repeatedly during July as 'in preparation', but did not make it to the Comedy Theatre stage until 27 August, after an interruption in the run when the company was, presumably, performing elsewhere.[54] Among the singers in *The Demon* was the young Joachim Tartakov (1860–1923), later to be the leading baritone and then director of the Mariinsky Theatre in St Petersburg. The conductor was Josef Truffi.

There have been a few world premieres of comic opera in the city, notably *The Sultan of Mocha*,[55] by Cellier, in 1874 (Cellier's less successful *The Tower of London* (1875), *Nell Gwynne* (1876) and *Belladonna* (1878) also premiered in Manchester), and *The Lancashire Witches* by Frederick Stanislaus (Cellier's successor at the Prince's Theatre: the vocal score of this was published by Forsyth's) in 1879. Others included John Crook's *The King's Dragoons* (1880), G. B. Allen's *The Wicklow Rose* (1882), Alfred D. Taylor's *The Bachelors* (1885), Edmond Audran's *Indiana* (1886), Joseph Batchelder and Oliver Gregg's *La Serenata* (1888), and A. H. Behrend's *Iduna* (1889). Cellier's later works also came to Manchester after opening in London: *Dorothy*[56] in 1887 (and repeatedly), *Doris* in 1889 and *The Mountebanks* in 1892.

---

[53] In fact it was not, as the opera had been performed at Covent Garden, in Italian, on 21st June, 1881, Rubinstein conducting (see The Times of that date and the following day).

[54] The break was apparently for a visit to Liverpool, where it has been observed that the company performed Mazeppa on 6th August, 1881 - "thus . . . the first of Tchaikovsky's operas to be heard in England". The company went on to London and hired the Royal Albert Hall for concert performances in national costume, with financially disastrous results. In October they took the Novelty Theatre for their three operas, ending destitute, and a public appeal had to be launched to get them back home to Russia. (Geoffrey Norris: Stanford, the Cambridge Jubilee, and Tchaikovsky (David & Charles, Newton Abbot, 1980), 255–6.

[55] The story of this work is told by Walker, 'A Manchester Connection', 93–101 (see also Thacker, 'Sullivan', 107). *The Sultan of Mocha* was revived in Manchester in 1876, 1878, 1879, 1880 and 1887. A further run, at Manchester's Comedy Theatre, in 1892, was probably of the revised London version mentioned by Walker at page 101.

But the century ended in glory with the Carl Rosa Opera Company's production, at the Theatre Royal, of *La Boheme*, a UK premiere, for which Puccini travelled to Manchester (22 April 1897), and, in 1896 and 1897, the company's premieres of two components of its English-language Ring cycle: *Die Walküre* and *Siegfried*. After his father's earlier work in building the Carl Rosa company, the second Eugene Goossens was to be found conducting in the city in the late 1890s – with the ambitious Arthur Rousbey Opera Company.

Two events to note, which were much thought of in their time were, like those Carl Rosa Wagner productions, first performances of English translations: Flotow's *Martha*, in English,[57] first heard at the Theatre Royal, on 2 October 1868,[58] and Hallé's first concert presentation of Berlioz's *The Damnation of Faust*, in his daughter Marie's translation, in 1881. Both were billed as 'first performances in England' but, since the works in question had been heard in their original languages earlier, do not qualify as UK premieres in the modern sense.[59]

But Hallé's edition of the Berlioz *Faust* did lead him – very near the end of his life, and the only recorded occasion after 1861 – back into the opera pit. The Carl Rosa Company staged the work in Manchester in 1894. They opened at the Theatre Royal on 19 March with a schedule which featured both the Gounod and Berlioz *Faust*s, and the first performance of the latter was 'conducted on this special occasion by Sir Charles Hallé'.[60] The Berlioz *Faust*, though quite familiar now as a concert piece, was, as a staged presentation, a source of some fascination. The day after Hallé's night, the *Manchester*

---

[56] A revision of *Nell Gwynne* (see Walker, 100–1): *Dorothy* was the most successful West End production of the nineteenth century, outrunning even *The Mikado*.

[57] Flotow included the Irish song *The Last Rose of Summer* in the score, which gave the piece great popularity, much as did the 'ballads' in the operas of Balfe and his contemporaries.

[58] It ran for fourteen performances and probably helped to take the gloss off the beginning of Hallé's second concert season, which was opening at the same time and suffered poor attendances.

[59] *Martha* was performed in Italian at Covent Garden on 1 July 1858. *La Damnation de Faust* was performed by Pasdeloup and French forces at Her Majesty's Theatre on 1 June 1878 (see contemporary reports and *The Times*' review of Hallé's first performance of his English version in London – 24 May 1880). Consequently, the Manchester performance on 5 February 1880 should be crossed off the list of Hallé UK premieres.

[60] *Manchester Guardian*, 17 March 1894. Other performances were conducted by Claude Jaquinot.

Guardian reported: 'It is a long time, indeed, since any musical event was regarded with such interest in Manchester.'[61] The house was crowded in every part, the band 'augmented', and the performance generally received with enthusiasm. The use of mechanical 'horses' for the last act ride was, however, 'at first received with scarcely concealed laughter, and it was almost a relief to arrive at Pandemonium', said the critic.

His main theme, though, was the respect accorded to the ageing conductor, who, he said, 'was received with ringing cheers as he advanced to the place in the orchestra which he filled with such credit to himself during a memorable season of opera forty years ago'. Rose-tinted spectacles were by now on universal issue.

---

[61] 21 March 1894.

Operas given in Manchester, 1848–1899 (titles are given in the form used for the first performance in any particular year)

1848 Local (1 day), Balfe and company [incl. Jenny Lind] (2 days), Theatre Royal
The Daughter of the Regiment, Lucia di Lammermoor, La Sonnambula

1849 Italian opera (local chorus and orchestra), Theatre Royal (16 days)
Norma (4), *Lucia di Lammermoor* (2), *Il Barbiere di Siviglia* (2), *I Puritani*, *L'Elisir d'Amore* (2), *Lucrezia Borgia* (3), *La Sonnambula* (2)

1850 Local: English opera (12 days), Italian opera (8 days), Theatre Royal
The Bohemian Girl (4), *The Bondsman* (2), *La Sonnambula* (3), *Maritana* (2), *The Bride of Lammermoor* (2), *Lucrezia Borgia*, *Norma* (3), *Il Barbiere di Siviglia* (3)

1851 Local (Loder) but with Clara Novello and Sims Reeves: Italian opera (7 weeks), English opera (3 weeks), Theatre Royal
La Sonnambula (5), *L'Elisir d'Amore* (2), *Lucia di Lammermoor* (5), *I Puritani* (2), *Il Barbiere di Siviglia* (2), *Lucrezia Borgia* (2), *The Bohemian Girl* (7), *Maritana* (5), *The Night Dancers* (6), *The Mountain Sylph* (5), *Masaniello*, *The Daughter of the Regiment*, *Norma* (4), *Don Giovanni* (5)

1852 Theatre Royal: *The Beggars' Opera* (2 days)

1853 Jarrett's company, with Formes: Italian opera (19 days), 'German and Italian opera', conducted by Anschutz (5 days), English opera (Loder) (10 days), Theatre Royal
Der Freischütz (2), *Norma* (3), *Lucrezia Borgia* (2), *Marco Tempesta* (13), *Les Huguenots* (3), *Fidelio* (2), *The Bohemian Girl* (2), *The Somnambulist* (2), *Fra Diavolo* (2), *The Bride of Lammermoor*, *The Crown Diamonds*, *Maritana* (2), *The Enchantress*

1854 Royal Italian Opera from Covent Garden (7 days), Local (Loder and Hallé) (10 weeks), Theatre Royal
Norma (6), *Ernani*, *La Sonnambula* (3), *Otello/Rossini)*, *Fidelio* (5), *Il Barbiere di Siviglia* (3), *I Puritani* (4), *Der Freischütz* (5), *Lucia di Lammermoor* (4), *La Favorita* (2), *Il Seraglio* (3), *Lucrezia Borgia* (6), *Les Huguenots* (4), *Semiramide*, *Die Zauberflöte* (4), *Robert le Diable* (5), *Don Giovanni* (2), *Masaniello*

1855 English opera (Loder) (30 days), Royal Italian Opera from Covent Garden (12 days), Theatre Royal
La Sonnambula (5), *The Bohemian Girl* (6), *The Bride of Lammermoor* (3), *Robert the Devil*, *Leonie* (6), *Mephistopheles* (5), *Raymond and Agnes* (5), *Don Giovanni* (2), *I Puritani*, *Il Barbiere di Siviglia* (2), *Il Trovatore* (2), *Semiramide*, *Norma*, *Don Pasquale*, *Lucrezia Borgia*

1856 – No performances

1857 Her Majesty's Theatre Company (6 days), Lyceum Company [i.e. former Covent Garden company] (8 days), Theatre Royal
Il Trovatore (2), *The Marriage of Figaro*, *Don Pasquale*, *Don Giovanni*, *La Traviata* (3), *Fra Diavolo*, *Rigoletto*, *I Puritani*, *La Sonnambula*, *Lucia di Lammermoor*, *Maritana*

1858 New National English Opera Company (6 weeks), Theatre Royal
Il Trovatore (2), *La Sonnambula* (3), *Norma* (2), *The Bohemian Girl* (3), *Guy Mannering* (6), *Louisa Miller* (2), *Maritana* (2), *Martha* (15)

1859 Italian opera [combined London company, cond. Arditi] (8 days), Theatre Royal
Les Huguenots, *Il Trovatore* (3), *Lucrezia Borgia*, *The Daughter of the Regiment*, *La Traviata*, *Don Giovanni*

1860 Her Majesty's Theatre Company (2 weeks), Theatre Royal
Il Trovatore, *La Favorita*, *Don Giovanni* (2), *Lucrezia Borgia* (2), *Norma* (3), *Macbeth*, *Orfeo*, *Rigoletto*, *Martha*

Magico (2), *L'Africaine*, *La Sonnambula*, *Le Nozze di Figaro*, *Il Barbieri di Siviglia*, *Semiramide*, *Lucia di Lammermoor*, *The Grand Duchess* (7), *La Belle Helene* (2), *Barbe-Bleue* (6), *A Mere Blind/Offenbach* (6), *Cox & Box* (10), *Martha/Reese* (6), *The Dancing Quakers* (5), *Kissi-Kissi/Offenbach arr. Burnand* (4), *Do Re Mi Fa/Offenbach* (6)

1874 Carl Rosa company (16 days), Her Majesty's Theatre Company (2 weeks), Theatre Royal
Crystal Palace English Opera Company (4 weeks), Sims Reeves company (3 days), Queen's Theatre
Metropolitan Opera Company (cond. Cellier: 2 weeks), Emily Soldene Company (2 weeks), London Philharmonic Company (1 week), Prince's Theatre
Maritana (5), *The Bohemian Girl* (8), *The Lily of Killarney* (5), *Il Trovatore* (5), *Don Giovanni* (2), *Fra Diavolo*, *The Crown Diamonds* (4), *Faust* (4), *Satanella*, *La Sonnambula* (3), *Dinorah*, *Il Talismano* (3), *Le Nozze di Figaro*, *Martha*, *Les Huguenots*, *Semiramide*, *Fidelio*, *The Rose of Castile* (3), *Lucia di Lammermoor*, *Lurline* (2), *The Beggars Opera*, *The Waterman*, *Guy Mannering*, *Cox & Box* (12), *The Contrabandista* (6), *La Fille de Madame Angot* (12), *Geneviève de Brabant* (6)

1875 Carl Rosa Opera (3 weeks), Theatre Royal
Her Majesty's Theatre Company (5 days), Queen's Theatre
Various incl. Royalty Company, Kate Santley Opera Company, Mme Dolaro Opera Company (10 weeks), Royal Italian Opera (1 week), Prince's Theatre (aka Prince's Opera House)
The Marriage of Figaro (2), *Fra Diavolo* (2), *Faust*, *Il Trovatore* (3), *The Bohemian Girl* (4), *Maritana* (4), *The Siege of Rochelle* (2), *Zampa* (2), *Semiramide*, *Rigoletto*, *Der Freischütz*, *Les Huguenots*, *Don Giovanni* (2), *The Sultan of Mocha* (?15), *La Fille de Madame Angot* (9), *The Grand Duchess* (12), *La Périchole* (9), *Trial by Jury* (9), *The Council of Ten* (6), *The Tower of London* (24), *La Sonnambula*, *Lohengrin* (2), *Dinorah*, *La Figlia del Reggimento*, *Un Ballo in Maschera* Act II

1876 Carl Rosa Opera (4 weeks), D'Oyly Carte company (1 week), Italian opera (based on Her Majesty's Theatre Company) (1 week), Theatre Royal
Special company (1 week), Queen's Theatre
Various incl. Campobello Opera Company (9 weeks), D'Oyly Carte company (6 weeks), Prince's Theatre
Zampa (4), *Faust* (2), *The Lily of Killarney* (4), *The Bohemian Girl* (5), *The Water Carrier* (3), *Fra Diavolo*, *Il Trovatore* (4), *Der Freischütz* (2), *The Porter of Havre*, *Maritana*, *The Grand Duchess* (6), *Les Huguenots* (2), *Don Giovanni* (2), *Martha*, *Norma*, *Pauline*, *Fidelio*, *The Flying Dutchman*,

Faust & Marguerite (6), *The Sultan of Mocha* (18), *Trial by Jury* (28), *Gi-roflé-Girofla* (12), *Le Nozze di Figaro*, *Il Flauto Magico*, *Gugliemo Tell*, *La Traviata*, *The Duke's Daughter* (2), *La Périchole* (2), *La Fille de Madame Angot* (6), *Genevieve de Brabant* (3), *Chilperic* (2), *The Big Judicial Separation Suit*, *Princess Toto* (6), *Cattarina* (6), *Nell Gwynne* (24)

1877 Grand Duchess Opera Company (1 week), R. W. South's Opera Company (1 week), Theatre Royal
Rose Hersee English Opera Company (2 weeks), Queen's Theatre
Carl Rosa Opera Company (11 days), Prince's Theatre
The Grand Duchess (4), *La Fille de Madame Angot* (4), *La Belle Hélène* (4), *Maritana* (4), *The Rose of Castile*, *The Lily of Killarney* (2), *The Bride of Venice*, *The Bohemian Girl* (3), *The Marriage of Figaro*, *The Huguenots*, *The Merry Wives of Windsor* (3), *Robin Hood*, *Satanella*, *Faust*, *The Crown Diamonds*

1878 Carl Rosa Opera Company (4 weeks), Theatre Royal
Italian opera (1 week), Rose Hersee and Walsham English Opera Company (2 weeks), Queen's Theatre
Various (6 weeks incl. The Comedy Opera Company 1 week), Prince's Theatre
The Lily of Killarney (4), *Faust* (3), *Maritana* (6), *The Golden Cross*, *The Flying Dutchman*, *The Bohemian Girl* (6), *The Huguenots* (4), *Il Trovatore* (3), *Lurline* (3), *The Merry Wives of Windsor* (2), *La Sonnambula* (3), *Linda di Chamonix*, *Ruy Blas*, *Der Freischütz*, *Le Nozze di Figaro*, *Il Flauto Magico*, *Norma*, *Martha*, *Fra Diavolo*, *Belladonna* (6), *The Sultan of Mocha* (6), *The Sorcerer* (14), *Trial by Jury* (10), *La Périchole* (6), *H.M.S. Pinafore* (4)

1879 Special company (5 weeks), Pyatt's Ballad Opera (3 days), Theatre Royal
Italian opera (Mapleson company) (1 week), Queen's Theatre
Various (4 weeks), Pattie Laverne's Opera Company (2 weeks), Cave-Ashton Company (1 week), Emily Soldene Company (4 weeks), D'Oyly Carte Opera Company (2 weeks), Carl Rosa Opera Company (2 weeks), Prince's Theatre
Faust & Marguerite (10), *Madame Favart* (6), *The Beggars Opera*, *The Lancashire Witches/Stanislaus* (18), *Carmen* (14), *Faust*, *Le Nozze di Figaro*, *Fidelio*, *The Sultan of Mocha* (12), *Babiole* (18), *Il Trovatore*, *The Lily of Killarney*, *Maritana*, *Martha*, *Fra Diavolo*, *Les Cloches de Corneville* (14), *Geneviève de Brabant* (5), *La Fille de Madame Angot*, *Chilperic*, *H.M.S. Pinafore* (12), *Maritana*, *Piccolino* (2), *The Bohemian Girl* (3), *The Lily of Killarney* (2), *Mignon* (3), *The Taming of the Shrew*

1880 Various (3 weeks), Frederick Archer English Opera Company (5 weeks), D'Oyly Carte children's company (1 week), Theatre Royal
Special company (2 weeks), Queen's Theatre
Various (3 weeks), Carl Rosa Opera company (3 weeks), D'Oyly Carte Opera Company (4 weeks), Soldene Opera Company (3 weeks), special company (2 weeks), Prince's Theatre
Maritana (3), *Il Trovatore* (2), *The Crown Diamonds*, *Fra Diavolo* (2), *Faust* (2), *La Sonnambula* (3), *The Lily of Killarney* (3), *Irene* (3), *The Sultan of Mocha* (18), *La Traviata*, *Faust & Marguerite* (6), *The Children's Pinafore* (6), *The King's Dragoons/Crook* (12), *Turn Out Again* (12), *Les Cloches de Corneville* (12), *Madame Favart* (6), *Carmen* (2), *Mignon*, *The Taming of the Shrew*, *Lucia di Lammermoor* (2), *H.M.S. Pinafore* (12), *The Sorcerer* (12), *Naval Cadets* (6), *La Fille de Madame Angot* (3), *Chilperic*, *Geneviève de Brabant*, *Carmen* (4), *La Fille du Tambour Major* (12), *Mignon* (2), *The Bohemian Girl*, *Zampa*, *Stradella*, *The Cadi* (2)

1881 Carl Rosa Opera Company (1 week), Theatre Royal
Various (5 weeks), Queen's Theatre
D'Oyly Carte Opera Company (4 weeks), special company (2 weeks), various (1 week), children's company (2 weeks), Wyndham and D'Oyly Carte Company (1 week), Carl Rosa Opera Company (1 week), Prince's Theatre
Carmen (2), *Mignon* (2), *The Lily of Killarney*, *The Bohemian Girl* (2), *Lohengrin* (3), *Faust* (2), *The Princess of Trebizonde* (6), *The Grand Duchess* (6), *Il Trovatore*, *La Traviata*, *Maritana* (2), *Lucrezia Borgia*, *La Sonnambula*, *The Curse of the Crusoes/Williams* (6), *Leah the Jewish Maiden* (6), *The Pirates of Penzance* (24), *La Fille du Tambour Major* (6), *Les Cloches de Corneville* (12), *The Children's Pinafore* (6), *The Children's Cloches de Corneville* (6), *Olivette/Andran* (6)

1882 Various (3 weeks), D'Oyly Carte Opera Company (5 weeks), Theatre Royal
Eldred's Opera Bouffe Company (2 weeks), Royal English Opera (1 week), Queen's Theatre
Special company (3 weeks), Kate Santley Opera Company (3 weeks), Emily Soldene Opera Company (2 weeks), Carl Rosa Opera Company (3 weeks), Prince's Theatre
The Lancashire Witches (12), *Patience* (18), *The Pirates of Penzance* (6), *Les Manteaux Noirs* (6), *The Grand Duchess* (4), *La Fille de Madame Angot* (4), *The Princess of Trebizonde* (6), *Faust* (2), *Maritana* (3), *The Huguenots*, *The Piper of Hamelyn/Nessler* (2), *Il Trovatore* (2), *Les Cloches de Corneville* (18), *La Mascotte* (12), *Geneviève de Brabant*, *The Wicklow Rose/Allen* (2), *Carmen*, *The Merry Wives of Windsor* (2), *The Bohemian Girl* (3), *Mignon*, *The Rose of Castile* (2), *Moro/Balfe*, *Fidelio*, *The Flying Dutchman*, *La Dame Blanche* (2), *Lucrezia Borgia*, *Boccaccio* (6)

1883 D'Oyly Carte Opera Company (6 weeks), Italian opera (2 weeks), Theatre Royal

D'Oyly Carte Opera Company (4 weeks), Carl Rosa Opera Company (2 weeks), Royal English Opera Company (1 week), Florence St John Opera Co (2 weeks), Prince's Theatre

Iolanthe (24), *Patience* (12), *Il Trovatore* (2), *Rigoletto* (2), *Lucrezia Borgia*, *Lucia di Lammermoor*, *La Traviata* (3), *Faust* (4), *Ernani*, *La Sonnambula*, *Rip van Winkle* (12), *Estrella/Searelle* (6), *Mignon* (3), *Esmeralda* (2), *The Bohemian Girl* (2), *Carmen* (3), *Maritana*, *The Piper of Hamelyn* (2), *The Lily of Killarney*, *Madame Favart* (4), *Barbe-Bleue* (4), *Lurette* (4)

1884 D'Oyly Carte Opera Company (8 weeks), Frank Emery's Comedy Opera Company (1), Theatre Royal

Royal English Opera Company (1 week), Tanner's English Opera Company (1 week), Comedy Theatre

Carl Rosa Opera Company (5 weeks), D'Oyly Carte Opera Company (1 week), Shiel Barry and W. Hogarth Company (1 week), Mme Soldene Opera Company (3 weeks), Alexander Henderson's Opera Company [Van Biene and Lingard] (1 week), Prince's Theatre

Royal English Opera Company (1 week), special company (1 week), St James's Theatre

Princess Ida (24), *Iolanthe* (18), *La Vie* (6), *Patience* (8), *The Pirates of Penzance* (2), *HMS Pinafore* (2), *Il Trovatore* (5), *Maritana* (5), *The Crown Diamonds*, *The Marriage of Figaro* (3), *The Lily of Killarney* (3), *Faust* (3), *Fra Diavolo* (2), *Carmen* (7), *Esmeralda* (3), *Colomba*, *The Bohemian Girl* (4), *Mignon* (2), *Lucia di Lammermoor*, *Les Cloches de Corneville* (6), *Chilperic* (3), *La Fille de Madame Angot* (3), *Olivette* (6), *Dick* (6), *The Canterbury Pilgrims*, *The Beggar Student* (3), *Esmeralda*, *La Favorita*, *Mignon*, *Flaka* (6), *Estrella* (5)

1885 Carl Rosa Opera Company (2 weeks), D'Oyly Carte Repertory Company (1 week), D'Oyly Carte Children's Company (1 week), D'Oyly Carte Opera Company (4 weeks), Cornelie D'Anka Company (1 week), Theatre Royal

Tanner's English Opera Company (3 weeks), Various (5 weeks), Comedy Theatre

D'Oyly Carte Opera Company (1 week), Various (1 week), Carl Rosa Opera Company (2 weeks), Van Biene and Lingard (2 weeks), Prince's Theatre

Royal English Opera Company (1 week), St James's Theatre

Carmen (2), *The Beggar Student*, *Il Trovatore*, *The Bohemian Girl* (7), *Mefistofele* (2), *Esmeralda*, *Mignon*, *The Lily of Killarney* (4), *Faust*, *HMS Pinafore* (4), *Patience* (6), *Children's Pirates of Penzance* (6), *The Mikado*

(14), *The Sorcerer* (13), *The Pirates of Penzance, The Grand Duchess* (13), *Mme Favart* (3), *The Crown Diamonds* (2), *La Sonnambula, The Marriage of Figaro* (3), *Faust* (2), *Peter the Shipwright* (5), *Don Giovanni, Fra Diavolo, Satanella, Maritana, Olivette* (6), *Les Cloches de Corneville* (6), *Children's La Fille de Madame Angot* (6), *Trial by Jury* (6), *The Bachelors/Taylor* (6), *Mignon, Manon* (2), *Esmeralda, Falka* (12), *The Silver Shield* (6)

1886 Carl Rosa (2 weeks), D'Oyly Carte's New York Company (2 weeks), Violet Cameron Opera Company (1 week), Her Majesty's Theatre Company (2 weeks), Captain Bainbridge's Company (1 week), Theatre Royal
Leslie's English Opera Company (1 week), Various (2 weeks), Comedy Theatre
J. W. Turner's English Opera Company (1 week), Queen's Theatre
Shiel Harry and Hogarth's Comic Opera Company (1 week), Carl Rosa Opera Company (2 weeks), Van Biene and Lingard (1 week), Prince's Theatre
Carmen, Mignon (3), *Ruy Blas* (2), *The Bohemian Girl* (6), *The Lily of Killarney* (2), *Faust* (4), *Esmeralda, Fadette, Nadeshda* (2), *Maritana* (3), *Il Trovatore* (2), *The Mikado* (12), *The Commodore* (6), *La Traviata, Il Barbiere di Siviglia, Lohengrin* (2), *Lucia di Lammermoor* (2), *La Sonnambula* (2), *La Favorita, Rigoletto, Don Giovanni, Martha, The Beggar Student* (6), *A Masked Ball, Der Freischütz, The Marriage of Figaro* (2), *La Fille de Madame Angot* (6)*, Indiana/Audran* (6), *Les Cloches de Corneville* (6), *Falka* (12), *Carmen* (3), *Il Trovatore* (2), *Don Giovanni* (2), *Nadeshda, Fadette, Fra Diavolo* (2)

1887 Carl Rosa Opera Company (4 weeks), Edgar Bruce's Company (1 week), Various (2 weeks), Her Majesty's Theatre Company (1 week), Theatre Royal
J. W. Turner Opera Company (1 week), Comedy Theatre
D'Oyly Carte Opera Company (6 weeks), various (5 weeks), Van Biene and Lingard's Company (2 wccks), Carl Rosa Opera Company (2 weeks), Barry and Hogarth's Company (1 week), Prince's Theatre
Carmen (9), *Maritana* (6), *Lohengrin* (2), *The Bohemian Girl* (8), *Don Giovanni, Esmeralda, Faust* (6), *Nordisa/Corder* (10), *The Lily of Killarney, Martha, Il Trovatore* (3), *Mignon* (2), *La Béarnaise* (6), *The Beggar Student* (9), *The Sultan of Mocha* (3), *Ernani, Don Giovanni, Il Flauto Magico, Fra Diavolo* (2), *The Mikado* (15), *Ruddigore* (18), *Dorothy* (18), *Pepita* (12), *Indiana* (6), *Patience* (3), *Lucia di Lammermoor, The Beautiful Galatea* (2), *Masaniello* (2), *Les Cloches de Corneville* (6)

1888
Carl Rosa Opera Company (3 weeks), Royal Italian Opera (1 week), Theatre Royal

Russian National Opera Company (3 weeks), Barry and Hogarth's Company (2 weeks), J. W. Turner's Opera Company (1 week), Comedy Theatre
D'Oyly Carte Opera Company (4 weeks), H. J. Leslie's Company (1 week), Carl Rosa Opera Company (1 week), Van Biene and Lingard's Company (2 weeks), Prince's Theatre
The Marriage of Figaro (6), *The Bohemian Girl* (4), *The Beautiful Galatea, Nordisa, Maritana* (3), *Carmen* (3), *Masaniello* (2), *Robert the Devil* (6), *Don Giovanni* (2), *Faust* (3), *Aida, Ernani, Lohengrin, Il Trovatore, Les Huguenots, A Life for the Czar* (6), *The Demon* (10), *Rigoletto* (4), *Mazeppa* (4), *Les Cloches de Corneville* (4), *The Gypsy Gabriel* (2), *Robin Hood* (2), *H.M.S. Pinafore* (2), *The Mikado* (10), *Patience* (2), *The Pirates of Penzance* (2), *Dorothy* (6), *The Yeomen of the Guard* (11), *La Juive* (2), *Mignon, Falka* (6), *Les Manteaux Noirs* (6), *La Serenata/Batchelder and Gregg*

1889 Carl Rosa Opera Company (4 weeks), Van Biene and Lingard's Company (1 week), special company (1 week), Theatre Royal
St John Opera Company (2 weeks), Horace Guy's Company (1 week), Various (3 weeks), Comedy Theatre
Valentine Smith and Company (1 week), Queen's Theatre
Carl Rosa Light Opera Company (2 weeks), H. J. Leslie's Opera Company (1 week), D'Oyly Carte Opera Company (3 weeks), Various (3 weeks), Carl Rosa Opera Company (1 week), Van Biene and Lingard's Company (3 weeks), Prince's Theatre
Robert the Devil (2), *The Puritan's Daughter* (2), *Mignon* (2), *The Bohemian Girl* (14), *Star of the North* (14), *The Jewess* (3), *Faust* (1), *The Marriage of Figaro, Maritana* (7), *Esmeralda, The Old Guard* (6), *Nanon* (6), *Delia* (6), *Carina* (6), *Fritz* (6), *Les Manteaux Noirs* (6), *Paul Jones* (12), *Dorothy* (12), *The Yeomen of the Guard* (18), *Doris* (12), *Carmen* (2), *Lucia di Lammermoor, The Brigands* (18), *Iduna/Behrend*

1890 Carl Rosa Opera Company (4 weeks), D'Oyly Carte Opera Company (5 weeks), Arthur Roberts' Company (1 week), D'Oyly Carte American Company (1 week), Carl Rosa Light Opera Company (1 week), Theatre Royal
Valentine Smith and Company (1 week), Queen's Theatre
H. J. Leslie Opera Company (2 weeks), Carrie Coste and Company (1 week), Carl Rosa Light Opera Company (1 week), special company (2 weeks), Carl Rosa Opera Company (2 weeks), Prince's Theatre
Romeo and Juliet (8), *Star of the North* (4), *Faust* (5), *Lurline* (6), *The Bohemian Girl* (5), *Mignon, Maritana* (2), *Carmen* (6), *Lohengrin, The Lily of Killarney* (2), *The Gondoliers* (30), *Guy Fawkes* (6), *The Mikado* (3), *The Yeomen of the Guard* (3), *Marjorie* (6), *The Red Hussar* (6), *Nadgy* (6),

Paul Jones (6), *Paola* (6), *Dorothy* (6), *La Traviata* (2), *Thorgrim*, *Martha*, *Lucia di Lammermoor*, *The Marriage of Figaro*, *La Sonnambula*

1891 Carl Rosa Opera Company (5 weeks), Horace Lingard's Company (1 week), D'Oyly Carte Opera Company (5 weeks), Theatre Royal
Various (4 weeks), Arthur Rousbey's Opera Company (1 week), Comedy Theatre
Carl Rosa Carmen Company (2 weeks), Carl Rosa Light Opera Company (1 week), Various (4 weeks), Carl Rosa Opera Company (1 week), Lingard's Company (1 week), Prince's Theatre
The Daughter of the Regiment (11), *The Huguenots* (5), *Carmen* (9), *The Bohemian Girl* (7), *Mignon* (3), *Lohengrin*, *Faust* (4), *Romeo and Juliet* (2), *The Talisman* (4), *La Traviata*, *Falka* (6), *The Mikado* (8), *The Yeomen of the Guard* (5), *The Gondoliers* (6), *The Match Girl* (6), *Iolanthe* (6), *In Summer Days* (12), *La Fille de Madame Angot* (6), *Martha* (6), *Marjorie* (12), *L'Enfant Prodigue* (12), *Fra Diavolo*, *The Black Domino*, *La Cigale* (12), *Fauvette* (6), *Maritana*, *Il Trovatore*

1892 Carl Rosa Opera Company (2 weeks), D'Oyly Carte Opera Company (7 weeks), special company (1 week), Georgina Burns' Company (1 week), Horace Lingard's Company (1 week), Theatre Royal
Various (3 weeks), W Hogarth's Company (1 week), J. W. Turner's Grand Opera Company (3 weeks), Arthur Rousbey's Opera Company (2 weeks), Comedy Theatre
Various (5 weeks), Carl Rosa Opera Company (3 weeks), Prince's Theatre
Valentine Smith Grand Opera Company (1 week), St James's Theatre
Special company (1 week) Palace Theatre
Rustic Chivalry (11), *Fra Diavolo* (2), *Romeo and Juliet*, *The Daughter of the Regiment* (8), *The Prophet*, *Carmen* (3), *The Bohemian Girl* (6), *Don Giovanni* (2), *Aida* (3), *The Mikado* (9), *The Match Girl* (2), *The Yeomen of the Guard* (3), *Iolanthe* (5), *The Waterman* (6), *The Vicar of Bray* (12), *Cinderella/Rossini* (6), *The Gondoliers* (4), *Patience* (4), *Falka* (3), *Pepita* (2), *The Old Guard*, *The Sultan of Mocha* (18), *The Princess of Trebizonde* (6), *Les Cloches de Corneville* (6), *Martha* (2), *The Bride of Lammermoor*, *Il Trovatore* (2), *La Sonnambula* (2), *Maritana* (5), *Faust* (4), *Un Ballo in Maschera* (3), *The Mountebanks* (18), *Brother George* (6), *Djamileh* (2), *L'Amico Fritz* (4), *La Cigale* (6), *The Blind Beggars* (6)

1893 Carl Rosa Opera Company (6 weeks), Van Biene's Company (1 week), D'Oyly Carte Opera Company (4 weeks), Horace Lingard's Comic Opera Company (1 week), Royal Italian Opera (1 week), Theatre Royal
Arthur Rousbey's Company (1 week), Queen's Theatre
Various (2 weeks), D'Oyly Carte Opera Company (1 week), Carl Rosa Opera Company (4 weeks), Prince's Theatre

Djamileh (4), *Rustic Chivalry* (17), *Aida, La Traviata, Carmen* (4), *L'Amico Fritz* (11), *Faust* (5), *The Bohemian Girl* (8), *The Daughter of the Regiment* (2), *Maritana, Tannhäuser* (9), *Fra Diavolo, The Postillion of Lonjumeau* (3), *Il Trovatore* (2), *Otello/Verdi* (2), *The Lily of Killarney, The Golden Web* (9), *Blue-Eyed Susan* (6), *The Gondoliers* (2), *Patience* (2), *The Mikado* (2), *The Pirates of Penzance* (3), *Iolanthe* (2), *The Yeomen of the Guard, Falka* (4), *Pepita* (2), *Orfeo* (5), *Pagliacci* (6), *Lohengrin, Carmen, Philemon et Baucis, I Rantzau* (3), *Les Huguenots, Haddon Hall* (6), *The Vicar of Bray* (6), *The Mountebanks* (6), *Haddon Hall* (6), *Nitouche* (6)

1894 Carl Rosa Opera Company (6 weeks), D'Oyly Carte Opera Company (10 weeks), Horace Lingard's Company (1 week), special company (1 week), Royal Italian Opera Company (1 week), Theatre Royal
Arthur Rousbey Grand Opera Company (1 week), Comedy Theatre
Carl Rosa Opera Company (3 weeks), Prince's Theatre
Special company (1 week), St James's Theatre
Faust (5), *Carmen* (7), *Lohengrin* (6), *Fra Diavolo* (3), *Romeo and Juliet, The Daughter of the Regiment* (7), *Rienzi* (5), *Faust/Berlioz* (5), *Lucia di Lammermoor* (3), *Orpheus and Eurydice* (5), *Rustic Chivalry* (4), *The Bohemian Girl* (7), *Il Trovatore, L'Amico Fritz, Tannhäuser* (5), *The Gondoliers* (5), *H.M.S. Pinafore* (7), *The Mikado* (7), *The Pirates of Penzance* (2), *The Yeomen of the Guard* (4), *Patience, Iolanthe* (2), *Utopia Ltd* (24), *Brother Pelican* (6), *Trial by Jury* (4), *The Gaiety Girl* (6), *Falstaff* (2), *Les Huguenots, La Navarraise, Die Meistersinger, Cavalleria Rusticana* (3), *Pagliacci* (2), *Martha, Maritana* (3), *Esmeralda* (2), *At Santa Lucia/Tasca* (2), *The Merry Wives of Windsor, La Fille de Madame Angot* (3)

1895 Carl Rosa Opera Company (6 weeks), D'Oyly Carte Opera Company (2 weeks), D'Oyly Carte Repertory Company (3 weeks), Theatre Royal
Arthur Rousbey's Company (3 weeks), Comedy Theatre
Special company (1 week), Carl Rosa Opera Company (2 weeks), Prince's Theatre
Faust (4), *Carmen* (5), *Martha* (2), *Esmeralda* (2), *Der Freischütz* (3), *Hansel and Gretel* (16), *The Bohemian Girl* (5), *Tannhäuser* (3), *Bastien et Bastienne* (3), *Maritana* (5), *Il Trovatore* (3), *Ivanhoe* (7), *The Daughter of the Regiment* (4), *Orpheus and Eurydice* (4), *Pagliacci* (6), *The Merry Wives of Windsor, The Chieftain* (8), *Cox and Box* (12), *The Vicar of Bray* (6), *The Pirates of Penzance, Trial by Jury, The Sorcerer* (4), *Iolanthe* (3), *Patience, H.M.S. Pinafore, The Mikado* (4), *The Yeomen of the Guard* (3), *The Gondoliers* (3), *Utopia Ltd* (4), *The Lily of Killarney* (2), *Cavalleria Rusticana* (2), *The Beautiful Galatea, The Marriage of Figaro* (3), *Love and War* (6), *The Flying Dutchman* (4), *Son and Stranger* (3)

1896 Carl Rosa Opera Company (4 weeks), D'Oyly Carte Repertory Company (3 weeks), D'Oyly Carte Opera Company (3 weeks), special company (1 night), Theatre Royal
Arthur Rousbey Opera Company (3 weeks), Comedy Theatre
Carl Rosa Opera Company (2 weeks), Prince's Theatre
Tannhäuser (10), *Mignon* (4), *The Flying Dutchman* (3), *Faust* (4), *The Bohemian Girl* (4), *La Vivandiere/Godard* (4), *Ivanhoe* (2), *Maritana* (4), *Son & Stranger*, *Rustic Chivalry* (2), *Carmen* (3), *Lohengrin*, *The Meistersingers* (4), *The Mikado* (5), *Iolanthe* (3), *Princess Ida* (2), *The Yeomen of the Guard* (3), *Patience* (2), *The Gondoliers* (3), *Trial by Jury*, *The Pirates of Penzance*, *H.M.S. Pinafore*, *The Grand Duke* (16), *Utopia Ltd* (7), *Shamus O'Brien/Stanford*, *The Lily of Killarney* (3), *Il Trovatore*, *The Daughter of the Regiment* (2), *The Marriage of Figaro*, *Don Giovanni* (2), *Pagliacci*, *Die Walküre* [company premiere] (2), *Romeo & Juliet*

1897 J. W. Turner Opera Company (1 week), Children's company, Regent Theatre, Salford
D'Oyly Carte Opera Company (3 weeks), Carl Rosa Opera Company (3 weeks), John Tiller Opera Company (1 week), Theatre Royal
Arthur Rousbey Opera Company (4 weeks), Comedy Theatre
Carl Rosa Opera Company (2 weeks), Prince's Theatre
Il Trovatore (5), *Maritana* (8), *The Bohemian Girl* (6), *The Daughter of the Regiment* (3), *The Waterman*, *The Mikado* (6), *The Yeomen of the Guard* (5), *His Majesty* (2), *The Meistersingers* (2), *Carmen* (5), *Tannhäuser* (6), *Don Giovanni* (2), *Romeo & Juliet*, *Faust* (7), *Mignon* (2), *The Valkyries*, *Rustic Chivalry* (4), *Pagliacci* (4), *Robert the Devil*, *The Bohemians* (4), *Children's Les Cloches de Corneville* (6), *La Poupée/Glover* (6), *The Gondoliers* (3), *The Pirates of Penzance* (2), *The Sorcerer* (2), *Lucia di Lammermoor*, *Martha* (2), *Le Villi* (2), *The Lily of Killarney* (2), *Siegfried*

1898 J. W. Turner Opera Company (2 weeks), Regent Theatre, Salford
Redmondt Opera Company, (1 night), Tiller Opera Company (1 week), Carl Rosa Opera Company (4 weeks), D'Oyly Carte Opera Company (3 weeks), Theatre Royal
Special company (3 weeks), Prince's Theatre
Arthur Rousbey Opera Company (2 weeks), Queen's Theatre
Moody Manners Opera Company (2 weeks), Comedy Theatre
The Rose of Castille (2), *The Bohemian Girl* (9), *The Daughter of the Regiment* (4), *Maritana* (8), *Faust* (9), *Il Trovatore* (8), *Hansel & Gretel*, *The King's Sweetheart/Glover* (5), *Cavalleria Rusticana* (2), *Pagliacci* (2), *A Poet's Dream*, *Carmen* (3), *The Martyr of Antioch* (2), *Tannhäuser* (4), *Tristan and Isolde* (3), *Son and Stranger*, *Mignon* (2), *Lohengrin*, *Diarmid/Hamish MacCunn*, *La Poupée/Glover* (18), *The Mikado* (5), *The Gondoliers* (6), *Iolanthe* (2), *The Yeomen of the Guard* (4), *Utopia Ltd* (2),

The Pirates of Penzance, The Sorcerer, Patience (2), *The Lily of Killarney* (4), *The Puritan's Daughter* (3)

1899 J. W. Turner Opera Company (3 weeks), National Grand Opera Company (1 week), Regent Theatre, Salford
National Grand Opera Company (1 week), D'Oyly Carte Repertory Company (3 weeks), D'Oyly Carte Opera Company (2 weeks), Carl Rosa Opera Company (2 weeks), Theatre Royal
Moody Manners Opera Company, Comedy Theatre (3 weeks), William Hogarth's Opera Company (1 week), Comedy Theatre
Special companies (5 weeks), Prince's Theatre
Faust (11), *The Daughter of the Regiment* (2), *Il Trovatore* (8), *Maritana* (7), *The Lily of Killarney* (5), *The Bohemian Girl* (7), *The Rose of Castille, Cavalleria Rusticana* (3), *Tannhäuser* (4), *Pagliacci* (2), *Hansel & Gretel* (2), *Don Giovanni, The Puritan's Daughter* (2), *The Amber Witch* (4), *The Yeomen of the Guard* (2), *The Gondoliers* (3), *H.M.S. Pinafore* (3), *Iolanthe* (2), *Utopia Ltd, Princess Ida, The Mikado* (3), *The Lucky Star/Caryll* (7), *Carmen* (2), *Lohengrin* (2), *San Lin, Les Cloches de Corneville* (6), *Falka* (6), *La Poupee* (6), *Haddon Hall* (7), *Trial by Jury, Paul Jones* (6), *Ma Mie Rosette* (14), *Masaniello* (3)

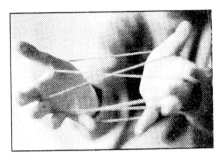

Henry Watson and the Manchester Gentlemen's Glee Club

ANDREW POULTER

IN 1906, the eminent Mancunian musician and benefactor Dr Henry Watson compiled a souvenir book celebrating the seventy-fifth anniversary of the founding of the Manchester Gentlemen's Glee Club, of which he was the music director.[1] Henry Watson's life and musical career are well covered by William Waterhouse in an earlier article in *Manchester Sounds*[2] and also in an article by June Tomlinson.[3]

By the 1890s Watson was a highly respected professional musician and much sought after, particularly by choral societies, which were very much in vogue at that period. At one time he was conducting eight different choral societies and preparing some forty-two different programmes each season. His musical interests ranged from the elite Manchester Vocal Society, with which he was associated for forty-three years – a select *a cappella* group of thirty-two singers whose repertoire included Bach's motets, Byrd's masses and, suitably augmented presumably, Tallis's forty-part *Spem in alium* – to the Manchester Gentlemen's Glee Club, of which he was music director for sixteen years. He also left a modest output of compositions, some published, others in manuscript, including a comic opera, works for solo voices and chorus, church music, solo songs and part-songs, incidental music for Shakespearian revivals and celebrations, and salon music for piano.

Henry Watson was particularly proud of his association with the Manchester Gentlemen's Glee Club. There was a long tradition of glee and catch singing in England. A similar club in London still active today, the Noblemen and Gentlemen's Catch Club, had been founded in 1761, and a London Glee Club existed between 1783 and 1857. Glee singing goes back to the seventeenth century. The term 'glee' derives from Anglo Saxon *gliw* or *gleo* – entertainment or mirth, especially in connection with the playing and singing of minstrels. Glee in its classic eighteenth-century form was an unaccompanied song in three or more parts for solo men's voices, including male alto,

[1] *A Chronicle of the Manchester Gentlemen's Glee Club* (Manchester, 1906).
[2] William Waterhouse, 'Henry Watson: Musician, Collector and Benefactor', *Manchester Sounds* 1 (2000), 47–63.
[3] June Tomlinson, 'Henry Watson (1846–1911): a Musical Life', *Aspects of Accrington* (2000), 76–90.

A Chronicle
OF THE
Manchester
Gentlemen's
Glee Club.

From
its Foundation
in 1830
to the Session
1905-6.

Together with
Complete Lists of the
Music performed at
the Meetings, and of
the Vocalists, Amateur
and Professional, who
have sung at the
Meetings; with other
incidents and features
of the Club's history.

Illustrated
with facsimiles, por-
traits, and views of
the premises in which
the Club's Meetings
have been held during
its progress through a
period of

Seventy-five years.

COMPILED BY
HENRY WATSON, Mus. D.,
Music Director of the Club.

Entered Stationers' Hall.   **Price Three Shillings & Sixpence Nett.**

COPYRIGHT. 1906 by HENRY WATSON.

(*Manchester Libraries and Information, Henry Watson Music Library*)

although later composers sometimes added women's voices. Texts were often about eating and drinking, but also included amorous and patriotic themes, and the hunt. Glees were usually fairly short and sectional, and homophonic or chordal rather than polyphonic (as opposed to catches, which were rounds or canons), but as time went on they increasingly contained contrasting contrapuntal sections. Although glee singing was essentially an amateur activity, the many glee clubs formed in the eighteenth century included both amateur and professional members. The singing of glees was much in vogue during the first half of the nineteenth century and continued into the twentieth. 'Glee' is by now perhaps too restricted a term to apply to much of what was being sung, as a glance at the repertoire of the Manchester club will show. Part-song might be a more accurate generic description. Henry Watson himself refers to the repertoire as 'glees and other part music'.

The Manchester Gentlemen's Glee Club was formed in 1830 with a membership of 60. By 1905 this had grown to 117. Henry Watson records in his introduction to the seventy-fifth anniversary souvenir that

> The only important organization in Manchester when the Glee Club was founded was the Gentlemen's Concerts, and there can be little doubt that at least indirectly the former sprang from the latter. Gentlemen and professional musicians associated with the Gentlemen's Concerts were concerned in the establishment of the Gentlemen's Glee Club; and the two institutions resembled each other at least in their private and subscription character. … It must be remembered that at the period with which we are originally concerned, part-singing constituted a direct feature in the programmes of the Gentlemen's Concerts.

To some extent the expansion of musical life in Manchester reflected the growing wealth of the city following the rise of industrialism and the burgeoning cotton industry and the city's associated social development. Looking through the rules of the club it is clear that, while music was the main interest, eating and drinking in a sociable environment were a major attraction. Thus, while Rule 2 states that 'eight Meetings shall be held on the *first Wednesday* in every month, from September to April … for the practice of Glees by such Members as are competent to take a part', Rule 1 says that 'the Club shall meet at some Inn or Hotel, where there is a room suitable for the purpose', and Rule 9 that 'a Supper shall be provided, to be paid for out of the Funds of the Club, the Members individually paying for what they, or their visitors, have to drink'.

Watson himself comments that

> the social characteristics of the Club … have formed an integral and designed part of its life and being from its first meeting to its latest … To the glee, more than to any other harmonised musical form, the social influences exerted by the charms of music belong … The Glee was born in a social atmosphere; and though times, and music with them, have greatly changed, it still loves best the social surroundings, and the social hour.

Rule 7 determines that 'the singing shall commence punctually at *seven* o'clock' and Rule 10 that 'the hour of supper shall be *ten* precisely, and that the Meeting shall be considered to be dissolved at twelve o'clock'. There is an interesting sociological and historical aspect here. Where in Manchester today, or indeed in London, could you find a hotel which would be prepared to lay on suppers for 60 or, by 1905, 117 men (each of whom was entitled to bring a friend under Rule 13), starting at 10 p.m.?

In 1830 Mr Hayward, a Manchester hotelier, built a room in his hotel expressly for the club, as later did the Albion Hotel when the club outgrew the facilities at Hayward's. Even the new room at the Albion proved hardly large enough for the first meeting there, prompting the composer Sir Henry Bishop, who was the distinguished guest, to remark that if 'their Architect would only give them with a little more *air,* they would give him a little more *harmony*'.

Mention of Bishop brings us to the music. The composition of glees and part-songs was taken up with enthusiasm by late Georgian and early Victorian composers, with Bishop the pre-eminent contributor. No doubt this was stimulated by the commercial popularity of such pieces and by the competitions offered by the glee clubs. The Manchester club's third rule states that 'one object of the Club shall be to offer premiums for Glees to be written for the Club', and the club first offered prizes for new glees in 1831. A newspaper advertisement proclaimed: 'The Committee of this Club, being desirous of encouraging the composition of English Glees, hereby offer a PREMIUM of FIVE POUNDS for the best SERIOUS GLEE, and another of similar amount for the best CHEERFUL GLEE.' This attracted seven entries. In following year the club offered prizes of £10 and received 46 entries, 25 serious and 21 cheerful. The serious prize went to Bishop and the cheerful one to Vincent Novello. Samuel Sebastian Wesley, at the time organist at Hereford Cathedral, won the prize for a cheerful glee in 1833 and the serious prize in 1834.

To return to Bishop: in his introduction, Watson observes that

The appreciation of the Madrigal, Glee, Part-Song, and Chorus, as comprising a branch of music instinctively British, and to which British composers were from the first, magnificent contributors, was at the moment greatly stimulated by the compositions in those styles – enlarged, differentiated, and trespassed upon by the composer's indisputable genius – of Sir (then Mr) Henry R Bishop, who in 1830 was, at 44 years of age, in the meridian of his fame.

1832.

The efforts of the Club in encouraging Glee composition had apparently become more widely known, and this fact, and the increase in value of the prize awards from £5 to £10 evidently produced their effect for the number of Glees sent in amounted to 46 -25 serious and 21 cheerful Glees. The awards were made as follows :

H. R. BISHOP (London)
    Serious Glee   " Where shall we make her grave."
VINCENT NOVELLO (London)
    Cheerful Glee   " Old May Morning."

These compositions were sung for the first time at the meeting held February 7th. 1833.

HENRY R. BISHOP

It is curious to state that though Sir Henry Bishop wrote other competitive Glees for other Clubs as well as for the Gentlemen's Glee Club, the only prize he ever won was that which the above composition secured him ; it is somewhat remarkable too, that 'Old May Morning' is the first and only prize Glee to which Mr. Vincent Novello's name was ever attached.

* VINCENT NOVELLO.

* The Photo. is reproduced by the kind permission of Alfred H. Littleton. Esq.

Amongst the other competitors worthy of special mention, the following should be noted :

'GEORGE HARGREAVES
    Glee   " Past is the race of heroes "
J. C. CLIFTON
    Glee   " Twas in the dark and dismal hour."
T. F. WALMISLEY
    Glee   "The wandering bird."
T. S. COOKE
    Glee   " Of all the boons."
JOHN PARRY
    Glee   " Come Fairies trip it."
G. HARGREAVES
    Glee   " Hence, smiling Mischief."
H. R. BISHOP
    Glee   " Oh, skylark, for thy wings."
*T. S. COOKE
    Glee   " Strike the Lyre."

Those marked thus * appeared in the programme, and were sung for the first time on February 7th, 1833.

The subsequent popularity of some of the Glees here mentioned, is sufficient to suggest once more, how often, and how completely, the public verdict supersedes that of the most competent and fair-minded judges.

(*Manchester Libraries and Information, Henry Watson Music Library*)

An appendix to Watson's anniversary chronicle contains a complete list of the pieces sung between 1830 and 1905–6. Bishop has more than twice as many as any other composer: 105. Given this, and the fact that Henry Watson can write about Bishop in such glowing terms fifty years after his death, it is clear that Bishop was held in high esteem throughout the nineteenth century. Two examples of his part-songs which featured in Watson's list of glees sung at the Manchester Gentlemen's Glee Club are included on a splendid CD of Bishop's music for productions of Shakespeare from Philip Pickett and the Musicians of the Globe.[4] These are 'Hark, hark each Spartan hound', a chorus of huntsmen for use in *A Midsummer Night's Dream*, and 'Under the greenwood tree', a song from *As you Like it*. The former, reflecting the popularity of hunting themes, is in a lively 6/8 style with fanfares and echo effects. It is mainly homophonic or chordal but with some brief sequential development. In 'Under the greenwood tree' Bishop uses a melody by Thomas Arne, himself a prominent composer of glees from the previous century. Again mainly homophonic, but with some contrapuntal and antiphonal writing, it also has some sequential development, and some simple word painting – a twittering figure in the accompaniment for 'tunes his merry note' and a plunge into the minor for 'winter and rough weather'.

Watson's list of compositions performed during the club's 75-year history contains over 1300 items – an astonishing number. Second and third in popularity after Bishop are Samuel Webbe with 47 pieces and John Callcott with 37, both specialist glee composers from a generation or two before Bishop. Webbe's 'Glorious Apollo', written for the London Glee Club, of which he was a member, generally opened the vocal proceedings of both the London and Manchester clubs, 'an appetising *hors d'oeuvre* to the musical feast', as Watson puts it. While Victorian composers were very well represented, the list ranges far and wide over musical history. So as well as Balfe, Barnby, Gaul, Goss, Hatton (with 31 pieces), Horsley (28), Macfarren (29), Parry, Smart (31) and Sullivan (18, including, of course, 'The long day closes'), plus Henry Watson himself (7), we find: Arcadelt and Marenzio; the English madrigalists Bennet, Gibbons, Morley, Weelkes, Wilbye and Dowland; Purcell, Handel, Haydn, Mozart and Beethoven, including the finale from *Fidelio* (!); also Bellini, Rossini, Gounod, Brahms and of course Mendelssohn (28). As the twentieth century dawns, some more modern English names appear, including Elgar and Edward German.

Who, then, sang? The Rules of the club state that its meetings are 'for the practice of Glees by such Members as are competent to take a part'. Watson comments, 'It was pleasant fiction perhaps … that every member of the Club should be, and was, capable of taking his share in the execution of the programmes.' He adds that

---

[4] Decca 470 381-2.

Even this fiction has vanished now; but at the outset … the number was a goodly one of the members who sang at the concerts, especially in pieces that needed choral reinforcement. The Club's records show for instance, that at one of the earliest Concerts, in 1830, eighteen of the members took part in rendering the programme … The Club at the outset, however, relied chiefly, as did the London Club, upon professional members, in rendering, as well as in rehearsing and accompanying, the pieces sung.

By 1859 the choir had changed from being 'self-contained amongst the members, as well as honorary in character', to being 'a paid organisation'. Watson goes on to say, no doubt with a characteristic twinkle in his eye, that

It sometimes delights the Presidents of the Club in our day, to twit good humouredly the members, and to picture for them the consternation that would possess them, if they were called upon, as their earliest brotherhood were called upon, to stand up, copy in hand, and sing 'Strike the Lyre', or any other glee the arbitrary President might select.

He notes, however, that members of both the Manchester and London Glee Clubs sang the canon *Non nobis Domine* attributed to Byrd when their meal had ended.

What of the ladies? As the club's name implies, membership was restricted to gentlemen. But in the early days an 'Extra Concert' was put on each season to which the public were admitted, 'the ladies being especially welcomed'. And from 1838 there were increasingly ladies present at the normal meetings, at least for the musical sessions. These were professional lady singers.

Watson names all the singers who had taken part over the seventy-five years. The list comprises 84 sopranos, including a few boys; 27 contraltos; 32 male altos (8 amateur and 24 professional); 54 tenors of whom 38 were professional; and 60 basses of whom 44 were professional.

Since the singing began at 7 p.m. and continued until supper was taken at 10 p.m., with a lighter programme of solo and concerted music after supper, the responsibilities falling to the music director for organising, rehearsing and accompanying the musical part of the proceedings each month from September to April were not inconsiderable. Notwithstanding all his other activities and commitments, Henry Watson appears to have taken all this in his stride during his sixteen years as music director. Indeed, it is clear from the way he writes about the club that it was an association in which he took great delight and of which he was immensely proud. Partly this is because he loved the glee and its sociable aspects. He writes:

The power of music to move the better feelings of our natures, to inspire with hope, to move to pity, and to set off the claims and pleasures of friendship, is perhaps more fully displayed when and where the music of the Glee enfolds us, than when we are addressed by any other form of the secular side of the art.

The club itself he describes as having 'preserved the appreciation, and enlarged the practice of a beautiful form of musical discourse, whose modest pretensions, while adding to its charm, expose it, from that very circumstance, to the perils of neglect'.

> Here every gen'rous sentiment awaking,
>   Music inspiring unity and joy,
> Each social pleasure giving and partaking,
>   Glee and good humour our hours employ,
>   Thus then combining,
>   Hands and hearts joining,
>   Long may continue our unity and joy.

ANDREW POULTER is a retired civil servant. He studied music at King's College, London, and is organist at Gospel Oak Methodist Church in Hampstead, London. This article is based on an extract from a lecture he gave in April 2004 to the London University Music Diploma Society, of which he is a founder member.

North West FILM ARCHIVE

Manchester Metropolitan University

Rescuing and ensuring the survival of moving images about the North West of England for the education and enjoyment of the region's people – both today and in the future.

The North West Film Archive is one of Manchester Metropolitan University's Special Collections, and one of the largest public regional moving image archives in the UK, holding over 31,500 reels of film and videotape – from early 'animated pictures' to BBC regional television collections and contemporary video productions. Life in the North West is illustrated through footage of work and local industry, leisure, holiday-making, sport and entertainment, local traditions and community activities, transport, housing, and wartime experiences. These include cinema newsreels, documentaries, educational films, travelogues, advertising and promotional material, alongside hundreds of films shot by local families and enthusiasts.

Further details and online catalogue at www.nwfa.mmu.ac.uk

The NWFA is pleased to contribute to this volume of *Manchester Sounds* by providing the DVD copy of *A City Speaks* – Manchester's Civic Film, sponsored by the William Alwyn Foundation.

Also supported by

AGMA GRANTS UNIT

·A·G·M·A·
ASSOCIATION OF
GREATER MANCHESTER
AUTHORITIES

NORTHWESTVISION

UK FILM | COUNCIL
LOTTERY FUNDED

North West Film Archive, Manchester Metropolitan University, Minshull House, 47-49 Chorlton Street, Manchester M1 3E
Phone: +44 (0)161 247 3097 Fax: +44 (0)161 247 3098
Email: n.w.filmarchive@mmu.ac.uk

THE WILLIAM ALWYN FOUNDATION
(Registered Charity No. 803294)

The William Alwyn Foundation was established by a Trust Deed dated 5th April 1990 at the instigation of the composer's widow Mary Alwyn (née Doreen Carwithen), with the intention of perpetuating the performance, recording and broadcast of Alwyn's work, thus furthering knowledge of the composer's achievements.

During 2005, the year which saw the centenary of the composer's birth, the Foundation was very active in sponsoring performances, broadcasts and recordings of Alwyn's music, in particular, a new series of recordings on the Naxos label which saw the release of Symphonies 1– 5, Piano Concertos 1 & 2, Harp Concerto 'Lyra Angelica', Sinfonietta, Overture 'Derby Day' and Sonata alla Toccata. Two of these recordings were an Editor's Choice in the Gramophone Magazine. The Chandos label released a third volume of film music, which was also an Editors Choice. Forthcoming on the Dutton Epoch label are two discs of chamber music, one of String Quartets the other of wind chamber music. Future recordings sponsored by the Foundation include four discs of orchestral music (two of which were recorded in January 2006), a vocal disc containing the major song cycles, a mixed disc of instrumental, vocal and chamber music and two discs of piano music.

Some fifty live performances were achieved around the UK during 2005: the most important of which was a concert at the Purcell Room on the South Bank (2nd May) in association with the Park Lane Group entitled Triple Centenary Concert which focused on some of Alwyn's chamber music in harness with that of Constant Lambert and Alan Rawsthorne, who also celebrated their respective centenaries in 2005. BBC Radio 3 in their 'Composer of the Week' programme broadcast a series of five programmes during the composer's centenary week beginning on Monday 7th November, which was then repeated the following week. Also on Radio 3 on the 7th November, in the 'Stage and Screen' programme, Edward Seckerson interviewed Ian Johnson (author of 'William Alwyn: The Art of Film Music,' published last August by Boydell & Brewer) about Alwyn's achievements in the field of film music, with many music examples. The publication of this book was also sponsored by the Foundation.

On the publishing front, with assistance from the Foundation, there was a collected edition of the mature piano works with a new cover and forward published by Alfred Lengnick & Co. Ltd. In preparation (also from Lengnick) are first publications of the Sonata for Flute and Piano, Trio for Flute, Cello and Piano, and Suite for Oboe and Harp. A biography of the composer is also being written and a collected edition of the autobiographical writings and essays and lectures into a one-book format is under way.

The Foundation has also funded the reproduction by The North West Film Archive of 1,000 copies of the documentary film 'A City Speaks' included with this issue of the Manchester Sounds Journal. This DVD accompanies an essay on the film that Ian Johnson has especially written for the journal.

The Foundation will continue to look into other aspects of Alwyn's creative output and determine how best they can be presented over the coming years.

The William Alwyn Foundation: Andrew Knowles, 30 Florida Avenue, Hartford, Huntingdon, CAMBS PE29 1PY
apkmusicprom@ntlworld.com

A City Speaks: The Story of Manchester's Municipal Musical

IAN JOHNSON

(*North West Film Archive at Manchester Metropolitan University*)

ONE OF THE BRIGHTER IDEAS put forward by Manchester City Corporation to celebrate its centenary in 1938 was to make a film. It was to be no ordinary film. It would be Manchester's 'Civic Film' and would record the *spirit* of Manchester. It would teach the city's young people how local government works, and infuse all generations with a sense of civic responsibility and pride.

The centenary year passed, war broke out, and the Blitz of 1940 and 1941 brought terrible damage and suffering to the city. The plans were briefly shelved – but not for long enough to gather dust. Such was the Corporation's enthusiasm that even the pressing needs of the hour could not to deter City Hall from stretching its resources in the cause of its propaganda project. So on the morning of 20 March 1944 the *Manchester Guardian* reported that the 'distinguished' documentary producer Paul Rotha would be attending that day a meeting of the Corporation's Civic Film Committee. It was 'expected that a decision will be reached about the production of the film depicting the contemporary life of Manchester'.

Rotha was celebrated as the author of the first English-language history of the cinema, *The Film Till Now* (1930), and had joined the industry in the early 1930s to work for the 'father of documentary', John Grierson. By 1944, when he met the Corporation's sub-committee, his reputation as a director dedicated to social purpose was secure. His company, Paul Rotha Productions, supported a group of young directors who between 1941 and 1943 made some 100 films on social problems for the Ministry of Information. In 1944 Rotha set up an additional company, Films of Fact, for which he personally directed films.

Before his sales pitch on that March Monday morning, Rotha laid the ground carefully. On the previous Saturday the Manchester and District Film Institute Society had held a reception at the Midland Hotel. Here Rotha met representatives of various Corporation departments, including – crucially – the Civic Film Committee. The next day, Sunday, he spoke at a film exhibition held at the Manchester News Theatre in Oxford Street, at which his highly acclaimed *World of Plenty* (1943) was shown.[1] It is hardly surprising therefore that a fortnight later we find the Civic Film Committee recommending the City Council to instruct Rotha to undertake a story outline for the making of an hour-long film. The cost of putting this proposal together was £1,000 (about £40,000 today), and any resultant film would be expected to be completed towards the end of 1945,[2] an estimate well out of touch with the final reality.

By the end of 1944 the draft script had been submitted, and in early January 1945 the Corporation gave its approval for Rotha Films–Films of Fact to go ahead with the 'Civic Film'. The unwieldy title of *Manchester Today – with a Hint of Tomorrow*, suggested at the initial meeting the previous year, had been speedily abandoned and the title

---

[1] *Manchester Guardian*, 20 March 1944; *To-Day's Cinema*, 24 March 1944, 62:5011, 15.
[2] *Manchester Guardian*, 25 March 1944; *Manchester Guardian*, 3 April 1944; *To-Day's Cinema*, 62:5015 (4 April 1944), 3 and 12; *To-Day's Cinema*, 62:5018 (12 April 1944), 15.

A City Speaks was chosen only in the final days of production. The cost was estimated at £16,134 (today, about £645,000), to be provided from the rates.[3]

The people of Manchester took a lively interest in 'their' film from the start. On 2 January 1945, before Rotha's contract had even been signed, and long before a composer had been commissioned, Richard Willcocks of Manchester 1 wrote to the *Manchester Guardian*:

Sir,– Your leading article today prompts me to appeal for the careful consideration of the musical accompaniment for the Manchester film – presuming, of course, that music has become necessary for 'documentaries'.

The strident, blatant, fortissimo stuff that is ground out with almost all modern films (and radio plays) will be decidedly out of place, and I sincerely hope that the directors will give some thought to a dignified musical sequence which may please the ear. The prestige of Manchester will not be enhanced if audiences in all parts of the world have to suffer the awful noise which has been shot at them with almost all films since 'Things to Come'.[4]

Rotha, the ink on his contract hardly dry, was quick to respond. On 6 January he wrote:

Sir,– Your correspondent Mr. Richard Willcocks does well to ask for careful consideration of music in the Manchester Civic Film. As its producer, I hasten to assure him that original music will be specially composed for the film.

I would add, on behalf of documentary film producers, that we have consistently tried these past fifteen years, wherever cost permitted, to use specially composed music for our films, as distinct from the 'strident, blatant, fortissimo stuff' favoured by most feature entertainment films. I recall that we have been privileged to commission music from, among others, Sir Arnold Bax, Darius Milhaud, Vaughan Williams, Benjamin Britten, Constant Lambert, William Alwyn, the late Walter Leigh, Ian Whyte, Richard Addinsell, the late Maurice Jaubert, Ernst Meyer, and Lennox Berkeley.[5]

Rotha decided he would direct and edit the film himself, although some of the scenes were handled by his assistant Francis Gysin, who had joined Rotha as assistant cameraman in 1943, soon after graduating from Cambridge. Rotha was impressed by his talent, and during

---

[3] *To-Day's Cinema*, 62:5011 (24 March 1944), 15. *Manchester Guardian*, 1 January 1945.
[4] *Manchester Guardian*, 5 January 1945.
[5] *Manchester Guardian*, 9 January 1945.

1944 and 1945 Gysin was appointed associate director with Rotha to work on the celebrated *Land of Promise* (1946).

The Civic Film's cameraman was Harold ('Hal') Young. Young was well established in the industry, having travelled to the United States as a young man to work as a cameraman for the Famous Players–Lasky Company. That was in 1919. He had returned to Britain soon afterwards, and was responsible for the photography of a string of feature films, with directors including Donald Crisp, Guy Newall, Graham Cutts and Walter Summers. Perhaps his most famous film was Alfred Hitchcock's *The Lodger* (1926). During the war he worked on documentaries, and just before filming the Civic Film he, like Gysin, had worked with Rotha on *Land of Promise*. In the final days of shooting, Rotha called in Cyril Arapoff to assist Young.[6] In his earlier life Arapoff had been a follower of Jean Cocteau in Paris, and subsequently had established a well-known theatrical portrait studio in Oxford. At the beginning of the war he made a career change to documentary films.

The documentary had two scriptwriters in addition to Rotha: Ara Calder-Marshall (whose husband, the better-known writer Arthur Calder-Marshall, worked on some of Rotha's other projects) and Walter Greenwood, who also spoke some of the dialogue in the film. Greenwood was a popular Salford novelist fondly remembered for his first novel *Love on the Dole* (1933), who contributed to *Picture Post*, the magazine with a 'human face'. The Corporation hoped the film would be shown abroad, as well as at home, and the commentary was designed to be easily translated.[7]

Graphics were to be provided by the Isotype Institute, which had been set up in Vienna by Dr Otto Neurath and his wife, and re-established in Oxford shortly before the outbreak of war. Rotha liked their work, used it in several of his films, and had established a happy relationship with the couple.

To compose the music Rotha commissioned, in February 1946, William Alwyn. At this time Alwyn was entering the years of his greatest creativity. Between 1946 and 1947 he completed six feature films (including perhaps his greatest film work, *Odd Man Out*), three documentaries, eight radio productions, a suite of Scottish Dances, an overture for wordless chorus and orchestra, a Piano Sonata, and four

---

[6] *Film Industry*, 1:4 (October 1946), 19.
[7] *Manchester Guardian*, 1 January 1945; *Manchester Guardian*, 25 August 1945; *Reynold's News*, 17 September 1945; *Manchester Guardian*, 16 January 1947.

songs. To add to his workload, Alwyn had his position to look after at the Royal Academy of Music, where he had been appointed professor of composition at the age of 21 in 1926.

Alwyn and Rotha had worked together since 1936 when, as producer-in-chief of Strand Films, Rotha had taken care of Alwyn's first film commission *The Future's in the Air*. Since then Alwyn had become a favourite composer and personal friend of Rotha's. They worked together on several productions, including three particularly significant titles. *World of Plenty*, for which Alwyn claimed to have suggested the title,[8] was the first British documentary film to condemn the systems of world food production, distribution and resultant malnutrition. *Land of Promise* preached a compelling Socialist sermon on the need to plan for decent housing in Britain, and *Total War in Britain* (1946) was intended to show that central planning was as important to winning the peace as to winning the war. One other title, *The World is Rich* (1947), was turned down by Alwyn because of the pressure of work. An attack on the problems of feeding the world in post-war conditions, it won the 1948 British Film Academy Award for best documentary.

Each of these films stressed the need for planning. With the end of hostilities in 1945, a wide social revolution engendered a mood for reconstruction, and expectations of a welfare state protecting the vulnerable from cradle to grave – a mood mirrored by the Labour landslide victory of July 1945. Now Rotha was about to show how the City of Manchester was planning for its post-war reconstruction.

Massive rebuilding strategies would be needed for both the inner city, where nearly 70 per cent of Manchester's Victorian and Edwardian buildings had been destroyed in air raids, and in the suburbs with their expansive areas of slum dwellings. The dream was to be realised in the visionary City of Manchester Plan conceived by the City Surveyor and Engineer R. Nicholas. Slum clearance projects were initiated, families moved into new housing in Wythenshawe and new dormitory towns. The leafy garden city of Wythenshawe, planned in the early 1930s by Barry Parker, the genius of Letchworth and Welwyn Garden Cities, saw its population grow from 8,000 to 100,000. The Plan projected its long-term vision not only in housing, but in transport, education, and in its people's leisure activities. It was a vision which was to be reflected by the Civic Film.

---

[8] William Alwyn, 'Ariel to Miranda', *Adam International Review*, 316–18 (1967), 44.

Shooting started around the beginning of September 1945, although the first 'official' filming took place at a Planning Exhibition in the City Art Gallery a couple of weeks later on 10 September. The Lord Mayor was present, together with the Town Clerk, members of the Civic Film Committee, and thirty children from local schools who were filmed inspecting the exhibition. In early October the outdoor work was virtually completed, and the unit returned to London to plan the winter programme of indoor shooting, and the soundtrack. But it was back to Manchester for the municipal elections at the end of the month, and after that the winter shoot began.

Filming was finally completed in the third week of June 1946.[9] Forty thousand feet of film had been shot, to be reduced to around 6,000 for the finished film:[10] it was a poor shooting ratio. In January 1947, the Civic Film Committee made a trip to the British Council Theatre in London to see a rough-cut of the film. There were criticisms at the expenditure 'at this time' on rail and hotel costs for fifteen to twenty people, 'when the film could easily have been shown in Manchester'.[11] But it seems the criticisms were misplaced, as Manchester lacked the equipment to project the unmarried print with its soundtrack. Alderman Wright Robinson, as Chairman of the Civic Film Committee, expressed the opinion that it deserved a 'world showing'. But another, less biased, councillor thought 'it all seemed a bit of a mix-up'. Perhaps, suggested the newspaper report, he 'did not appreciate that it was the cutting copy he had seen'.[12]

Rotha had decided to edit the film personally, and the film partially reflects the supercharged cutting style he had favoured for several of his more highly regarded films. In *World of Plenty*, *Land of Promise*, *Total War in Britain* and an earlier production, *New Worlds for Old* (1938), he had experimented with 'every trick and device of the movie medium – stock library footage, diagrams, cut-in interviews, an argumentative voice track, trick optical effects and so on'[13] – until the technique became virtually formulaic. On these films the composer Alwyn, conspiring with Rotha, had choreographed the visuals with instrumental and sound effects of all kinds, including short punctuations of explosions, brass and percussion clashes, rising and falling

[9] *Manchester Guardian*, 25 August 1945; *Manchester Guardian*, 11 September 1945; *Reynold's News*, 17 September 1945; *Manchester Guardian*, 20 October 1945.

[10] *Manchester Guardian*, 18 June 1946; *The Cinema*, 66:5358 (19 June 1946), 24.

[11] *To-Day's Cinema*, 68:5448 (17 January 1947), 68.

[12] *Manchester Guardian*, 16 January 1947.

[13] Paul Rotha, *On the Film* (London: Faber, 1958), 100.

glissandi, drum rolls, beats, and rattles, bursts of harp, bells, the chimes of Big Ben, drum and other fancies including recordings of musical phrases played backwards. It must have been great fun to do. Commenting on one of the backward-played recordings Rotha observed, tongue in cheek, 'Alwyn was quite charming about this, saying his music sounded much better that way'.[14]

To sustain interest in *A City Speaks* Rotha called to his aid some of the punctuation tricks of these films, such as a dispute between two voice-overs, dramatised action, and graphics and charts, but shunned Alwyn's short musical chords and sound effects. They were unnecessary for he had a prestigious source of music – nothing less than the Hallé Orchestra, now climbing from a low point in 1943 to a peak in esteem, owing to the appointment that year of its permanent conductor John Barbirolli. All the music contracts – Barbirolli's, the Hallé's, Alwyn's – were signed in February 1946.[15] A couple of weeks later the film unit was seen in action shooting scenes of the Hallé Concert Society at the King's Hall in Belle Vue, as Cyril Smith enchanted an audience of 5,000 with Rachmaninoff's First Piano Concerto.[16] By August 1946 Alwyn had finished the main score,[17] and it was recorded in a day and a half at the Houldsworth Hall on 23 and 24 August. Present were Alderman Wright Robinson, representing the Civic Film Committee, and, of course, the composer.[18]

The Hallé Orchestra added glitter to a film which was designed to impress. The mood is established under the main titles which are superimposed across the Corporation's coat of arms ('concilio et labore') and accompanied by a ponderous roll of timpani and majestic horns, soon to be joined by orchestra *tutti*. A calmer passage follows, to announce the motto: 'What is the city but the people?' The motto is important, for the intention of both the Corporation and the film-makers was that this film was actually to belong to Manchester people, to involve them in the Corporation's vision of the model city of the future.

The music falls silent for a minute or so, as the words mix to the first moving pictures and we are taken on an aerial journey from the southern suburbs, passing over Wythenshawe, the Mersey Valley and

---

[14] Paul Rotha, *Documentary Diary* (London: Secker & Warburg, 1973), 226.
[15] *The Cinema*, 66:5304 (13 February 1946), 37.
[16] *To-Day's Cinema*, 66:5312 (5 March 1946), 15.
[17] Alwyn's completion date on MS. Alwyn Archive, University of Cambridge Library.
[18] Hallé Archive; *Daily Dispatch*, 25 August 1946.

Hough End fields, towards the centre of Manchester, 'the great mother of the common life and weal' as the commentary declaims. Then, as rows of back-to-back terraced houses and the chimneys of factories sprawl below, Alwyn's opening motif is repeated *moderato* until we discover the city centre and the dark silhouette of the Town Hall rising high above bleak bomb-wasted streets. The music ceases, supplanted by the chimes of the town clock as a small boy looks up at the statues of Manchester's pioneering scientists James Joule and John Dalton.

(*North West Film Archive at Manchester Metropolitan University*)

Even Alwyn's compositions for the wartime propaganda films had shunned the rhetoric of this imposing opening. On the large cinema screen, picture and music must have thrilled the cinema audiences of 1947. The music's grand motivation is demonstrated by comparison with other council-led commissions – for example, Malcolm Arnold's *Fair Field* (1973), John Scott's *A Colchester Symphony* (1995) or Alwyn's own *Festival March* (1951) for the Arts Council.

In fact, Alwyn's contribution to the film was considerable. Rotha's film is organised as a series of sequences, or blocks, each illustrating a different aspect of the city of Manchester; instead of drawing on his customary techniques as a film composer, Alwyn contributed five concert pieces, or movements (of which the main title music was the first piece), to match five of these blocks. Alwyn's movements were a

(*North West Film Archive at Manchester Metropolitan University*)

cousin to the film or stage musical's technique of freezing the plot while players and orchestra burst into song. It was not a new idea for Alwyn, who years earlier had set colourful shots of spinning and weaving to music in a wartime documentary called *Queen Cotton* (1941). For Rotha the attraction was in displaying Barbirolli and the Hallé, the stars of his film, without the necessity of tiresome commentary writing. So, having little more to say at this stage than that Manchester is 'built on cotton' and also that 'there are other and equally important industries', how much easier it was to leave Alwyn alone to illustrate Manchester's industrial scene. And Alwyn soars away in his second concert piece with his flutes and strings in a rhythmic and propulsive march, dignified with timpani, against which Rotha fast-cut a myriad of industrial processes and close shots of workers (in a film about 'the People').

The music rests for nearly two minutes now as the commentary enthuses about a dawning 'new age of materials and fluids, all the products of scientific discovery'. After scenes including the Stock Exchange and the Royal Exchange the commentary explains that 'Manchester men and women produce many of Britain's exports', for which overseas customers come back for more 'because the quality of the stuff turned out is like the people who made it'.

Another voice-over comes immediately, announcing that 'Homely: that's the word for Manchester folk', and Alwyn's attractive third

(*North West Film Archive at Manchester Metropolitan University*)

movement follows. Over domestic scenes showing a man trimming his hedge, his wife contentedly knitting at the hearth, people relaxing in the park, flower-sellers, and densely populated streets ('all of us', says the track, 'citizens of a great city'), plucked strings rise and fall in contrapuntal cascades in a simple galop, delightfully lightened by flutes and piccolos. It resembles, and may have been an inspiration for, the punting music that Alwyn composed for the film *The History of Mr Polly* (1949).

There follows a long nondescript and gloomy organ solo, *moderato serioso*, against an instructional narration of the history of Manchester. This was composed in addition to the concert pieces, and was completed after them. Unlike the concert pieces it was written to the pictures. There still exists a letter sent by Francis Gysin straight from the cutting room to 'Bill' Alwyn at his home in North London. It accompanied dialogue sheets, marked with the relevant footages, for this sequence. On the back of Gysin's letter Alwyn has scribbled, in pencil, various further cues and timings. Gysin finished his letter hoping that his timings would give Alwyn 'enough information to get on with'.[19] Evidently it was enough, for the archive folder contains three manuscript pages, again in pencil, noted with various timings and alternative timings. This sequence could, of course, have been relatively easily recorded at a different time and place from the Hallé's orchestral contribution. The organist is unnamed.

The unremitting dourness of Alwyn's composition for this sequence is only partially effective. Serving as appropriate illustration of the troughs of Manchester's unhappy history, a 'cesspit of human

---

[19] Gysin to Alwyn, 4 September 1946. Alwyn Archive, University of Cambridge Library.

misery' as the commentary puts it, the score spurns the peaks of interest, such as pictures of machinery in motion, the Luddites, the Peterloo Massacre, and Manchester's social reformers. A variation in rhythm need not have detracted from the message of the evils of Manchester's industrial development, but could have stirred more passion about its injustices and raised the inner tension of the sequence.

After an equally long and detailed explanation of the workings of local government against mainly mute pictures, the film returns to Alwyn's galop over scenes of the council's community services: buses, library, parks, police, road-sweepers, art galleries, fire brigade, public laundry, housing inspectors, sewers and – finally – crowded lifts descending from the town hall's administrative offices.

Alwyn's fourth movement follows almost immediately: 'Manchester generates all the electricity she needs...' proclaims the commentary, and the Hallé's turbulent timpani bound in with rhythmically energetic and intricate brass and strings over pictures of rows of dials, gas and steam. The music calms, becomes rhapsodic, and a harp arpeggio conducts us to the mountains, to reservoirs ('masterpieces of engineering and design') and to hillsides where foresters harvest fir trees against a brief flute tremolo and a plaintively beautiful violin solo.

More mute scenes follow as the film resumes its instructional purpose to explain the building of the Ship Canal and how local

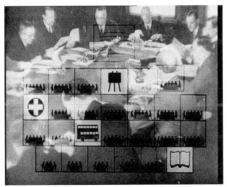

(*North West Film Archive at Manchester Metro-politan University*)

government is 'administered by the largest business undertaking in the City – the Town Hall'. Improvements in health care and slum clearance are outlined, and, in a two-way voice-over filmic conversation, a technique Rotha favoured, the slums of Hulme, with its 84,000 population and its accumulation of 270 tons of soot and dirt in one square mile in a single year, are compared with the modern comforts of Wythenshawe where 120 tons of soot accumulate (not ideal, says the film, but better).[20]

To fulfil the Plan, explains the film, most of Manchester will have to be rebuilt in any case and two-thirds of the people will have to move elsewhere. But will people themselves pay this price? It will mean an extra £300,000 on the rates. ('There you are, I told you so', argues a resident in the local pub. 'Look here,' comes the reply, 'the money's being spent for your benefit …'.)

It's up to the people of Manchester, says the commentary, to take a lively interest in their local affairs, and love their city. Nevertheless, 'It isn't all work and no play, Manchester folk see to that', says the soundtrack, and now – well before the end of his 69 minutes – Rotha introduces his editing *tour de force*. The Hallé Orchestra is shown tuning up, almost certainly the scene filmed in the King's Hall early in 1946. There follows a performance not of Alwyn's music, but of that film editor's friend: Wagner's rousing *Ride of the Valkyries*, racing to scenes of the city at leisure. Inter-cutting fast between Hallé, Belle Vue, Old Trafford, music hall, trapeze artist, horse race, pub, speedway, wrestling, dance hall and rugby, the sequence whirls to a finish as it flies off the big dipper to mix with a tracking shot over the

(*North West Film Archive at Manchester Metropolitan University*)

---

[20] There had been a proposal to use infra-red film to cut through Manchester's smoke haze when filming buildings on dull days. *Manchester Guardian*, 11 September 1945. The aerial shots may have been filmed with infra-red film stock.

(*North West Film Archive at Manchester Metropolitan University*)

rooftops. The music finishes and Barbirolli acknowledges his applause. The sequence was very much admired by critics of the time: 'a beautiful reel',[21] 'delightfully integrated'.[22] It was remembered, too. In February 1950 Rotha discussed his editing of the sequence with the critic Richard Winnington for the BBC's television programme *Montage*.[23]

(*North West Film Archive at Manchester Metropolitan University*)

Nevertheless, without denying Rotha's fine editing, which builds an exhilarating speed and tension, the sequence is overlong and sits unevenly and uncomfortably with the rest of the film. Indeed, it detracts from the message. After the audience has left the cinema, will it remember most the lesson on local civics, or a breathless recreational spin? The relief is tangible when the film adjourns to the local pub with its more ordinary singer, and the reel finishes with moody contrast shots of wet cobblestones against the sound of the last tram, while simple pictures and simple sound effects evoke the city at rest.

For the finale, the script writers return to the people, repeating the film's opening sentiment: 'What is the city but the people?' They are shown at work in industry, the university, the Rylands Library, 'proud of their ancient skill in trade and industry, proud that they are going to use their skill to create a new city out of the old'. Musically, the sequence is Alwyn's fifth movement, and commences with a long deep pedal point with faint timpani beats exciting feelings of expectation, even apprehension. Slowly more strings and the woodwind join

---

[21] *Documentary News Letter*, 6:56 (April–May 1947), 89.

[22] *Monthly Film Bulletin*, 14:165 (30 September 1947), 126.

[23] 13 February 1950, 9.45–10.15 p.m. It represented over a quarter of the whole evening's viewing, as during that period the BBC broadcast only 1¾ hours of television in the evening. *Radio Times*, 106:1374 (10 February 1950).

in as a melodically vague but ceremonial theme emerges, becoming stronger, higher and increasingly fervent. Weaving a musical texture attesting civic pride, the theme is now pierced with horn fanfares and drum rolls as Manchester's achievements are declaimed; now hushed – perhaps with harp arpeggio – as the commentary becomes thoughtful. Increasingly affirmative, however, the musical composition coalesces with the spoken word to proclaim 'the world is on the threshold of a new revolution' and outline the Mancunian's sense of rights and justice. Rotha's socialist conscience replays pictures seen earlier, but this time the mood is in striking contrast to the earlier historic review mourned then by Alwyn's dismal organ. Now the script is uplifting, a positive socialist vision of the city of the future. 'Night is over, to be refreshed again', declaims the commentary, a view soon reversed as pictures of children in slum conditions are revealed and the composer discovers a plaintive musical mood: 'but this, this is not fresh, it is the rotten left overs of yesterday. In our new city-to-be it can have no place.' Then a horn fanfare ushers in a repetition of the rousing opening music as the commentary brings home the lesson of the film: 'From the very centre of our city let us resolve that the lessons of yesterday shall not be forgotten in our plans for tomorrow … Let us not forget that this is our city, to make of it what – we – will.' And as aerial views glide backwards from the city hall, Alwyn's music, optimistic and resolute, is left to sway emotions, while a caption has the final say: 'This film is dedicated by the citizens of Manchester to all those whose courage and energy will create the cities of the future.'

The first showing of the finished film was in July 1947, and – like the viewing of the rough-cut in January – in London. Harry Thorneycroft, the Labour member for Clayton, had been anxious that other MPs would see what Manchester had been up to, and be 'stung with envy'. He therefore arranged a showing to over fifty members in Westminster's Grand Committee Room, which served part-time as the 'Palace of Westminster Cinema'. A large representation from the Manchester area prompted one member to observe that all that was lacking was the Manchester City Police Band. MPs from other industrial cities, including Liverpool, Leeds and Plymouth, also came to take a look, and Tom Driberg brought a party of German prisoners with him.[24]

---

[24] *Manchester Guardian*, 17 July 1947; *Manchester Guardian*, 23 July 1947.

Three days later, on 25 July 1947, J. Arthur Rank was in Manchester to join city councillors for a private preview of the film.[25] It was another three weeks before the film opened to the general public. Civic leaders from Manchester and other towns attended the premiere on 11 August at the Odeon Cinema in Oxford Street. It was followed by a week's run at the cinema, then by screenings in other Odeon and Gaumont cinemas in the Greater Manchester area.[26]

Not everybody was pleased with the film. 'Mr Manchester' writing in the *Manchester Evening News* Diary thought people would get the impression that the city consisted of 'slums, smoke, councillors, speedway racing, all-in wrestling, the "bobs" and John Barbirolli', in that order.[27] A letter to the *Manchester Guardian* regretted 'how much of our real Manchester Paul Rotha has missed. We deserve another film to correct wrong impressions. There is beauty in our city, especially in the suburbs, for those with eyes to see it.'[28]

Comments like these were answered by Stephen C. Wallwork of the Oxford University Scientific Society, who thought

It is natural that some indignation should be felt at the number of aspects of Manchester life which are not represented in *A City Speaks*, but condemnation on these grounds is not justified.
The treatment of the subject matter which your correspondents seem to desire would result in nothing more than a travel film in which the audience's attention is directed first to one interesting feature and then to another with no possibility of synthesis. Such a treatment would leave no lasting impression.
By concentrating on the two main themes of local government and housing, the Manchester man is deprived of the pleasure of seeing many familiar places on the screen, but the film assumes a greater significance for the outsider.[29]

A balanced evaluation had been made earlier by R.J. of the *Manchester Guardian*, who correctly discriminated between the 'light relief' and the 'lecture on history, organisation, and statistics' which it was intended to 'sweeten'. 'The lecture itself is accurate, balanced, and rather long: the sweetening chosen for its appeal to youthful audiences.' He went on as follows:

---

[25] *Manchester Guardian*, 26 July 1947.
[26] *Manchester Guardian*, 9 July 1947; *To-Day's Cinema*, 69:5517 (11 July 1947), 31.
[27] Quoted in *Manchester Eyewitness*. On-line summary of the week's news for week ending 16 August 1947. http://www.manchesteronline.co.uk/ewm/mew/mew133.html
[28] *Manchester Guardian*, 16 August 1947.
[29] *Manchester Guardian*, 1 September 1947.

By any standards, this is a polished essay in documentary which faces squarely the problems of Manchester's slums and present lack of planning. The photography is uneven: the sequences from the air, in the Town Hall, and in the Royal Exchange are excellent; those in the factories and the Thirlmere flat and conventional. The commentary, spoken in various dialects, is admirable, though the chief Lancastrian seems to have spent some time in Yorkshire. The humour is unforced and apt.

It is the quality of imagination which is lacking. Love Manchester or hate it, few people can maintain a detached view of it, and there have always been some citizens who saw magic in its warehouses and perverse beauty under its dirt. Mr Rotha steers a middle course, as befits a Londoner, and is not one of them.[30]

In the early days of 1944, when the film was simply a gleam in the eye of Manchester's Civic Film Committee, one of the bedrock proposals to the Corporation had been that 'a key or foundation film' would be made, 'followed later by a shorter film in continuation of the ideas propounded in the key film, to show in some detail particular activities or aspects of local government'. This would be for general circulation outside the Manchester area.[31] The proposal was brought up again in early December 1946,[32] and in the spring of 1947, the *Documentary News Letter* in its review of *A City Speaks* discussed at length the intention to make this shorter version which would last about 45 minutes. It would be done, said the journal, by omitting the centre reels dealing with Manchester's particular problems.[33] We next learn of the proposal in January 1948, when 'Our London Correspondent' announced in the *Manchester Guardian* that the Ministry of Health had 'taken over the guardianship of the Manchester proposals to cut the film to 40 minutes'. The new film, said the report, would combine the Manchester film with footage of locations in Norwich, and be distributed by the Central Office of Information's Central Film Library.[34]

News of this emasculation elicited a tart response from Rotha:

Sir,– I was interested to learn from today's *Manchester Guardian* that the civic film *A City Speaks* is to be shortened. I should be even more interested to learn who is to do the shortening.[35]

---

[30] *Manchester Guardian*, 26 July 1947.
[31] *To-Day's Cinema*, 62:5015 (4 April 1944), 3–4.
[32] *The Cinema*, 67:5430 (4 December 1946), 6.
[33] *Documentary News Letter*, 6:56 (April–May 1947), 89.
[34] *Manchester Guardian*, 29 January 1948.
[35] *Manchester Guardian*, 30 January 1948.

For his answer Rotha had to wait for over three years, when in 1951 the shortened version entitled *City Government* was released by Data Films. The Norwich footage was forgotten, and at a running time of 13 minutes the film nowhere approached the old proposal of a 40- or 45-minute documentary. The editor was Francis Gysin (with Eric Pask), the former assistant director of *A City Speaks*.

If civic authorities elsewhere looked enviously at Manchester's achievement, they may nevertheless have been discouraged by the cost. Even as *A City Speaks* was released, Lambeth Council was shelving its plans, announced several months earlier, for a film costing £5,000 (equivalent currently to £200,000, less than a third of Manchester's bill), to educate Londoners on how their boroughs spent the rates. Lambeth had tried hard to persuade other London councils to participate, 'but when the cost was considered enthusiasm died'.[36]

It was natural that London's devastation by enemy bombings should have been seen as an opportunity to document that city's plans for ideological reconstruction schemes. Indeed, a few short films were produced, including *The Proud City* (1945), an important film explaining the visionary Greater London Plan, and *The Plan and the People* (1945), described as presenting 'the human angle on the LCC plan for London'.[37] Both of these films had scores by Alwyn. A short film was also proposed by the Corporation of Eastbourne,[38] and the Corporation of Glasgow managed to complete a 20-minute documentary telling the story of the city's civic housing schemes.[39] But only the City of Portsmouth managed to match in ambition and achievement Rotha's mighty *A City Speaks*. There, Jill Craigie's 64-minute-long *The Way We Live* (1946) documented the arguments in favour of the Watson-Abercrombie plan for the re-creation of that ruined city. Ordinary Portsmouth citizens acted out roles, and the music was by Gordon Jacob. Filippo Del Giudice's influential Two Cities Films produced the film, and J. Arthur Rank put it out on general release, beating the Manchester Civic Film by a year.

Rotha's company Films of Fact closed down soon after the release of *A City Speaks*. It was forced to do so, according to Rotha, by the

---

[36] *To-day's Cinema*, 67:5437 (20 December 1946), 7; *The Cinema*, 69:5519 (16 July 1947), 29.
[37] *Documentary News Letter*, 6:51 (1946), 8.
[38] *The Cinema*, 66:5343 (15 May 1946), 27.
[39] *The Cinema*, 67:5439 (25 December 1946), 14.

inefficiency and lack of policy of the Ministry of Information's successor, the Central Office of Information.[40] But there was no let-up in Rotha's energy. Until 1963 he was involved in a number of film enterprises, including two years as Head of the BBC's Documentary Film Department, and the direction of three feature films, one of which, *No Resting Place* (1950), was scored by William Alwyn and received wide critical acclaim and screening at the Venice Film Festival – but minimal distribution. His film *World Without End*, made in co-operation with Basil Wright and completed in 1953 for UNESCO, won the British Film Academy Award. As he himself complained, however, 'Since … 1963 I have not made another film not because I did not wish to, but because no-one asked me.'[41] Rotha's friendship with Alwyn lasted until well after both had retired from the business of making films. In later years when Rotha had fallen on hard times, and with a sick wife to support, Alwyn never refused a request for financial assistance, so grateful was he for the chances Rotha had given him.

As for the rest of the film's technical staff, most left Rotha within a year or two of its release, to found a new co-operative called Data Films. Francis Gysin became a producer and director with the company, and ultimately headed the film unit of the National Coal Board (NCB) – probably the largest unit in Europe – from 1963 until its demise in 1986 following the pit closures of the Thatcher years.

The photographer Harold Young had been the oldest member of Rotha's Manchester film team and he continued in work for various companies for a few more years. His last production that I can trace was a second feature made in 1954, by which time he was 65 years old and ripe for retirement. The other cameraman, Cyril Arapoff, worked for a time with Cavalcanti in Brazil. On his return to Britain he joined Gysin at NCB Films, where he served as senior cameraman for two decades.

For the composer of *A City Speaks*, the film had long-term consequences. At the time of the film's recording, Alwyn was planning his first symphony, but because he was, in his own words, 'an individual-

---

[40] Herbert G. Luft, 'Rotha and the World', *Quarterly of Film, Radio and Television*, 10:1 (Fall 1855), 89–99; David Pearson, 'Multi-voice Commentary, *World of Plenty* and *Land of Promise*', in *Paul Rotha*, ed. Paul Marius, BFI Dossier No. 16 (London: BFI, 1982), 80–81; Paul Rotha, *Films and Filming*, 12:10 (July 1966), 66; Paul Rotha, *Films and Filming*, 12:11 (August 1966), 66.

[41] Quoted in Eva Orbanz, *Journey to a Legend and Back: The British Realistic Film* (Berlin: Volker Spiess, 1977), 193.

ist, a "loner" more or less content to go my own way',[42] he was reluctant to approach a conductor to sponsor a performance of his work. As a result of coming into contact with John Barbirolli, 'fortune smiled on me and opened the way to the performance of my symphonic cycle'.[43] At first, however, their relationship was cool, as Alwyn recalled:

At the first recording session Barbirolli was very much aloof, and cold in his attitude to me. He quite obviously regarded me as yet another hack film composer and unworthy of his attention. But as the music evolved he gradually warmed towards me, and at the end of the week's recording he called me up to the rostrum and, addressing the orchestra to heart-warming applause he said what a great privilege it had been for him and the Hallé to play my music. At a convivial lunch with Paul and me, and after the discovery of our mutual adoration of Puccini, John asked me what I was composing. I told him: 'My first symphony.' 'When will it be finished?' 'At the end of this year.' 'Then,' said John, 'I shall give it the first performance at next year's Cheltenham Festival.' He was as good as his word, the work was duly performed at Cheltenham (1950) where it received a great reception, and the following year he brought it to London for performance at the Royal Festival Hall. Thus began a fruitful association, for John commissioned my Second Symphony for a world premiere with the Hallé, and followed it by the first performance of my Symphonic Prelude *The Magic Island*. Later, John's wife, Evelyn Rothwell, introduced my *Oboe Concerto* to London at the Proms.[44]

Perhaps the experience of working with Alwyn influenced Barbirolli's opinion of film composers. In an interview in *The Gramophone* in 1947, when *A City Speaks* was fresh in his mind, he was asked whether he thought British composers spent too much time writing for film. He replied:

No, it's all good practice for them and, as you say, the composer must live. Mozart was commissioned to write music for all sorts of social occasions, some of which is very beautiful, but people very probably didn't listen to it. They are a little snobbish about film music today. It may not be great music, but who knows?, some day a composer might write a really good score that can stand alone from the film. Besides, background music helps people to cultivate an ear for good orchestral texture – William Alwyn has written some beautiful music for the Manchester Civic Film.[45]

[42] William Alwyn, *Winged Chariot* (Southwold: Southwold Press, 1983; 1997), 13.
[43] Alwyn, *Winged Chariot*, 13.
[44] Alwyn, *Winged Chariot*, 13.
[45] *The Gramophone*, 24:284 (January 1947), 117.

In November 1947, Alwyn's *Suite 'Manchester' for Orchestra* was performed by Barbirolli and the Hallé at the King's Hall.

By early 1956 Alwyn's third symphony was ready for showing to Barbirolli. On Sunday, 19 February Alwyn recorded the occasion in his diary. He was still chafing from his turning down a prestigious appointment as Head of Music at BBC Television, and the weather was bitterly cold:

Yesterday afternoon I took the sketches of the symphony to show to John Barbirolli. I ascended several flights of creaking, uncarpeted stairs in a decayed house in a bomb-damaged square in central London to find John huddled in a wicker chair in a room overlooking a grave-yard. The surroundings were not without dignity, and the neighbourhood, although fallen on bad times, still preserved something of its classical period – the snow-shrouded tombstones were the solid caskets of a more opulent era. John looked tiny and wisp-like; he had a chill, and his burnt-up, haunted hollow-eyed visage seemed more strained than ever. It is so difficult sometimes to get at the man behind the mask, but this time the mask melted and he was as human as his conducting. He thumbed through the sketches, singing phrases and making various suggestions and asking questions about scoring. The outcome was that he liked it – better than No 1 or No 2 – and he has agreed to conduct the first performance as arranged. But I am worried about John. I fear that he has more than a chill; he looks like a man on the verge of a serious illness.[46]

Alwyn's Symphony No. 3 was given its first performance at the Royal Festival Hall on 10 October, but Barbirolli was not there. Because he was seriously ill, Barbirolli had cancelled his engagements and could not complete his sequence of performances of Alwyn's symphonies. The symphony was performed instead under Sir Thomas Beecham.[47]

And so the aftermath of Manchester's Civic Film played itself out over the years. And it still does, for the film is in constant demand by the local general public who take a nostalgic pleasure from it: for example, towards the end of 2005 it was screened in the Town Hall, and the North West Film Archive has included the scenes contrasting the city slums with leafy Wythenshawe in a sampler DVD called *Moving Memories*. The film is also in demand by architects and historians: its record of the old city has been seen as a 'priceless document' on buildings lost in the spate of post-war reconstruction after the 1950s.[48] But although at that time there was little concept of

---

[46] Alwyn, 'Ariel to Miranda', 53.
[47] Alwyn, 'Ariel to Miranda', 84.
[48] Anon. http://www.manchesteronline.co.uk/ewm/mew/mew126city.html

the conservation of the old and valuable, there was a vision, and that vision was bold, ambitious, enlightened, beautiful, and planned. The vision embraced Manchester Corporation's compassion for its people, its determination that they should be involved in their local society. It embraced, too, its dedication to moving them from inner city slums – where local people took for granted the grimy and soot-blackened buildings – to the light, open and airy, leafy garden city, and shunned the continental concept of high-rise buildings, with their consequent social problems. Manchester became a model, not just for housing, but also for health care, education, and education for leisure, and though it by no means met all its aspirations, its optimistic, integrated, vision set an agenda for other cities too. That vision was recorded in *A City Speaks*.

A City Speaks (1947)

Sponsor: City of Manchester Corporation. Production Company: Films of Fact. Produced and Directed by Paul Rotha. Associate Director: Francis Gysin. Script: Walter Greenwood, Ara Calder-Marshall, Paul Rotha. Photography: Harold ('Hal') Young, Cyril Arapoff. Production Assistants: Michael Orrom, H. Martyn Wilson, Peter Bradford, Mary Beales, John Reid. Maps and charts: Isotype Institute. Animation: Diagram Films. Unit Manager: Sydney Sharples. Commentary by Valentine Dyall. Among the voices: Deryck Guyler, Alexander Grandison, Walter Greenwood, A. Robins MP.
Among the players: Members of the Unnamed Society
Music played by Hallé Orchestra conducted by Barbirolli
Duration: 69 minutes
Commercial 35 mm release arranged through the J Arthur Rank Organisation, non-commercial 16 mm distribution by Central Film Library. Transmitted on BBC Television: 11 February 1952.

Suite 'Manchester' for Orchestra (1947)

From *A City Speaks*, in five movements:
   1 Prelude
   2 March
   3 Interlude
   4 Scherzo
   5 Finale

Duration: 14 minutes
Instrumentation: 2 flutes, 2 oboes, 2 clarinets. 2 bassoons, 4 horns, 3 trumpets in C, 3 trombones, tuba, timpani, percussion (side drum and cymbals), harp, strings

First performance: Hallé Orchestra/Sir John Barbirolli, King's Hall, Belle Vue, Manchester: 30 November 1947

City Government (1951)

A re-edit of *A City Speaks*. Sponsors: Central Office of Information and Ministry of Health. Production Company: Data Film Productions. Edited by Francis Gysin and Eric Pask.
Duration: 13 minutes
16 mm distribution by Central Film Library

My grateful thanks to Marion Hewitt (North West Film Archive), Andrew Knowles (The Alwyn Foundation), Michael Redhead, and Eleanor Roberts (The Hallé Archive).

IAN JOHNSON's *William Alwyn: The Art of Film Music* was published in 2005 by Boydell & Brewer at £25. ISBN: 1 84383 159 7.

The Royal Society
of Musicians
of Great Britain

FOUNDED 1738 INCORPORATED BY ROYAL CHARTERS 1790 & 1987

The Royal Society of Musicians of Great Britain was founded by Handel and others to support professional musicians and their families when in distress because of illness, accident, or old age. Its charitable work has continued, responding to increasing need and acting swiftly in cases of emergency.

If you know a musician needing help
please let us know at once.

If you wish to help us
please send a donation or arrange for
Gift Aid or GAYE donations or a legacy.

For details please contact: The Secretary
The Royal Society of Musicians of Great Britain
10 Stratford Place, London W1C 1BA
Telephone 020 7629 6137

Registered Charity Number 208879

Curved Air: L. W. Duck and the Henry Watson Music Library

MARTIN THACKER

I FIRST MET Leonard Duck on a Thursday evening in January 1982, in surroundings which were new to me but habitual to him. At that point, he had been retired for nearly a year, whereas I had only just taken up his vacated post. The long balcony lounge of the Free Trade Hall, with its queues for refreshments, was the background against which he and his wife were pointed out to me, drinking coffee and watching the music-loving world go by.

The Hallé concerts were an essential part of Leonard Duck's world, and his programme notes (of which more later) were in those days a characteristic part of the Hallé experience. He was of a retiring disposition, and my greeting caused a look of real alarm to pass over his face. I feared that in over-compensating for my own shyness, I might have done more harm than good, but not many weeks later he and his wife invited me to dinner at their home in Wilmslow. They had qualities that tend to be in short supply today: they were unassuming, courteous and friendly; engaged in their retirement in a variety of creative pursuits. Some of these were habitual to them: playing the piano and composing for him, painting for her, hill walking for them both; but they took full advantage of the adult education available at the Wilmslow Guild: Edith took up wood-carving; Leonard also became a painter in both oils and water-colour, and a photographer, and he took classes in local history, religion and astronomy. He was particularly keen to increase his understanding of the connection between science and religion.

He had been born on 6 February 1916 at Sutton Coldfield in the West Midlands – slight evidence of this could be heard in his speech all his life. He first learned music from his mother, who was an accomplished amateur pianist. At the age of ten he won a scholarship to Bishop Vesey's Grammar School. As well as music he enjoyed the strategic challenge of chess, and during his teenage years began his lifelong love of hill walking and cycling. A great deal of his profound knowledge of classical music and other subjects must have been gained by self-education: like some other outstanding music librarians of his generation he went neither to university nor to conservatoire.

By the outbreak of the Second World War he had served his apprenticeship in various libraries in Birmingham, gaining his ALA in 1937. Already an independent thinker, he felt that he must register as a conscientious objector, and immediately began a tough outdoor life on the land. Three years in civil defence followed, during which he drove ambulances in blitz-torn London, as he did later in Liverpool. In the latter city he discovered the Society of Friends (Quakers), finding in their reflective method of worship, and their Peace Testimony, a mirror of his own ideals. In 1943 he married Edith Speirs, a member of an established Quaker family. After the war he returned to the West Midlands and worked for a while in the Dudley public libraries. Then, in 1948, he and his wife moved to Manchester, where he took up an appointment as sub-librarian in the Henry Watson Music Library.

This was the vintage age of the Henry Watson (which had also had a veteran period), for it had recently moved to spacious accommodation, only half of which it still occupies, on the second floor of Manchester Central Library. Re-opening it on 16 September 1947, Sir John Barbirolli had referred to it as 'the most living library I have ever had the good fortune to use'. The floor plan was highly unusual, the building itself being a rotunda. Writing in 1952, Leonard Duck described it as 'a long, wide, curved corridor: it extends half-way round the circumference of the Central Library building'.

Space was used with a prodigality verging on abandon, as can be seen from one of the accompanying illustrations. Watson's second collection of instruments, the first having been given to the Royal Manchester College of Music, was at last able to be displayed, with a degree of public accessibility that would nowadays be out of the question. Included were an Italian virginal of circa 1600, a Tschudi-Broadwood harpsichord of 1791, a three-quarter Stradivarius violin, five pianos dating from 1771–1830, viols, a serpent, an ophicleide, some Bach trumpets, and much more. Duck warned, however, against putting the cart before the horse: 'The library houses all these because it happens to have room for them: it does not consider itself to be a museum, and will not thank you for referring to it by that title.'

Somewhere among all this was a den occupied by John F. Russell, who, having been employed by the City Council since 1902, was content to allow Leonard Duck to do most of the day-to-day work, while he himself wrote programme notes and received friends among

2nd floor, Manchester Central Library, circa 1952. (*Manchester Libraries and Information*)

resident and visiting musicians: many of the famous names of the day made a point of visiting him in the library when they came to Manchester. Russell had been Watson Music Librarian since 1920, but his knowledge of the library went back to Henry Watson's own day, when it had operated from the latter's house in Chapel Street, Salford. Russell had been one of the earliest city council staff sent to the library after Watson's death in January 1911. In his outgoing, friendly way, Russell inspired many, including the young Michael Kennedy, who wrote of him thus:

'Johnnie' Russell was a great librarian. The thousands of people who have used the magnificent library over which he presided with such geniality probably know little of the administrative genius needed to ensure that their varying needs were met. Johnnie had this genius, which he concealed by a seemingly casual, un-erudite approach. He always remembered, too, that a library is a humanitarian place, and he enjoyed helping his friends to run a fact to earth or to choose a book, often, as I well know, suggesting something off the beaten track which invariably proved to be a stimulating choice. When he retired he missed his work dreadfully.

In the same way Leonard Duck, in his more self-effacing way, was to inspire a slightly younger generation.

Duck spent five years as Russell's deputy, at the end of which he was 37. He had been married for ten years and had a two-year-old daughter, Barbara. Coronation year, 1953, would be a milestone in his own life for several reasons. On Russell's retirement, he finally succeeded to the Librarianship of the Henry Watson Music Library. In this year he published his only full-length book: *The Amateur Orchestra*, a concise but thorough treatment of all aspects of its subject; historical, administrative and artistic. He had in print by this time several arrangements and editions of eighteenth-century music, and had recently published a lengthy illustrated description of the Watson library in the *Musical Times*. And on 23 March he was present at the meeting that led to the foundation of the UK branch of the International Association of Music Libraries, Archives and Documentation Centres (IAML), becoming the Library Association representative on the committee.

The following April, the branch Annual General Meeting was held at Manchester Central Library: committee minutes of 10 March 1954 include the following vital preparations: 'We should book 30 teas at 1/6d per head, through Mr. Duck, with an outside caterer, and allow 3d per head for an urn of tea to be provided by the Manchester Libraries Catering Department.' At that AGM, the first ever certificate of honorary membership was presented to John Russell: a mark of respect which had been proposed by Duck himself at a committee meeting on 22 October 1953. Russell spoke to the meeting about the early years of the library and the personality of Henry Watson. Leonard Duck then spoke about the present-day HWML, after which the meeting divided into two groups, to be given guided tours of the library, presumably by Russell and Duck themselves.

Leonard Duck remained on the IAML committee, representing the Library Association, for twenty-two years until 1975, speaking seldom, but ready to contribute when he felt that something needed to be said. When IAML was preparing a memorandum for submission to the Committee on Public Libraries in England and Wales, in February 1958, he wrote to Walter Stock (the redoubtable secretary/treasurer) as follows:

Since I shall not be present I feel that I should query two points in the memorandum … Two statements in the third section strike me as being questionable. The first is 'a high proportion of these twelve thousand [music] students borrow records from public libraries'. Can this really be true, in view of the fact that the majority of gramophone libraries are situated in the metropolitan area?

Secondly, in the paragraph following, *is* it notorious that since the war a good many societies have had to cease their activities for lack of music which is expensive and often hard to obtain? This is not my experience. In every case where societies known to me have ceased to function it has been because of lack of interest in their community. Moreover, as a matter of fact, although admittedly expensive, it surely is not hard to obtain (except of course certain recondite items).

Although he sat silent through the majority of meetings, he would often produce a sample of dry humour which showed that he was wide awake. One day in the late 1970s, the Central Library Briefing Group were hearing a report of the proceedings of the Cultural Services Committee, which in those days usually included a lengthy list of the

Leonard Duck shows the Henry Watson Collection's Italian virginal to a visitor in the 1950s. (*Manchester Libraries and Information*)

travels and social contacts of Timothy Clifford, then Director of Art Galleries. At the words 'the Director had the privilege of lunching with Lord and Lady Sainsbury', Duck murmured to his neighbour 'I often have a Sainsbury's lunch'.

The Watson Music Library never included recorded music (except, long after Duck's time, a closed-access collection of vinyl from 1994–2003, which though extensive was by that time obsolete, and a few CDs for a short time in the 1990s). Duck's strenuous efforts to establish a record library nearly succeeded in October 1962, when his thoroughly costed proposal was quoted verbatim in the City Librarian's own report to committee. But the Council feared legal complications. A further report was submitted in September 1964, after the passing of the Public Libraries and Museums Act of that year, but by that time the City Librarian had decided to split the collection among various other departments and branches. In other ways, too, this library was different from most others represented in IAML. Though neither a national nor an academic library, it had a large collection of early printed music and, from 1965, a sizeable quota of manuscripts. And it ran the most extensive of all national services of choral and orchestral sets: in effect it was a mail-order warehouse in the best Manchester tradition. Duck described the stress-ridden nature of this side of the operation in 1952:

The success of the scheme may be said to depend on these representatives [of borrowing societies], who may jeopardize a whole season's plans by not returning music to time. Real calamity is often averted by the ingenuity of the staff, but there are times when the air is thick with trunk-calls and telegrams.

Hilda Walsh, his sub-librarian from 1962, remembers him arriving hurriedly in the stacks with the cry, 'If I can't find six more Vivaldi Glorias, we're sunk!' To anyone who has tried running such a service these quotations do not sound like exaggerations; and he of all people was the least inclined to make a drama out of a crisis. Nowadays trunk-calls and telegrams have become emails and faxes, and Manchester limits its service to the North West of England, lending about ten percent of what was usual in Leonard Duck's day and the decade following his departure.

All these characteristics of the Watson Music Library made the experience of Leonard Duck and his staff essentially different from that of colleagues elsewhere. Developments of the 1950s and 60s further combined to ensure that the IAML Annual General Meeting of 1954 would remain the high-water mark of the fortunes of the library. In 1955 a new City Librarian, the dynamic and colourful David I. Colley, soon began to show an interest in measuring the impact of the Music Library. The Chairman, Alfred Logan, was of the same mind, but they sometimes seized the wrong end of the stick. Colley to Duck, 28 March 1956: 'A detailed explanation of the 25% decrease in issues

which you reported to the Chairman is required.' Duck's reply was a
tasteful blend of Jeeves and Sir Humphrey Appleby:

I have not made a report to the Chairman at any time; my report to you dated
6 January did however point out that 'the issue of anthems was 7,453 in the
quarter October-December 1955, compared with 9,709 in the corresponding
quarter of 1954. This accounts for two-thirds of the drop in issues during the
last quarter'. Is this the matter referred to, please?

Colley urged greater contact with the users of the Music Library, a
good effect of which was a civilised series of 'at homes' – talks and
chamber recitals, held in the late 1950s to publicise the library and its
instruments. The first, in 1955, was planned as a forum in which to
discuss ways of 'increasing the usefulness of the Music Library'.
Colley to Duck, 19 July 1955:

I want you to start planning your arrangements for this, which should include
    (a) Some kind of display
    (b) Perhaps a short recital on the harpsichord
    (c) A list of guests. The Chairman suggests that the principal guest should
be Sir John Barbirolli, who might be asked to speak for ten minutes or a
quarter of an hour.

There followed a list of nineteen suggestions for guests, including 'the
Dean of Manchester', 'someone from the B.B.C. Northern Region',
'Full press support', 'The Parks Band Master' (against this Duck
wrote in pencil '!???'), 'Mr. Iles, Belle Vue Band Contest Organiser'
(Duck annotated this 'Deceased, 1951'), and 'A representative of the
Co-operative Union of Choirs' ('what's that?' he wrote). The 'at
homes' meant that for several years Leonard Duck now added the
duties of concert manager to his schedule. We find him writing to
Maurice Aitchison, of Manchester University Music Department, on
21 November 1958: 'The harpsichord is kept up to modern concert
pitch and tuned regularly by contract and again of course on the day
of a concert. Facilities for practice could be made available on Tuesday evenings.'

    On the whole, Colley's undoubted zeal was unfortunate in its
effects. He pushed up the use of the mail-order service to a level which
at peak times was simply unsustainable: urgently needed sets would
be hidden among literally hundreds of identical brown paper parcels.
He initiated his infamous 'packet of tea' policy, which had sets issued

April 1962: Anne Ransley confronts a mountain of returned music in the library stacks. (*Manchester Libraries and Information*)

and received through a hatch at the bottom of the library stairs by staff who were not equipped to deal with queries (needless to say, queries almost always arose). An organization and methods review of 1959 (Colley was abreast of all the fashionable management trends) removed staff from the Music Library and showed an insensitivity to the special nature of printed music which caused the highly efficient sub-librarian, Jean Hickling, to leave Manchester and return to London (before coming north, she must have worked for Westminster Libraries, since we find her representing Lionel McColvin at a IAML (UK) committee meeting on 22 October 1953). Worst of all, in a manifestation of the 50s craze to open more and more subject departments, the Music Library lost half its floor space on the foundation of a Fine Arts Department in 1960. No longer was there room to display the instruments, which mouldered for years in storage at Wilbraham branch library; and never again would the Music Library be an integral department: it had thenceforth to share a counter, and the duties of its clerical staff overlapped with the Arts Library.

An initiative of David Colley's in 1965 did, however, add a dimension to the Watson Music Library which greatly increased its international reputation. On the death of Sir Newman Flower, formerly Chairman of Cassell, Colley successfully negotiated the purchase of his Handel collection, containing manuscripts originally copied for Charles Jennens, Handel's patron and librettist. More interestingly still, the collection had an Italian section which later proved to contain previously unknown Vivaldi violin sonatas, and a version of *The Four Seasons* which differs in important respects from the previously known text. Asked to examine and report on the collection, Duck initially advised against its acquisition, on the grounds that the HWML had not previously contained many manuscripts, and that many of the printed Handel scores were simply duplicates of items in Watson's own collection. However, very shortly after the arrival of the collection, he had prepared and published an efficient finding list. And he was given full credit by Michael Talbot for leading him to the uncatalogued part of the collection, where Talbot made the Vivaldi discoveries:

I was delayed, however, by the Music Librarian, Mr. Leonard Duck, who, knowing, naturally, of my general interest in late Baroque music, asked me whether I would like to have a look through some uncatalogued material from the same collection … Mr. Duck's offer was of a kind that one does not easily refuse, so I went down into the stacks with him.

Duck's philosophy of service was expressed in the introduction to a talk he gave in about 1950, while still sub-librarian. This introduction, deleted in pencil on the typescript, must have been important to him, since it appears again in a draft of his first annual report to the Libraries Committee, 1953–4, though there too it is deleted, with a comment in the margin: 'put in next year'. His thesis was that modern production methods had robbed work (i.e. what people do for a living) of its creative aspect. Not only that, but

as the diversions which are available for leisure hours are too often themselves commercialised and mass-produced, the workers are frustrated and find in them no relief or fulfilment. There follows a seeking after easy ways of self-forgetfulness, leading to an undue love of the sensational, the violent and the superficial, and typified by the cult of the motion-picture.

The music librarian's task, therefore, was 'not to supply facts, but to release the imagination and to correct the false sense of values to which I have referred'. This would not be an inappropriate mission for a librarian today, who would, however, have to embrace many more types of music than Duck envisaged in the early 1950s: 'The library has no "speciality", or any aversions, apart from the world of jazz, which it does not attempt to cover.' Beyond jazz there were, of course, forms of activity that he did not stoop to mention at all. But before labelling him elitist, one must remember that these views were fairly typical of their time, and that he did eventually introduce a jazz piano section, creating for it a new number within Russell's classification scheme.

Duck inherited from John Russell the task of writing programme notes for the Hallé concerts, though the conservative Hallé continued to use Russell's notes whenever they played a work which he had previously annotated: in 1964–5, Russell's notes were still far more numerous than Duck's. Their styles were those of different eras: Russell had frequent recourse to formulations such as 'a heavenly melody is first announced by the cellos', whereas Duck was more terse, factual and analytical. He made use of examples in music notation, and his writings are often of real value when an analysis of a work is requested by a student. His humour, variously described as 'dry' or 'impish', often appears in the notes. Quoting the line 'Deemest thou praiseworthy wedlock's breach, then prate thou yet farther and call it holy that shame now blossom forth from bond of twin-born pair!' from *Die Walküre*, he commented: 'Her reactions are expressed with force if not brevity.' He wrote with authority, his judgements backed up by wide reading, and he did not mince words. Later in the same note, he speaks of 'a moment in which the paste-board figure of Wotan comes to life in music that causes the creaking mechanics of the plot to fade away'.

Leonard Duck retired in 1981 after thirty-three years at Manchester Central Library. In various ways he had had a considerable influence, and had helped many scholars, creative artists and ordinary citizens. Interviewed on BBC radio in 2000, Sir Peter Maxwell Davies referred to him by name as someone who had helped him in his youthful quest for self-education among the scores of the Watson Music Library.

He flourished during an active retirement of twenty years, though saddened by his wife's death in July 1991. He learned to use an early version of Sibelius, and his output as a composer increased as he got older: at the end of his life he had, and still has, as many as twenty original compositions in print. He wrote for a wide range of instrumental ensembles: a Concertino for piano and strings, a Concerto Grosso for trumpet, piano and strings, string quartets, and a work for five winds, two violins and cello, entitled *Equilibria*. Among many works for wind instruments are *Impressions and Inscapes* for oboe and piano, *Tone Sketches* for trumpet and piano, *La Cloche* for flute

Retirement day, February 1981. Left to right: Anne
Ransley, Leonard Duck, Hilda Walsh. (*Chris Ransley*)

and piano, *The Silver Huntress* for horn and piano, a *Partita* for
woodwind quartet, and, in lighter vein, *Concertissimo!* and *Knight
Errant* for flexible woodwind ensemble. At least one of his pieces was
used in the Associated Board grade syllabuses. Altogether he mus-
tered forty entries in the British Library catalogue.

Leonard Duck died on 6 March 2002, aged 86. The memories of
his friends, family and colleagues are remarkably synoptic: all speak
of his efficient mastery of his field of activity, his quiet authority, his
wide reading and his knowledge of diverse subjects. As well as all
this, there is a collective memory of his most important trait of all: 'He
was there when you needed him!'

Thanks are due to Barbara Whiteford (née Duck), some of whose notes on
her father's life and compositions are quoted verbatim in this article; and to
Hilda Walsh, Anne Ransley and David Taylor, erstwhile colleagues of
Leonard Duck.

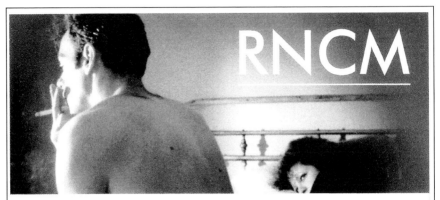

An Aldeburgh Memoir: 1968

DAVID DUBERY

*To William Delafield, to whom I shall be for ever indebted for his generosity
and for giving me the opportunity to realise a dream*

I FIRST VISITED Aldeburgh on 9 June 1968 and attended the opening concert of the twenty-first Aldeburgh Festival in the year-old Maltings Concert Hall at Snape. I was 19, a music student in my second year at the Northern School of Music in Manchester. I had been acquainted with the music of Benjamin Britten for several years, having been introduced to it in 1961 by a most enthusiastic and encouraging music master, Roger Fowler, at the High School of Art. He was a kind, friendly giant who inspired and nurtured my early efforts in composition. Britten's music was challenging, individual, and strange at first; but I persevered and discovered a rich and enthralling musical personality.

During a music lesson at school Roger played *A Ceremony of Carols* Op. 28, in the 1953 10-inch mono recording of the Copenhagen Boys' Choir accompanied by Enid Simon on the harp. The combination of treble voices and harp had a certain enchantment, and I admired the procession and recession at the start and close of the piece, an idea that Britten used later in the *Three Church Parables*.

Roger lent me two of his own long-playing records so that I might become better acquainted with two other works that he thought interesting. The first was *The Young Person's Guide to the Orchestra*, written to accompany the Board of Education's 1946 film *Instruments of the Orchestra*. I was immediately impressed and I played it often, admiring Britten's dazzling orchestration, and revelling in that remarkable fugal finale which brings the work to a glittering and majestic D major conclusion. The *Nocturne* for tenor, strings and seven obbligato instruments was a dark, atmospheric piece, unlike anything I had previously heard. Completed in 1958 and dedicated to Gustav Mahler's widow, Alma, it was premiered at the Leeds Festival in October of that year. This recording was made in 1959, and on repeated hearings I was lulled into its world of dreams, each of the eight song settings linked by a hypnotic gentle breathing of the strings. The finale is a beautiful and haunting setting of Shakespeare's Sonnet 43.

On 30 May 1962, Britten's *War Requiem* Op. 66 received its premiere and was broadcast live from Coventry Cathedral on BBC television in black and white.

I remember being totally enthralled. The occasion was a celebration of a new Cathedral, the old one having been bombed in the Second World War in 1940. The event attracted a great deal of media coverage, not least because of an unexpected change when Heather Harper was brought in to replace the soprano Galina Vishnevskaya who, on political grounds, was refused permission to appear by the Russian Minister of Culture. Heather Harper, appearing as Helena in Britten's *A Midsummer Night's Dream* at the time, had only ten days to prepare the Requiem's taxing soprano part.

In 1964 the Covent Garden company visited Manchester for an extended season while its opera house in London underwent renovation. I attended Britten's opera *A Midsummer Night's Dream*. Composed in 1960, it was first performed at the thirteenth Aldeburgh Festival in the newly enlarged Jubilee Hall. The role of Oberon was created for the countertenor Alfred Deller, who also appears on the 1966 Decca recording; but in Manchester Russell Oberlin's was the first countertenor voice I had ever heard, and it was an unearthly and curious experience.

Eager to discover more about Britten and his music, I started building my own collection of recordings, not difficult during the 1960s as Decca led the way in issuing Britten's new works. I became addicted, read reviews, books, articles, bought the monthly *Gramophone* magazine, and regularly raided the second-hand records at the excellent Gibb's Bookshop in Manchester.

In January 1968, at a dinner party given by my friend Neil Salveson, I was introduced to William Delafield. He was very fond of music and our conversation soon led to a discussion about Britten's compositions and the Aldeburgh Festival, which William had visited on several occasions. Listening to his accounts I longed to experience the Festival for myself. He invited me to stay at Cambridge for a weekend in June and arranged a visit to Aldeburgh and tickets for the opening concert at Snape on the Sunday. I was bowled over at the prospect; June could not arrive soon enough.

Spring was a busy term at music college, where I was caught up in long rehearsals singing in the chorus of Verdi's *Otello* for Sir John Barbirolli's three farewell performances with the Hallé Orchestra at the Manchester Free Trade Hall. The international cast of soloists included Piero Miranda-Ferarro, who had recorded *La Gioconda* with Maria Callas. I was also studying and memorising the first movement of Mozart's Piano Concerto No. 9 in E flat for performance in the college piano recitals in May, immediately after a third *Otello* performance in Sheffield. Music exams would follow and rehearsals for a production of Vaughan Williams's *Hugh the Drover*.

On Friday 7 June, Neil drove me to his lodgings in Hale Barns and at 7.20 the next morning we set off in the rain for Cambridge. By the time we arrived at 11 a.m., the sun was shining gloriously. William had booked rooms at the Royal Cambridge Hotel and Neil would lodge at his college rooms. Since William would not arrive until later in the day, Neil delighted in showing me the sights of the city, its remarkable architecture, beautiful gardens with huge copper beech trees, and the riverbanks flanked by willows gracefully bending to the water's edge. We visited many of the colleges including Clare, King's, St John's, Queens' and Corpus Christi. Students sporting straw boaters were punting along the river enjoying the early summer sunshine and passing beneath the Bridge of Sighs. We examined some of the treasures of the Fitzwilliam Museum, a fine palace housing manuscripts by Scarlatti and Handel and collections of unique paintings and pottery.

William arrived in time for dinner at the Club restaurant; it was decided afterwards that a stay in Cambridge could not be complete without seeing the famous Cambridge Footlights Review, a selection of comedy sketches with plenty of silliness, and when that was over we were invited to join music students at a party in their college.

On Sunday, Neil remained in Cambridge to visit college friends and professors. William and I set out for Aldeburgh in style in his Bentley with its comfortable leather seats and walnut dashboard. We stopped for morning tea at the fifteenth-century Bull Hotel in Long Melford, a dignified old wool town with views of green parkland and great manor houses. The town is noted for its Holy Trinity Church, which of all the churches in Suffolk has the finest proportions and flushwork, a type of decoration using flints. William told me that the Bull was known to be the preferred place of residence during the Bach weekend, an event engineered by Benjamin Britten.

We continued our journey, the Bentley gliding along exceptionally straight roads, presumably Roman in origin, which offered intriguing views of windmills, canals and flat reedy marshes and endless sky. Because of coastal erosion there is no coast road, and separate roads branch off from the A12 to reach the various seaside towns. Suddenly we arrived in Aldeburgh and a seascape replaced the countryside.

Aldeburgh is a small seaside town of endearing charm. It was surprising to learn that in the sixteenth century it had a thriving ship-building industry and was the place where Sir Francis Drake's ship *The Golden Hind* was built. The industry went into decline when the River Alde silted up, and from the nineteenth century Aldeburgh became a fishing village. In 1968 it had a High Street with shops, pubs and a tiny cinema, one tourist hotel, the Festival Club, and public gardens. Along the promenade we saw terraced houses covered in pebbledash and painted in white or pastel colours; at the far end of Crag Path, where it merges with Crabbe Street, stands the seventeenth-century Old Moot Hall which features prominently in Britten's *Peter Grimes*. On this Sunday it housed a highly rewarding exhibition of paintings and drawings by James McNeill Whistler.

After a buffet lunch at the Festival Club we walked along the shingle beach where young people were enjoying the sunshine and sea. The ocean was very deep and dangerous for swimming, so the Lifeboat Station was always alert and ready to put to sea. Britten captured this atmosphere superbly in *Peter Grimes.*

We viewed another exhibition at the Parish Church on a hill above the town, this time of photographs, news cuttings, programmes and posters from all the past Aldeburgh Festivals. It strongly emphasised the level of co-operation and contribution made by the local community to every festival.

Before proceeding to Snape we drove out of Aldeburgh and turned into a country road leading to the golf club. William slowed the car down and stopped outside the drive of the Red House so that I could see the home of Benjamin Britten and his partner Peter Pears. The architectural style possibly dates from the early seventeenth century and at one time it had been a large farmhouse. The frontage was double-gabled, partially covered in creeper, and in the centre of the tiled roofs there stood unusually tall chimney stacks. The sash windows were painted white, as was the wooden slatted fence that protected the property. The gate, bearing a sign with the name of the house, stood open, and we were amused by the collection of home-made signs nailed to wooden posts at each side of the pebbled drive that read 'welcome' in a vast assortment of languages. The drive was circular with a green lawn in the centre, and at the left-hand side of the building was an unpretentious front door.

The concert at the Maltings was due to begin at 3 p.m. The building had once been a huge malt barn where barley was dried for the brewing of beer. Now it was transformed into a glorious concert hall with financial aid from the Gulbenkian Foundation, the Arts Council, the Decca Record Company, the Pilgrim Trust and subscriptions from private individuals. It was opened by Queen Elizabeth with due ceremony on 2 June 1967.

We drove along rough roads past several of these characterful buildings and parked the car. A first impression of the concert hall was that it still looked like a collection of storage barns. The hall was covered by an enormous roof with four chimney stacks, and joined to one side was another smaller barn. At the entrance stood a sculpture presented by Sir Henry Moore. The interior of the hall maintained the original red bricks of the old barn and an expanse of varnished wood that constituted the lining of the roof, the floors, seats and low-level stage. On either side of the foyer there were two staircases, one leading to the upper hall and the other to the bar.

With glasses of chilled Prosecco in hand, we stepped outdoors and onto a wooden bridge leading to a terrace which was already peopled with smartly dressed concert-goers. The other side of the bridge took us over a narrow canal onto a strip of land along the banks of the River Alde with a wonderful view of the fenlands and reedy marshes which brought to mind the scenery described in *Curlew River*.

William encountered old friends and I was introduced to Bim who was at the festival on a Princess of Hesse Scholarship, and to the countertenor James Bowman whom William knew from his Oxford days when James was a chorister at New College. During conversation, James suggested that I write something for him. I spent hours that summer composing a set of songs to Chinese poetry, hoping they would be complete when he returned from his American tour. Would that I had been a better and more experienced composer in those days! James was one of the artists taking part in this opening concert and, as it was nearly time to start, we wished him well and re-entered the barn to locate our seats.

The hall seated around 800 in an area raked at an angle so that everyone had a good view of the stage. To one side of the stage was a glass windowed room, rather like a recording facility, where Britten was seated with his guests Peter Pears, Imogen Holst and the librettist William Plomer. Over the years the festival had gained an international reputation and the audience was often peopled with notables from many countries. Sitting immediately in front of me was the veteran actor Sir John Gielgud and to my right Don Garrard, a fine singer with the Sadler's Wells Opera.

The concert opened with Henry Purcell's 1683 *Ode for St Cecilia's Day*, for voices, strings and continuo. The singers were Susan Longfield, Jane Manning, Meriel Dickinson, James Bowman, Martin Lane, Ian Partridge, Christopher Keyte and basses from the Ambrosian singers. The strings of the English Chamber Orchestra were directed from the harpsichord by Philip Ledger. (Meriel Dickinson had been my music tutor at the High School of Art after Roger Fowler left, and was responsible for my first performance at the Manchester Free Trade Hall in 1963 when I was 14 years old, playing two of my own compositions and accompanying a singer in an aria by Handel in front of an audience of 1500.)

The acoustic of the hall enriched everything that we heard, and the concert, Five Centuries of Occasional Music 1519–1968, was recorded by BBC Radio 3. Following the Purcell we heard two songs from the time of King Henry VII, 'England be glad' and 'Pray we to God'. The first half ended with John Blow's *Ode on the death of Mr Henry Purcell*, a long virtuoso piece with florid intertwining passages well suited to the flexible and magical voices of James Bowman and Martin Lane.

After an interval the concert continued with Schubert's rarely performed *Gesang der Geister über den Wassern*, scored for four tenors, four basses and lower strings to a text by Goethe. Contrasting with this profound and unusually moving piece there followed the 1964 *Elegy for JFK* by Stravinsky, which appeared even more poignant on this occasion since John Kennedy's younger brother, Robert, had been assassinated a week before the concert. It was here that Meriel Dickinson was able to employ her dramatic mezzo accompanied by three clarinets. For me it was thrilling to watch her perform at so auspicious a concert, her rich, deep-toned voice filling the hall. (I remembered her bringing some compositions by her brother, Peter Dickinson, for me to read and play at school.)

The Stravinsky was followed by Britten's *Alpine Suite* for three recorders. It had been composed in 1955 and was played on 26 June that year at Thorpeness Mere by members of the Aldeburgh Music

Club. But in 1968 it was unknown; and it certainly delighted the audience, who responded with glee to the happy sounds that bubbled forth from the sweet-toned instruments played by David Munrow, John Turner and Richard Lee. The piece had been composed to cheer up the painter Mary Potter, who had broken her leg while on a skiing holiday in Zermatt with Britten and Pears. The final piece, commissioned by Britten's Aspen fund, was the *Occasional Suite* by John Gardner,[*] composed for the occasion and scored for the forces deployed in the rest of the programme: three recorders, three clarinets, harpsichord and strings.

All the performances were of exceptional quality and gave us immense pleasure. Here there was a sense of occasion and a feeling that music was truly valued and respected, a journey of discovery that could satisfy both the intellect and the heart. Soon it was time to make the return journey to Cambridge for 7.30 dinner at the Garden Hotel with Neil, to say our goodbyes and then drive back to Manchester where I arrived home at 1.30 a.m. My visit to Aldeburgh had made a huge impact on me, and I couldn't wait to return.

---

[*] John Gardner (born in Manchester in 1917) is the composer of, among other works, a particularly attractive Flute Concerto, recorded by Jennifer Stinton and the Royal Ballet Sinfonia on ASV WHL2125.

Jaunting Car: Peter Hope and his Music

JOHN TURNER

Peter Hope in September 2003. (*John Turner*)

PETER HOPE celebrated his seventy-fifth birthday on 2 November 2005. The event was joyously marked the next day on BBC Radio 3 with a special edition of *Brian Kay's Light Programme*. This took the form of an extensive conversation with the composer, punctuated by performances of several of his pieces, including some specially recorded for the event by the BBC Concert Orchestra under Barry Wordsworth. The same format had been used in 2004 for the eightieth birthday of Ernest Tomlinson, a composer whom Peter Hope regards as his mentor, and who came from the same Mancunian stables.

The name of Peter Hope is less well known to the general musical public than that of almost any other composer of his generation, but the same certainly cannot be said of his music. His compositions and arrangements were broadcast almost daily in the 1950s and early 1960s (and his title music for the BBC Television News continued to be used until 1980). But the tight stratification of music broadcasts by the BBC left him and many other composers of light music stranded. The same thing of course happened with a good number of distinguished serious composers who had elected to write in a tonal, approachable style; and it is heartening that the changed climate of the present decade has encouraged some who gave up composition as a result to start writing again. Peter Hope was never silent, as he forged new ways of earning a living, and his skills as an arranger were highly valued.

He was born at 15 Cashmere Road, Edgeley, Stockport, in 1930. His father and aunt (father's sister) owned a ladies' and children's outfitters shop, which had been started by their mother. They traded under the name of Clarkes, in Castle Street, then a lively and diverse secondary shopping area of the town. Sadly today it is run down, with tattoo parlours, discount furniture shops and many 'to let' signs, a situation exacerbated by the pedestrianisation of the road and the proximity of a booming Morrisons supermarket. The family shop itself was demolished to make way for the roundabout by the Armoury.

Peter's father died when he was still young, in 1935, and his mother had of necessity to take over his place in the shop, which she continued to run in partnership with her sister-in-law. Peter's mother was born in Toronto and had come to England when she was 16 to live with her mother and stepfather in Shaw Heath, Stockport. After her husband's early death she eventually took up with David Neave, a car mechanic by profession, but when the Stockport clothing business was sold in the mid 1950s they moved to Appleby, in Westmorland. In the early 1970s they sold up again and moved south to Wareham in Dorset, not too far from Peter's present home. This was Peter's happy introduction to the area where he now lives, and it was his inheritance from his mother that first bought Peter and his wife Pamela a cottage in Dorset, allowing him the peace and quiet to compose away from his busy schedule in London.

When Peter was growing up in Stockport in the 1930s, there was no piano in the house and his parents were not musical, but the young boy spent many hours in the local cinemas (there were two fleapits in

Castle Street: the Alexandra and the Edgeley), whiling away the time before his mother came home from the shop. So movie scores were an early influence. His first school was the local Edgeley Park Primary School, but at the age of seven he entered Cheadle Hulme School (then known as Warehousemen and Clerks') as a day-boy, as had been his father's wish. A later entrant to the same school was the composer Gordon Crosse, whose parents also lived in Stockport. Music entered Peter's life in a big way only when, at the age of thirteen, he heard and was transfixed by Schubert's Unfinished Symphony, played by the teacher Miss Young (he's never forgotten her name) on a wind-up gramophone. In his enthusiasm he asked for piano lessons, and was able to practise on an old upright at his step-grandfather's house in Shaw Heath. One of the school's two peripatetic piano teachers at the time was the celebrated Dora Gilson, who was also on the staff of the Royal Manchester College of Music. She gave him his first lessons. He recalls her now as being an inspirational figure, who impressed him as much by her unconventional appearance (tall and elegant with a grand cloak, which she used to swirl around) as by her strong personality and musicianship.

Peter had completed all the Associated Board piano exams by the time he reached the sixth form, and his gift for improvising at the piano led him to start composing. He remembers that his first piece was performed in a school concert (very crude, he now says, mainly tonic/dominant in C major). When he was in the sixth form he composed a 'sort of piano concerto – a crib of Rachmaninov 2 and the Warsaw Concerto', which he played with the school orchestra. He won a County Scholarship on the basis of his examination results and, following in the footsteps of three older cousins, entered Manchester University. There he started on the three-year Joint Course run by the Music Department with the Royal Manchester College of Music. The University's full-time music staff consisted of the professor, Humphrey Procter-Gregg, and Maurice Aitchison, a greatly gifted pianist, and there were only six students in Peter's year reading music. Of his contemporaries one of the most gifted was the Rossendale-born Philip Lord, who later did doctoral research at Cambridge, where he was in the Footlights, became a Lecturer in Music at Aberdeen and Sheffield Universities, and was becoming known for his compositions before his early death in 1969.

Peter was much in demand for writing incidental music for university drama productions, and his graduation work was a Quartet for

Manchester University days. Left to right: Philip Lord, Humphrey Procter-Gregg, Peter Hope, Michael Hirst.

flute and string trio, its whereabouts now unknown. He was awarded a fourth-year composition scholarship to study under Procter-Gregg and deferred his RAF service in order to take it up. In this year (1952) both Peter Maxwell Davies and Elgar Howarth joined the Department. Peter was encouraged to start a Trumpet Concerto for Elgar Howarth, which subsequently received several performances including a broadcast by the Hallé principal trumpet William Lang with the BBC Northern Orchestra. Another work written at this period was a Quartet for flute, oboe, clarinet and bassoon. There was also a continuing profusion of incidental music.

On leaving the University in 1953 he was unexpectedly turned down for military service, and through the good offices of Ernest Tomlinson, a former student of Procter-Gregg at the University, obtained work as a copyist at Mills Music in Great Pulteney Street (and later Denmark Street – tin-pan alley), London. These were the days before photocopiers, and so multiple instrumental parts all had to be written out by hand. The big name in Mills Music at that time was Leroy Anderson, and Peter, during his first year with the firm, copied out hundreds of orchestral parts of his works. The Mills arranging department consisted of Ernest (as full-time arranger), Pam Mellers (who later became the wife of Ernest's brother Fred) and Peter. When Ernest Tomlinson left Mills to pursue his aim of becoming a full-time

PROGRAMME

SYMPHONY No. 5 IN B FLAT . . .   *Schubert*

Allegro
Andante con moto
Menuetto
Allegro vivace

CONCERTO FOR TRUMPET AND ORCHESTRA
Peter Hope

Allegro moderato
Andante con moto
Allegro

This concerto was in the first place specially composed
for the coming-of-age of the Music Club, and is being
given its first performance to-night. The composer,
incidentally, took his Mus.B. 'with distinction' here in
1952.

The music has obviously been written with enjoyment
and for the pleasure of the performers, especially the
solo trumpeter, for whose instrument the available
repertory is unfortunately small. The work is laid out
on sound, classical foundations and, unlike most music
of to-day, explains itself.

Interval

during which coffee is provided for Club
members and their guests

Page of programme from Manchester University Music
Department concert, 17 May 1956.

composer (the impetus being a BBC commission for his operetta
Cinderella), Peter left too (in 1954), as the prospect of endlessly
rescoring Leroy Anderson potboilers was not appealing.

Lady Luck then played a part in his career, in that the BBC wanted
new arrangers for their Concert Orchestra, and set up two sessions
with a section of the orchestra to test out applicants. Again at the
suggestion of Ernest Tomlinson, Peter was, with others, asked to
submit two arrangements for the orchestra to play through. He submitted *Flamingo* and one other (he cannot now recall which!) to the
producer Charles Beardsall. These found favour with both orchestra
and producer, and resulted in the commission of a few more arrangements for the Concert Orchestra, performed under Vilem Tausky.
There then ensued a more formal agreement whereby he was retained
on a yearly basis to produce a certain number of arrangements for the

orchestra. As often as not these were, in his own words, 'flashy openers' for pre-recorded broadcasts, and included several which have now became well known: *Mexican Hat Dance*, *Marching through Georgia*, *The Camptown Races* and *La Cucaracha*. Arrangements these may have been, but Peter give full rein to his imagination in their preparation and scoring, and they can really be regarded as original compositions even if the thematic material was not his own. The works were published by the London firm Josef Weinberger, who specialised in light music (indeed still do – they publish *Yanomamo* and other highly successful musicals by the Blackburn schoolteachers Pete Rose and Anne Conlon). Through the extensive connections of Joe Cohen the works went into the repertoire of light orchestras nationwide (at a time when such orchestras still existed). Indeed it was usually Joe Cohen who suggested the material that Peter might arrange, and it was his idea that Peter should write an original work: the *Momentum Suite* for string orchestra, recently recorded by the Northern Sinfonia under David Lloyd-Jones.

Joe Cohen left Weinberger's in the late fifties to set up his own publishing company, Mozart Edition, and it was for them that Peter composed what is probably his best-known piece – *Jaunting Car*, later to be joined by three other movements to form the *Ring of Kerry Suite*. It became extremely popular and won an Ivor Novello Award in 1968/9. This was the heyday of light music on the air, and Peter's music was regularly broadcast not only by the BBC Concert Orchestra but also by the BBC Midland Light Orchestra, the BBC West of England Light Orchestra, the BBC Welsh Orchestra and others. In addition he was producing quantities of library music for both Weinberger's and Mozart Edition. Other original works from this period include *Irish Legend* (intended as a follow-up to the *Ring of Kerry Suite*), *Four French Dances*, *Kaleidoscope* (a mini-concerto for orchestra composed for the BBC's Festival of Light Music in 1970) and several shorter orchestral works, including *Petit Point* and *Playful Scherzo*.

Peter was asked by Weinberger's in 1968 to submit examples of title music for the BBC Television News. In fact he submitted 'a whole sheaf' and fortunately one was chosen for regular use (thus following in the footsteps of another eminent Mancunian, Alan Rawsthorne, who in 1942 had composed the titles music for the BBC Radio Newsreel). It remained on air until 1980, and naturally became his most instantly recognisable music.

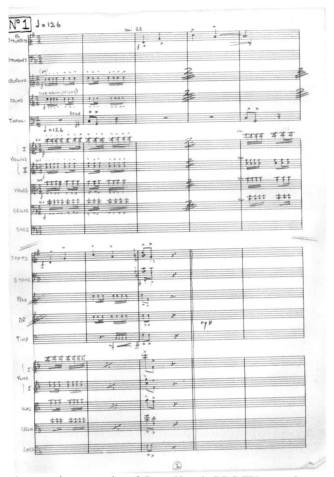

Autograph manuscript of Peter Hope's BBC TV news theme

Until the end of the 1960s Peter had something broadcast almost daily, but things were to change drastically and very suddenly. Pirate radio stations such as Radio Caroline and other pop broadcasters forced a change in the BBC's attitude towards and treatment of light music; and the reign of Glock and Keller at the Third Programme meant that the genre fell between two very tall stools and suffered a catastrophic and near-fatal decline. This sudden change coincided with a crisis in Peter's personal life. At the same time as his performing royalties fell drastically, his marriage was disintegrating in some acrimony, and at the age of forty he still had two young children to maintain. For two years he lived alone in flats in London, with no heart for either composition or arrangement – in his own words, 'doing nothing'. In any event there was nothing to do as the work had dried up.

In 1971, at a party given by a friend, he met Pamela Zinnemann, a poet whose parents had been forced to flee Nazi Germany. Her father, Prof. Kurt Zinnemann of Leeds University, had been interned on the Isle of Man with a congenial group of German and Austrian intellectuals including Hans Gál, Franz Reizenstein, members of the Amadeus Quartet and others. Peter's relationship with Pam and eventual marriage resulted in a determination to rekindle his career, but this time perforce merely as an arranger.

Fortunately the arranging work soon built up and over the following years Peter worked extensively for Dutch TV and German radio. He also worked for Charles (Chuck) Gerhardt, the conductor who made many productions in this country for Reader's Digest, often using large orchestras at a time when record companies were making do with smaller ensembles. In 1979 the Dutch record company Phillips asked him to arrange *An Album of Tosti Songs* for José Carreras, which was recorded with the English Chamber Orchestra under Edoardo Müller. *An Album of Neapolitan Songs*, also with Carreras and the ECO, followed the next year. So commercially successful were these that many albums have ensued over the last thirty years, noteworthy among them being *Sacred Songs* (for Jessye Norman and the Royal Philharmonic Orchestra under Sir Alexander Gibson), *The Spirit of Christmas* (carols recorded by the John Alldis Choir and the London Symphony Orchestra under Sir Colin Davis, but originally intended for the Hollywood Bowl, and indeed subsequently performed with the Boston Symphony Orchestra), collections for Dennis O'Neill and Stuart Burrows (both of these being offshoots from television programmes for which Peter was the main arranger), and orchestrations for Dame Kiri te Kanawa. Although Peter has not himself composed music for feature films, other composers have relied on his consummate facility for scoring: his orchestrations include John Williams's score for *Raiders of the Lost Ark* and James Horner's for *Willow*.

The Carreras connection has led to regular commissions for arrangements of Spanish traditional material and popular hits to be performed and recorded by both the Orquesta Sinfónica de Tenerife and the Orquesta Sinfónica de Galicia. These arrangements include orchestral settings of pop tunes by the Spanish group Meccano, whose

for James Bowman

A HERRICK GARLAND

1. I SING OF BROOKS

ROBERT HERRICK

PETER HOPE

star Nacho Cano has been responsible for yet more Hope arrangements (or rather compositions). On tunes provided by Nacho Cano Peter produced two large-scale scores, one for the wedding of the Crown Prince of Spain (2004) performed by the Orquesta Sinfónica de Madrid, and one for the Spanish 2012 Olympic bid recorded in London at the Abbey Road studios in 2003.

Despite his involvement with the commercial side of music, Peter Hope has always been devoted above all to more serious music, and he gave considerable help to his fellow composers as Chairman in 1969 and co-Chairman (with Anthony Hedges) in 1971 of the Composers' Guild of Great Britain. The impetus again came from Ernest Tomlinson, who wanted the Guild to make itself more professional and tighten up its admission procedures, and suggested a composer with commercial talents for that reason.

Since 2000, when he reached seventy, Peter Hope has concentrated more on his first love, original composition. Although the works he has produced in the last few years are more serious than his earlier light music, they are still in a readily accessible idiom, with great melodic charm, immaculate and grateful writing for the instruments, imaginative orchestration, and often complex but beguiling rhythmic tricks. Although the harmony breaks no ranks with tradition (he disparagingly refers to his works as using 'the three-chord trick') it is employed in a memorable and striking way. The influence of modern popular music is to be heard in the *Bramall Hall Dances* (written for performance in a medieval/Elizabethan manor house near his home town of Stockport), the influence of blues and Latin American music in both the Concertino for bassoon, harp and string orchestra and the Concerto for recorder, harp and string orchestra, the style of the baroque trio sonata in *Four Sketches* for oboe, bassoon and piano, and the influence of Dowland and the Elizabethan lute composers in the delicious song cycle *A Herrick Garland*, composed for and frequently performed by the countertenor James Bowman.

Since 2000 most of the early light music has been recorded thanks to the work of Philip Lane and the conductor Gavin Sutherland. Both the Bassoon Concertino and the Recorder Concerto have been recently issued on CD. Most of the chamber music will shortly be released on disc to celebrate Peter Hope's birthday in 2005.

COMPOSITIONS

ORCHESTRAL

Concerto for trumpet and orchestra (1952) (Arcadia Music)

Momentum: Suite for string orchestra (1959) (Inter-Art)

Suite: Ring of Kerry (1961) (Mozart Edition)

Petit Point (1962) (Mozart Edition)

Playful Scherzo (1962/3) (Mozart Edition)

Overture: Scaramouche (1967) (Arcadia Music)

Suite: Irish Legend (1967) (Mozart Edition)

Four French Dances (1968), Ms

Kaleidoscope (1969/70)

Champagne Festival (1981), Ms

Speedbird Salutes the Few: March commissioned by British Airways (1990) (Quatermass Music)

Concertino for bassoon, string orchestra, harp and percussion (2000) (Emerson)

Concerto (Birthday Concerto) for recorder, string orchestra, harp and percussion (2003) (Peacock)

ORCHESTRAL ARRANGEMENTS OF TRADITIONAL OR NON-COPYRIGHT MUSIC

Three American Sketches: Marching through Georgia, Black is the Colour of my True Love's Hair, Camptown Races

The Bells of Aberdovey for recorder and string orchestra

Cantos Canarias

Cielito Lindo

Cockles and Mussels

La Cucaracha

Hollywood Concerto for 2 pianos and orchestra (for Rostal and Schaefer)

The Lark in the Clear Air

Majorcan Fantasy

Mexican Hat Dance

The Nightingale, by John Parry (Bardd Alaw), for recorder and string orchestra (originally arranged for recorder and piano)

O Waly Waly

Waltzes of Offenbach

Christmas carols (in order of appearance on the LP *The Spirit of Christmas*): Joy to the World; In Dulci Jubilo; Silent Night; God

Rest Ye Merry, Gentlemen; The Holly and the Ivy; What Child is This; Deck the Halls; O Tannenbaum; Patapan; We Three Kings; Away in a Manger; I Saw Three Ships

CHAMBER MUSIC

Quartet for flute, oboe, clarinet and bassoon (1951)

Quartet for flute and string trio (1952)

Divertimento for guitar and string trio (2002)

Bramall Hall Dances for recorder and guitar (2003) (alternative versions for recorder and piano, and recorder, cello and harpsichord) (Forsyth)

Four Sketches for oboe, bassoon and piano (2003) (Emerson)

Overture to 'The Rivals' for recorder, bassoon and harpsichord (or piano) (2004) (Peacock)

Serenade for violin viola and cello (2005)

The Nightingale, by John Parry (Bardd Alaw), for recorder and piano (2006)

VOCAL MUSIC

Original works

A Herrick Garland for countertenor, recorder, cello and harpsichord (2004) (Peacock)

Cantata: Along the Shore for soprano, choir and orchestra (2005)

Beaminster, song for low voice and piano (2005)

Arrangements of traditional and non-copyright songs (collections)

Sea Shanty Selection for baritone, choir and orchestra (Ms BBC Music Library)

Stephen Foster Selection for soprano, baritone, choir and orchestra (Ms BBC Music Library)

Christmas Carols for choir and orchestra: Hark the Herald Angels Sing; Coventry Carol; The First Noel; Good King Wenceslas; I Wonder as I Wander; O Come, All Ye Faithful; The Twelve Days of Christmas

Songs by Francesco Paolo Tosti, as recorded by José Carreras (1979): La serenata; Segreto; Marechiare; Vorrei morire; Malia; Chanson de l'adieu; L'ultima canzone; L'alba separa della luce l'ombre; Aprile; Ideale; Sogno; 'A Vucchella; Non t'amo piu; Goodbye

Neapolitan Songs, as recorded by José Carreras (1980): Funiculi, funicula; I' te vurria vasa; Core 'ngrato; 'O paese d'o sole; Dicitencello vuie; Silenzio cantatore; Santa Lucia luntana; Tu, ca nun chiagne!; Torna a Surriento; 'O sole mio; Passione; 'Na sera 'e maggio; 'O surdato 'nnamurato

The composer has made different versions of several of these (and similar) songs for other singers, e.g. Dennis O'Neill, who has recorded *O sole mio*, *Santa Lucia*, *Catari* and *Come Back to Sorrento* with the BBC Welsh Symphony Orchestra. There are also versions of *Parlami d'amore* and *Musica proibita* in the BBC Music Library.

Arrangements of individual traditional or non-copyright songs with orchestra

Some of the following exist in various versions; where there has been a recording the artist's initials are included (*AJ* – Aled Jones, *JN* – Jessye Norman, *MA* – Moira Anderson, *RW* – Robert White)

All Through the Night *AJ*; Amazing Grace *JN*; Aye Walkin' o *MA*; Aye Fond Kiss *MA*; Danny Boy *RW*; Foggy Foggy Dew *RW*; Galway Bay *RW*; Gesu bambino *JN*; He's Aye Kissing Me *MA*; A Highland Lad *MA*; Holy City; I Wonder as I Wander *JN*; John Anderson, my Jo *MA*; Last May a Braw Wooer *MA*; Last Rose of Summer *RW*; The Lea Rig *MA*; Let us Break Bread Together *JN*; Macushla; Molly Malone *RW*; Myfanwy; My Heart is Sair *MA*; My Love is like a Red, Red Rose *MA*; Oft in the Stilly Night *RW*; O Holy Night *AJ*; O Kenmures On and Awa', Willie *MA*; O Whistle and I'll Come to you, my Lad. *MA*; A Rosebud by my Early Walk *MA*; The Rowan Tree *MA*; She is Far from the Land *RW*; Star of Bethlehem; Star of the County Down *RW*; What Child is This; Where Cart Rims Rowin' to the Sea *MA*; Y Cymro; Ye Banks and Braes *MA*

INCIDENTAL AND MEDIA MUSIC

Chips Comic, 2 series of children's programmes for Channel 4 (with Juliet Lawson)

Gala Concert Hall, signature tune for BBC radio programme

Newsroom 1, for BBC1 television news, 1969–80

The Rivals, for RADA production, 2004 (see also CHAMBER MUSIC)

Numerous items of library music

North West Composers'
NWCA
Association
Affiliated to the British Academy of
Composers and Songwriters

The North West Composers' Association
Information: The Secretary, NWCA,
Joanna Treasure, 4 New Acres, Newburgh, Lancashire, WN8 7TU
tel: 01257 464320 email: jotreasure@compuserve.com

In addition to its principal aim – to raise and maintain the profile of new music – the Association promotes the talents of North West-based performers through its concerts and recordings.

These CDs can be ordered from the NWCA, or from local music shops, distributors, and on-line at:

www.dimusic.co.uk

www.dunelm-records.co.uk

www.ascrecords.co.uk

Currently available recordings on CD:

The Wagon of Life - to mark the centenary of the birth of **Thomas Pitfield** a CD of songs performed by **MARK ROWLINSON** (baritone) and **PETER LAWSON** (piano) is now available, including music by Stuart Scott, Geoffrey Kimpton, Stephen Wilkinson, Joanna Treasure, John R. Williamson, Sasha Johnson Manning, Kevin George Brown, David Golightly, Philip Wood and David Forshaw.   DUNELM RECORDS DRD 0220

Contemporary British Piano Music (Vol.1) – **JONATHAN MIDDLETON**   ASC CS CD 1
Music by Golightly, Jeremy Pike, Scott, Colin Bayliss, Treasure, Margaret Wegener.

Contemporary British Piano Music (Vol.2) – **JOHN McCABE**   ASC CS CD 3
Music by Alan Rawsthorne, Pitfield, Forshaw, Williamson, Christopher Beardsley, Golightly.

British Clarinet Music – **ROGER HEATON & STEPHEN PRUSLIN**   ASC CS CD 2
Music by Kevin Malone, Pike, Forshaw, Stephen Plews, Kimpton, Golightly, John Reeman.

British Violin Music – **ANDREW LONG & STEWART DEATH**   ASC CS CD 4
Music by Walton, Geoffrey Kimpton, Stephen Plews, Pitfield, Stuart Scott, Jeremy Pike.

An Image of Truth – **WILLIAM BYRD SINGERS, KEITH SWALLOW, JOHN TURN-ER, PETER LAWSON, ALISON WELLS, COULL QUARTET.**   ASC CS CD 6
Music of David Ellis.

Manchester Accents – **NCO directed by NICHOLAS WARD**   ASC CS CD 45
Music by Pitfield, Anthony Gilbert, James Langley, McCabe, John Manduell, Terence Greaves.

Fast Forward – **LINDSAYS, CAMERATA, COULL and NOSSEK**   ASC CS CD 11
Quartets for the new millennium by Kevin Malone, David Ellis, John Casken, Robin Walker, Geoffrey Poole and Anthony Gilbert.

Old City–New Image – CAMERATA ENSEMBLE   CAMPION CAMEO 2027
Music by John McCabe and David Ellis (String Quartets and Trios).

Songs of Love and Loss   CAMPION CAMEO 2047/2048
Music by Geoffrey Kimpton performed by Mark Rowlinson and Peter Lawson & Georgina
Colwell, Sasha Johnson Manning and Nigel Foster.

Thirteen Ways of Looking at a Blackbird – **JOHN TURNER / CAMERATA**   Olympia
Music by Leonard Bernstein, Robert Simpson, Richard Arnell, Matyas Seiber &   CD 710
NWCA members Beth Wiseman, Philip Wood, David Forshaw and David Ellis.

The Music of Thomas Pitfield – TRACEY CHADWELL, JOHN McCABE,   RNCM TP3
DENNIS SIMONS, RICHARD & JANET SIMPSON, KEITH SWALLOW

John and Peter's Whistling Book – JOHN TURNER & PETER LAWSON   Forsyth
Includes music by Geoffrey Poole, David Ellis and Kevin Malone.   FS OO1/2

Colin Bayliss – DAVID MARTIN (piano) & RONALD FROST (organ) NCC 2001 & 2002
Sonatas for piano and the complete organ music – separate CDs.

Songs of Solomons – STEPHEN TAYLOR & JONATHAN LEONARD   NCC 2003
Music of David W. Solomons.

Twelve Housman Songs – NIGEL SHAW & JOHN WILLIAMSON   DUNELM DRD 0133
The music of John Williamson with the composer as accompanist.

Music for Piano (2 volumes) – MURRAY McLACHLAN   DUNELM DRD 0134 & 0176
The music of John Williamson.

Jigs, Airs and Reels – JOHN TURNER & CAMERATA   CAMPION CAMEO 2034
Music by Malcolm Arnold, Edward Gregson, Ernest Tomlinson, Robin Walker etc.

Hat Box – JOHN TURNER & NEIL SMITH   CAMPION CAMEO 2020
Music for recorders and guitar celebrating the sights and sounds of Stockport.

Earth and Moon & Move – TUBALATE   [2CDs]   ASC CS CD 21 & TCD 4
this popular group plays music by Colin Bayliss, Stuart Scott and David Solomons.

Music for organ : volume 5 – RONALD FROST   DUNELM DRD 0244
Recorded at St Ann's Church, Manchester – includes works by Ronald Frost and David Ellis.

Into the Light: music for orchestras in the community   ASC CD86
NCO and Camerata Ensemble. Includes works by Philip Wood, David Forshaw, David Ellis &c.

4 x 4 – North West: music for string quartet UK Composer series CAMPION CAMEO 2049
Manchester Camerata Ensemble & Tavec Quartet. Music by Anthony Gilbert, Duncan Druce,
John Reeman and David Ellis – all premiere recordings.

*The composers are grateful to Manchester Musical Heritage Trust, the Pitfield Trust, the Ida
Carroll Trust, and Arts Council England for their generous support of specific NWCA projects.*

The 'American' Music of Sasha Johnson Manning

PHILIP BARNES

FEW SUBURBS in the Greater Manchester area have enjoyed such a rich musical heritage as Bowdon, located on its southern edge overlooking the Cheshire plain. Among its more celebrated residents have been musicians associated with the Hallé Orchestra and Manchester's various colleges and universities. A century ago the conductor Hans Richter welcomed to his Bowdon home several foreign luminaries, including Grieg and Bartók, while close by the composer John Ireland spent some of his childhood. The distinguished violinist Adolph Brodsky lived close to the parish church, as did – later – the composer Thomas Pitfield. This parish church, dedicated to St Mary the Virgin, has long attracted outstanding organists and choir directors, many of whom have gone on to glory further afield. In the past three decades alone we find a remarkable roster of talented musicians.

That roster begins in the late 1960s with the multi-talented James W. Dickenson, trained in both law and music, and a highly gifted jazz musician in addition. As his article in the last issue of *Manchester Sounds* mentioned, he emigrated to Norway, to work as a kantor and organist. He was followed at Bowdon by Stuart Pedlar, a superb keyboard player who subsequently worked extensively in musical theatre, most notably for Millicent Martin and Stephen Sondheim. One of Pedlar's immediate successors was the distinguished organist Graham Barber, now Professor of Performance Studies at Leeds University. His high standards of organ playing were maintained first by Jeremy Spurgeon (now Organist of Edmonton Cathedral, Alberta, Canada) and then by Gordon Stewart, who went on to serve Manchester and Blackburn Cathedrals as organist, a position he currently holds at Huddersfield Town Hall.

During the 1970s two of the many choristers in the Bowdon parish church choir were myself and Sasha Johnson Manning. Little did we realise then that our paths would cross significantly more than twenty-five years later. Sasha left Bowdon to attend the Royal Academy of Music, where she studied cello and composition, the latter with Roger Steptoe. Upon graduation she pursued a career as a singer and a composer, eventually returning to Bowdon to become its choir direc-

tor. For this choir, as well as her students at Withington School, she began to write occasional pieces, gradually establishing a reputation in the north-west as an imaginative composer, sensitive to the needs and expectations of the performer. Certainly, her own experience as a choral vocalist has served her well in knowing what does and doesn't work with different levels of singer.

My own departure from Bowdon led eventually to my being appointed the artistic director of the St Louis Chamber Chorus, one of oldest independent professional choirs in the USA. Although the Chamber Chorus has performed just about all the works of the German Romantic School, from Schubert to Wolf, and naturally is well versed in major American composers, such as Barber, Copland and Schuman, British music has always played a significant part in its programmes. Doubtless, this is because Ronald Arnatt, its founder (in 1956) and conductor for more than twenty years, is English; he studied at Trinity College, London, and Durham University. With my appointment, as its fourth conductor, the tradition was resumed, and we have now established significant ties with many British composers.

The Chamber Chorus has given numerous American or world premieres by British musicians, some of whom may be more familiar in England than in the USA. These include Sir Richard Rodney Bennett, Judith Bingham, Geoffrey Burgon, Anne Dudley and David Matthews. However, the composer with whom we have worked most closely and consistently has been Sasha Johnson Manning, appointed our 'composer-in-residence' in 1996.

Though readers of *Manchester Sounds* can refer to some of her premieres given in north-west England, this article describes how she has carved a niche in the American Midwest. In many ways, St Louis and Manchester complement one another, both being industrial giants of the nineteenth century, rusting behemoths of the twentieth, and reinvigorated cultural capitals of the twenty-first. Both cities can boast world-class orchestras and a long tradition of fine choral singing. Both cities have enviable reputations for top educational institutions, with St Louis boasting no fewer than eight colleges and universities within its borders. Thus the city enjoys a large base of trained musicians and educated audiences, people always open to music and musicians from abroad. Although Sasha Johnson Manning's music was introduced to St Louisans by the Chamber Chorus, other performers have subsequently commissioned pieces from her, attracted by her infectious melodies, rich use of harmony and insistent rhythms. Among her more prominent commissions have been songs for the Parkway North High School, directed by Brian Reeves. The group has performed both in St Louis and on concert tours to Britain as well as at the annual convention of the state's music teachers – a huge event. Sasha has written anthems, carols and canticle settings for several professional church choirs, including the Episcopal Churches of St Peter's (Ladue) and the Holy Communion (University City). For the latter church she also composed *He Came All So Still*, an exquisite rhapsody for strings and harpsichord based on the French carol 'Quelle est cette odeur agréable?' Most recently, a sizeable body of solo songs has been commissioned by singers, singing teachers and even a university department (for its postgraduate recitals).

The compositions for the Chamber Chorus – scored for unaccompanied mixed voices – have included an elegiac setting of James Elroy Flecker's poem 'Mary Magdalen' and four songs (two from 2001, joined by two more in 2004) from *Love's Labours Lost* for a programme of Shakespeare settings. These were warmly received: the chief classical music critic of the *St Louis Post-Dispatch*, Sarah Bryan Miller, commented in her review of 12 October 2004:

A quartet of settings by Johnson Manning - two from 2001, as well as the new pair - ranged from the slightly jazzy to the purely ravishing. Barnes was right: The additions make for a more complete and multifaceted group. Johnson Manning has a rare gift for choral composition; her relationship with the Chamber Chorus is a fortunate one for all of us.

This is the fourth movement of
'REQUIEM FOR ST. LOUIS' for the
St.Louis Chamber Chorus, Missouri.

IV

Let Down The Bars, O Death!

Text
Emily Dickinson

Music
Sasha Johnson Manning
© 10th February 2001

A page from the seventh movement of the Requiem, 'Toward the Unknown Region'.

Sasha's most substantial work for the Chamber Chorus, though, is a Requiem sequence that she has been writing incrementally over a period of eight years. A final movement, 'Lux Aeterna', will receive its premiere on 28 May 2006, when for the first time the 'Requiem' will be performed in its entirety.

The 'Lux Aeterna' is preceded by an interesting variety of texts that enhance the individual nature of this Requiem. The first two movements, 'Requiem Aeternam' and 'Dies Irae', like the final 'Lux Aeterna', are conventional texts for the burial service, and are scored for SATB choir with some divisions. The third movement is an extensive setting for SSAATTBB of Psalm 130, 'Out of the deep have I called unto Thee, O Lord'. The growing tension created by the opening three movements is then alleviated by the men's voices (TTBB) singing resignedly 'Let Down the Bars, O Death' (words by Emily Dickinson). The women follow, with Oscar Wilde's 'On Hearing the "Dies Irae" in the Sistine Chapel', in which the composer quotes her own earlier setting of the 'Dies Irae'. With the division of the choir into male and female voices now established, the sixth movement juxtaposes a Spanish poem by the mystic St John of the Cross (sung by the women), describing the aged Simeon witnessing Christ's presentation in the Temple, with the Latin Song of Simeon (the 'Nunc Dimittis') sung by the men's voices. For the penultimate movement the eight voice-parts are reconstituted into two SATB choirs for a more conventional piece of antiphony, setting Walt Whitman's famous lines, 'Darest thou now, O Soul, Walk out with me toward the Unknown Region?' After an ecstatic passage on the words 'Then we burst forth – we float, In time and space', the piece ends enigmatically on a hushed open fourth that leads into the sublime conclusion to the Requiem, the 'Lux Aeterna'.

How the entire Requiem will be received remains to be seen, but after hearing the Whitman movement Sarah Bryan Miller wrote as follows (16 May 2005):

The seventh (and penultimate) installment of British composer Sasha Johnson Manning's 'Requiem for St. Louis' had its world premiere on Sunday. 'Toward the Unknown Region' is a gorgeous piece, reflecting Manning's growth as a composer, and it was beautifully sung. The entire Requiem will be performed in the final concert of the Chamber Chorus' 50th anniversary next May; judging by the existing movements, it should be a highlight of the season.

Another page from 'Toward the Unknown Region'

PHILIP BARNES was awarded a master's degree in music from Manchester University in 1985. He sang in several English cathedral choirs before moving to America in 1988 to chair the Classics Department of John Burroughs School, St Louis. Since his appointment to the St Louis Chamber Chorus, he has conducted all the major works of the unaccompanied choral repertoire, and given numerous premieres by American, Australian and British composers. He has already recorded some of the Requiem: the opening two movements are on *Singing St. Louis* (SLCC 006), available directly from the Chamber Chorus http://www.chamberchorus.org, while the sixth movement, 'Romança', is included on the Chamber Chorus's recent disc on GUILD (GMCD 7272) entitled *Songs of the Soul*. An inspection score of the entire Requiem may be available from the Chamber Chorus or from the composer herself, following the May 2006 premiere.

Cellier Encore une Fois

DUDLEY DIAPER

AS A GENEALOGIST, I was asked during the preparation of Raymond Walker's article[1] for the previous *Manchester Sounds* to investigate the origins of Alfred and François Cellier. Was their father really French? Where exactly did they spend their early years? Unfortunately, I did not gain access to the full run of the newly-available online census returns for Victorian England in time to settle these matters before the publication of the article. But better late than never, for the returns not only answer these questions but also tell us a good deal else about this musical family.

Following the standard advice always to work backwards in family history, I began by examining the 1901 census. However, lest you grow weary during the slow journey backwards, let me say at once that yes, their father was really French. Arsène Cellier, born in Normandy about 1797, came to live in Hackney, north-east London, at some point before the 1841 census. The index of marriages shows that he was conjoined with Mary Anne Peacock, in Hackney, in the third quarter of 1842, and that she was from Dover. The first lady he met when he got off the boat, one wonders? How romantic! They had four children: Adeline, Alfred, Charles Herbert, and François Arsène. The three boys all served, before their voices broke, as Children of Her Majesty's Chapel Royal. Arsène himself died at a ripe age in the third quarter of 1880, in the district of Lewisham, south London.

But now, to begin at the end in approved fashion. Alfred does not appear in the 1901 census, having died in his forties nearly ten years before. François, however, is there, and on census night, 31 March 1901, was *chez lui* at Belmont, Cranes Park, Surbiton, south London, with his Bristol-born wife Clara [née Short: they had married in the second quarter of 1873 in Hackney] and their children Lily Marie, Rose Clara, Marguerite and François. Born 51 years earlier in Hackney, François senior was identified as a musical director and composer. Lily was a teacher of music, and Marguerite an actress. François junior was, perhaps disappointingly, a merchant's clerk – although, as

[1] Raymond Walker, 'A Manchester Connection: Alfred Cellier (1844–1891), composer and conductor', *Manchester Sounds*, 5 (2004–5), 89-104.

we shall see, his father had spent some time as a banker's clerk thirty years before.

On 5 April 1891 François spent census night at an earlier house, Aubrey, King Charles Road, Surbiton, and he was listed then too as a musical director and composer. Brother Charles was a music teacher living near the Crystal Palace in Sydenham, south-east London, with his American wife Adèle. I cannot find Alfred in this census either. We know he was to survive for a few months more, but either he was abroad, or the records have so mangled his details as to make him untraceable.

Census day 1881 – 3 April, found François as a professor of music dwelling at 9, St Andrews Road, Surbiton. He certainly seems to have found this area congenial, probably because it offered quick access by train to Victoria Station, from where a short cab ride would bring him to the Savoy Theatre, or the Opéra Comique, or Sullivan's flat in Victoria Street. His three daughters had not yet been blessed with a baby brother. Alfred, yet again, was abroad – or hiding from the census – and brother Charles was an organist residing at Cedar Cottage, Sydenham.

1871 is our year of discoveries. In the census of 2 April Alfred Cellier, professor of music (i.e. music teacher), is staying with the George family of Lonsdale Villa, Lower Richmond Road, Putney. Also present is one Harriett Greenhill, and a sidelong glance at the index of marriages for that year tells us that Alfred married Harriett Emily Greenhill on 29 August at the church of St Martin in the Fields. Brothers Charles (no employment given) and François (a banker's clerk) were at 2 Gothic Terrace, Kent House Road, Sydenham, with their parents Arsine (sic) and 'M. A. P.', and Adeline– this last an imbecile, in the language of the day. Father was an annuitant, 74; mother was 63.

The 1861 census on 7 April shows Arsène, teacher of languages, and Mary Anne at home at 7, Cassland Crescent, South Hackney, with Alfred and Adeline, but Charles and Françoise (sic) were still in the Chapel Royal choir, housed at 6 Cheyne Walk, Chelsea – the home of the formidable Reverend Thomas Helmore, Master of the Children of the Chapel Royal.

On 30 March 1851 Arsène, styling himself a professor of languages, was in a crowded house in Mare Street, South Hackney with Mary Ann, all four children, four visitors and three servants.

Finally, the 1841 returns. On 6 June Arsène, professor of French language, was living alone in Mary Bowman's lodging house, Clarence Place, Hackney.

I should like to know more of Alfred's movements between 1871 and 1891, which the census returns seem not to record. However, as the information above has been found despite the mis-spelling of the Cellier name, either by Victorian enumerators or by recent transcribers, as Collier, Callier, Pellier, Celli and even Bellile, the truth may, as they say, be out there somewhere. At least I can now say exactly how French (that is, half) the Cellier brothers actually were.

New from Forsyth:

Basil Howitt: *Walter and his Daughters: The Story of the Carroll Family of Manchester*. 559 pages: illustrated; paper-pack. ISBN 0-9514795-2-0. £18.95.

The Carroll family were at the heart of Mancunian music making for over a century and their influence extended to all corners of the globe. This intriguing narrative sets the achievements of the family, from Walter's imaginative piano miniatures for children to Ida's guiding hand in the formation of the illustrious Royal Northern College of Music (not forgetting Elsa's work for the Girl Guides) in their social and historical context, with incidental vignettes of many distinguished Mancunians.

Forsyth Brothers Ltd. 126 Deansgate, Manchester M3 2GR
Tel: 0161 834 3281 Fax: 0161 834 0630   Email info@forsyths.co.uk   web www.forsyths.co.uk

Reminiscences of Ida Carroll in her Centenary Year

MICHAEL KENNEDY and many others

(*Royal Northern College of Music*)

These tributes to Ida Carroll were assembled for the concert presented at the Royal Northern College of Music on 24 September 2005.

I REMEMBER SO CLEARLY the day I auditioned for the Northern School of Music, just back from Germany and Africa doing National Service with an army band, followed by a summer season in the Isle of Man. This formidable but kindly lady was the only other person in the room, and accompanied me in a couple of pieces including the Adagio from

Mozart's Clarinet Concerto. At the end, Ida pronounced: 'Well you certainly can play the clarinet, but you don't know much about Mozart.' She proceeded to arrange a grant for me there and then on the telephone, and I started my studies the following week.

Ida had a saying: 'We don't have red tape here, only green elastic'; and that was how she ran things. I was pleased to join her staff four or five years later, first in the Junior School, and later teaching two days a week in the senior college following the untimely death of my own teacher, Ronnie Wright. Ida was always such a supportive colleague, and this continued for many years, right up to the setting up of the new college in which she was so influential. Certainly I and many others owe her a great debt of gratitude, and retain so many memories of her.

Neville Duckworth

IT WAS MY GOOD FORTUNE that, when the Schools' Music Service could no longer supply bass lessons, Percy Welton, my school music teacher, sent me to Ida. She took me in, like a poor double-bass-playing waif, to the Northern School's Saturday morning Junior School. To become one of Ida's pupils was a privilege and the start of a long friendship. I think she saw her students as her children and would, in turn, refer to our pupils as her grandchildren. Her interest in our careers continued long after we had left the Northern. If Ida recommended you for any job there was no question but that you would do it well.

She was a truly inspirational teacher. Scales became lovely pieces of music, yes, even on the double bass, as Ida, seated at the grand piano, accompanied the rumblings with beautiful harmonies. I progressed to the Graduate Course. There was so much to learn and it was wonderful to be on such a broad-based course covering many musical skills. Sol-fa was a useful tool and, in later years, Ida found it handy for remembering phone numbers and the entry/exit code for the front door of the nursing home where Griff and, later on, Ida herself stayed. She was still playing the bass when a group of us would go with her to the Parr Hall in Warrington. She could play most of *Messiah* from memory and watch the clock in the 'Amen' chorus to keep up the tempo from the bass end so we wouldn't miss the train home.

Ida set a standard not only as a teacher but also as a person: be generous and gracious; be the same with everyone, rich, famous, poor or ordinary; don't complain, be cheerful; and be thankful for your gift of music.

Gladys Williams (née Kallenberg)

IDA WAS A WONDERFUL FRIEND. I have many marvellous memories. When I went for my audition at the NSM she immediately told me that I had a place to study piano and singing. She noted that I did not have an orchestral instrument. 'You'll play the double bass,' she said, 'and I'll teach you.' I was no great shakes but lessons were always full of fun. Ida accompanied with great vigour at the piano. One piece I was playing went very high and I couldn't play all the notes so I sang some of them in my best double bass tones. At the end of the piece Ida simply turned to me and said, with a gleeful smile, 'Very nice, dear!'

Ida was a great support to me during my student days, helping me to make lots of contacts in the concert world. She also got me a job at the new Northern College of Music and found me a position as a director of a Saturday Morning Music School at the Manchester High School for Girls. When Ida knew I was going to get married she called me into her room and said, 'Michael, I think I've found a house for you.' It was a splendid house but I could not possibly afford the deposit. 'How much are you short?' she said, and immediately proceeded to write a cheque for the said amount. 'Don't worry about paying me back – I know you will when you can.' Of course, I did so, about a year later.

I used to be chairman of a music society in south Manchester. Ida was president, a very active one who was always asking what she could do to assist the society. Each year a president's evening took place. Ida not only provided all the refreshments but also booked and paid for the artists.

I have a lovely photo of Ida, which looks over the beautiful Bösendorfer grand that she insisted I should have, a few years before she died. She came up to Carlisle with the piano in Forsyth's van just to make sure everything was all right and to see her lovely piano in its new home. Ida really did care for all her students individually. She was a truly remarkable woman. I miss her terribly and will never forget her.

Michael Hancock

I FIRST MET IDA when I was a part-time piano student at the NSM in 1945. Hilda Collens was the Principal, ruling with quiet determination and authority, but Miss Carroll was the Secretary, fixer of everyone's timetables, the always busy mopper-up of anything that needed doing, and with an incredible memory for what everybody *ought* to be doing, at all times. My RAF service then intervened and when, two and a half years later, I became full-time I encountered her aural training course – five grades (years, unless you dropped by the wayside or were sufficiently able to compress them), and a revelation illustrating her true forte as a teacher. Then, whichever orchestra one played in, there was Ida again, wielding the baton; many others will share my memories of thrilling dashes through Borodin, impeccably timed to finish just before the canteen down in the basement closed, and the mad dash down three flights of stairs with IGC in the lead – and not easy to overtake!

I never lost touch with her; never left, in a sense, for I took some of the evening classes when I worked in the schools. Then I discovered that she, and the faithful, patient Griff, toiled on until midevening – at least a twelve-hour day. I used to take them home in my car, dropping Griff off at his little house just off Kingsway, despite his protests *en route* ('No need to go further, Mr Welton. I could easily catch a bus from here.'), then on with Ida to Lapwing Lane. Even so, she had some spare time, apparently, for she organised the OSA, right down to writing and licking the envelopes calling the faithful to the various area gatherings around the country and to the annual lunch in Manchester. I acted as chauffeur for these trips up to Glasgow, down to Bristol, across to York and so on. As a passenger she occasionally dozed (though she would deny it); when we travelled by train – to the London tea-party at the Charing Cross Station restaurant   she seized the opportunity to write new aural tests or to catch up with correspondence, for she never left letters without a prompt reply.

She seemed indefatigable. Students earning a few extra pounds playing in a show or a *Messiah* might glance around to find Ida giving them a little smile from the bass section – just helping out, with Ebenezer. She knew her students as individuals and was always there to support them – in many ways, as needed. Her Friday mornings were surely unlike any other student gathering; parish notes included news of forthcoming weddings and the like; she would just as certainly be there if one was hospitalised with an accident or illness. There just couldn't be another like IGC. I still miss her and I'm sure I am not alone in that.

Percy Welton

I FIRST MET MISS CARROLL in 1947 when I applied to study at the Northern School of Music. She was already known to me as she had played the bass in orchestras with various members of my family and I am sure that this helped me to obtain a place at the School. There were eight of us starting at that time, all ex-servicemen like myself, and one or two of us found it difficult adjusting to civilian life after years away in the services. Miss Carroll saw our difficulty and would spend time with us talking about life, telling us how to plan our work and practice, calm us down mentally and generally rehabilitate us into the community. I am sure no one knows of this extra work she took on her shoulders, but I for one will never forget her kindness and under-standing at a very sensitive time in my life. A very special person altogether.

Erik Knussen

IDA WAS FOND OF HER FOOD. Apart from our first encounter at the old place on Oxford Road – when as an arrogant young ignoramus from the *Manchester City News* I was greeted on her behalf by the bursar Geoffrey Griffiths ('Griff'), who I thought was a porter – we rarely met again without having something to eat. This would very often have been in caffs of low degree, such as the one in Albert Square, opposite the town hall, and some on Oxford Road between the North-ern School and the University. Sometimes she would invite me to join her and the ever-present, ever-helpful Griff. One of her favourite restaurants in the 1960s was on Cross Street, again very near the town hall and just round the corner from Tib Lane (where my paternal Yorkshireman grandfather once worked as an estate agent's chief clerk and rent collector on the two floors above what was then the Town Hall Hotel). Ida in those days had succumbed to the current trend for Mateus Rosé. Very often, when I returned from a stint on the *Scotsman* in Edinburgh to become music critic of the *Manchester Evening News* she met me (without Griff) for lunch, usually in the cellar restaurant of the Thirty Nine Steps in South King Street. She always paid the bill: that was always understood, because she was beholden to no man or millionaire. But her hospitality at home in Lapwing Lane was lavish. It was there I was welcomed when my marriage and my family was breaking up. When I was writing *Northern Accent* (the story of the NSM) for her (for no fee or royalties) Ida was a hard taskmaster and chided me about the delay. I said I had to get home for an evening meal (then known in north-west parts as tea). Rubbish, said Ida, have it here. So I did for many weeks, even early on Sundays when I shared a lavish breakfast fry-up with Ida, her sister Elsa and, yes, Griff, when she recommended Lewis's food hall as her source of ready roasted chicken. Ida knew my problems but was not judgmental, and on one Christmas day she invited me to Lapwing Lane for the meal she had prepared. It included all the seasonal goodies, cooked to perfection. Ida knew that I was trying to recover from a drink problem and that I had to be elsewhere that night. I was then in my late fifties and I was by far the youngest person at her party. Without my family after a painful divorce, Ida was indeed a friend in need. It was a very happy Christmas – one of the best of my life. I'm honoured to call myself her friend.

John Robert-Blunn

FIRST IMPRESSIONS are important. Just prior to the opening of the new College, auditions were held to select fifty young musicians from the existing Junior Departments to form the new Junior School. I arrived at the RMCM at 8.30 a.m., only to be informed that two ladies were already waiting for me in the Lecture Theatre – Ida Carroll and Eileen Chadwick. Hurrying in, I put on a bright smile and introduced myself: 'Good morning ladies you are nice and early. Would you like a coffee and biscuits before we begin?' 'Ah,' said Ida: 'a girl after my own heart!' We never looked back, and became firm friends. Ida continued to teach aural and theory lessons in the Junior School long after her retirement from the Senior College and her pupils' results were always first class. Chocolates always resided on top of the grand piano at Christmas and Easter. Needless to say, she was a very popular teacher and she dealt with unruly youngsters in her own charming way. One young man insisted on wearing a baseball cap during his lessons and she did not approve. One Saturday morning, a member of staff came into my room and asked: 'Has Miss Carroll gone completely round the bend?' 'Why?' I asked: 'What is the matter?' Came the reply: 'She is giving an aural lesson seated at the piano wearing a baseball cap back to front.'

Shirley Blakey

IDA WAS VERY QUICK to assess a situation. I remember playing Liszt for Louis Kentner on a hot summer's day during the 1949 Holiday Course. I learned in later years that Kentner had requested that his expenses for accommodation at the Midland Hotel should also cover his friend. One can only imagine Ida's response. In September 1976 Ida came to Wales for an ISM meeting in Cardiff. She had stayed with us *en route* and on the morning of the meeting we had travelled by car.

Ida and Ebenezer, probably in July 1949 at Queenswood School, Hertfordshire, where she took a party from the NSM to join a summer school orchestral training course under the direction of Ernest Read. (*Royal Northern College of Music*)

Unfortunately it rained all day and the returning journey was a nightmare, with much flooding. At one stage Ida said, 'Do you think I shall have to swim?' Having arrived back safely we had a jolly good laugh.

Eugène Collins

I EXPECT THAT MANY of us have been in receipt of Miss Carroll's kindnesses at some time or other, and this is one of several occasions I remember well. In the Christmas vacation, after all the staff and students had gone, Miss Carroll used to have a day off and stayed at home to prepare a Christmas dinner for the domestic staff.

Mrs Grundy and her daughter Joan, in the canteen, Mrs Dunn, the cleaner, Mr Kirkham, the caretaker, and his wife, and of course Griff, joined us. No work for them that morning and we all arrived at Miss Carroll's home at mid-day, drinks being dispensed by Griff and then we all sat down to dinner. I think we had goose with all the trimmings including home-made stuffing, and then trifles. Nothing was spared. Mrs Dunn so loved Miss Carroll's trifles that she used to make one especially for her to take home. We finished the meal with coffee, tea etc., and then we were all given Christmas presents. No one was allowed to help with the washing up and so we all went home having had a lovely time. As the years went on, Miss Carroll became even more busy as the new building was nearing completion so she used to take us to the Sidney Hotel across the road for our Christmas dinner until 1972 when we went into the new building.

Pamela Stones

I RECALL AN AMUSING REMARK Ida made to me not long after I left. She had wanted me to teach rather than perform, and we used to have slight differences of opinion on this subject. Finally she suggested that I came back to do a performer's year, and then I was taken on as a pupil of Otakar Kraus (as were Ian Comboy and several other students – all men, I think). Ida came to a recital I gave about a year later, and remarked, 'You've improved a bit since you left, haven't you!'

Joyce Parker

WHEN THE NEW College building opened in 1973 there was much to finish, outside as well as inside. Ida was walking towards the entrance in Booth Street when she tripped and fell heavily on the pavement, which was not completely level. She grazed her knees badly but got up without a grumble. To our sympathetic concern her rebuff was, 'Oh, don't fuss. You should see what I've done to the pavement.' This was the sort of spirit and good humour that was typical of Ida. As co-dean with Dr Wray and me she was always as straightforwardly positive and constructive – and apparently always one step in advance.

I noticed how well she was respected by her students and staff. There seemed to be nothing she didn't know about what was going on, academic, domestic or personal. This respect had obviously grown because of her intelligence, ability to lead, kindness and sympathy, coupled with a strict expectation of the conduct of others to whom she set such an admirable example.

What a capacity for work she had! After 'retirement' she trained as an examiner for the Associated Board of the Royal Schools of Music at an age beyond the normal retirement age for examiners and soon developed a great reputation. I frequently had the unenviable luck to be examining in centres where she had just examined during the previous week and had to get used to hearing, 'That was a wonderful woman we had here last week.' They were right!

Terence Greaves

IT IS EXTRAORDINARY to understand how the Northern School of Music could be run by a total administration of three. They controlled, and I mean controlled, 250 full-time students and 850 part-timers. I include in the *administration* the Principal, universally known, though not to her face, as Ida. One of the most curious of her abilities was to be where you should have been but weren't. Choir was compulsory on Wednesday evenings for every student. Miss a rehearsal because Wimbledon was gripping or England was in the World Cup, and Ida would also happen to be standing at the entrance when you arrived the following morning with a wry comment. Few of us missed more than one rehearsal.

At the beginning of every academic year, we were given Ida's standard pep talk from which the most important message was, 'It doesn't matter if you're the soloist, if the piano needs dusting, find a duster and dust it. We all do.'

And we weren't allowed to wear jeans.

Nick and Sally Smith

MY FIRST ACQUAINTANCE with Ida Carroll happened while I was in Africa. In 1977, my husband Jim, a Lancashire lad, had accepted the post of Director of the Rhodesian College of Music and conductor of the Salisbury City Orchestra. All was not well, however, and no matter how much one wished otherwise, the political situation was in direct contrast to the animated order and beauty within the walls of the College.

As it happened, a friend of Jim's was in Salisbury at that very time, examining for the Associated Board. Peter Element said: 'I know who might be able to help you – Ida Carroll.' So he wrote to her. She responded to the call with typical vigour, and before long – between Ida and Percy Welton – Jim was assured of part-time work at RNCM. Much could be said about Ida and many will recall that she could be fun-loving and charming and hugely enjoyed social occasions. I was soon introduced to Ida's older sister, Elsa; then came Griff, with his beautiful, deep voice, her ever-loyal friend and companion. Ida could be a generous host: 'Have a sherry'; 'Would you like a chocolate?'; 'Have a cake'; 'Just help yourself to biscuits': familiar snippets of conversation I remember well, along with 'Man proposes …' and 'Everything's under control'. I had initially been somewhat overawed in Ida's presence, but I needn't have feared, for there was always a warm welcome waiting for me at Lapwing Lane. I clearly remember the first time Jim and I were shown the music room: it was a very busy room, a worked-in room, crammed with two grand pianos, an abundance of manuscripts, papers and packed bookshelves. On the walls hung Heath Robinson originals. There were dinner parties, too, at that time. Ida was an inventive cook, it has to be said, and we were introduced to many varieties of food, including the renowned 'Duck à la Ida'; and she had her own unique way with salmon, too.

Ida had a plan for me: she wanted me, guided by her, to write a fictional story about an imaginary College of Music. I was assured that she had plenty of ideas and an abundance of material, but sadly, as her health failed, the venture never got off the ground. As the years passed and Elsa grew frailer, my daytime visits occurred with increasing frequency and then came the time when Ida, too, was 'at home' to receive me. Despite her failing health, the conversation was always lively and there was much reminiscing and laughter; occasionally, even a tear or two; but never a dull moment.

Valerie Eastham

WHEN WE CAME BACK to Manchester in 1971 Ida's influence was everywhere in the Manchester music scene, including here at Forsyth's. She was, of course, always interested in how the sales of her own and her father's publications were doing and reminded us that her father's music was 'the goose that laid the golden egg'. For us as Walter Carroll's publishers she always made life difficult at the end of each financial year. No matter how many times we explained that we needed three months to physically count the enormous stocks of publications (no computers in those days) and have them audited in order to compute the copies sold, she always expected her royalties to be paid immediately after the end of the financial year. Each year we waited in trepidation for the arrival of her inevitable letter calculating how much interest she was losing. Nevertheless we all loved her dearly and knew that she often went out of her way and used her money generously to help young musicians in various ways, a matter in which we were always sworn to secrecy.

During the Second World War and resultant paper shortage it had become necessary to drop the elaborate full-colour covers by well-known artists which were such an integral part of Walter Carroll's vision. However, Ida made it very clear she did not wish us to tamper with the existing impoverished covers and for many years we obeyed. It was once more with trepidation therefore that we unveiled to her our secretly prepared new edition using the original full-colour artwork but in a slightly more contemporary format. This was one of the few times we remember her being lost for words and almost moved to tears of pleasure: an enormous relief to one and all. We knew such approval, coming from Ida, was genuine: plain speaking was perhaps one of her most characteristic and endearing qualities. We all remember Ida with great affection.

Dr Robin Loat, Managing Director

IT IS UNIVERSALLY ACKNOWLEDGED that Ida Carroll was a wonderful, inspirational teacher and a brilliant musician. For myself I know that, with her positive encouragement and constant support, my early musical education developed rapidly and shaped the first steps of my career.

Lessons with Ida were always such happy occasions, though always a challenge ('Come on, Gerald, you can do better than that!'): she had an uncanny knack of making you exceed your expectations. For example, she encouraged me to join a local amateur orchestra when I lacked the self-confidence to take that step myself. Ida's concern for the wellbeing of her students can be illustrated by two personal memories: she arranged for me to have a two-week holiday in the Cotswolds with her close friend's family, as she was concerned that I was practising too intensely (eight to ten hours daily!) and she felt that I needed a break; another sensitive memory was when I damaged my first good bow and, without any show, Ida presented me with a new bow at my next lesson.

I'll never forget Ida, how much she did for me, and all the happy events of those early years. Her infectious enthusiasm really paid off: after a year or so I was in the National Youth Orchestra, and my eventual career had begun.

Gerald Brinnen

I KNEW IDA on many levels over the years. Of course, as well as many enjoyable events and situations with her there were some that were exceedingly confrontational. When I was 13, she made me Librarian of the Northern School of Music Junior School. This involved having to stand at the top of the dark old staircase sorting piles of music, making absolutely sure that nothing was missing or had fallen down the back of the big steel cabinet on which I was working. At that time I had superb eyesight, but even so, there was only one tiny window and the place was almost in darkness, and the 40-watt bulb did precious little to alleviate the stress caused to my eyes. So much so that one day I had the audacity to search inside the aforementioned cabinet, and to my astonishment found a new 150-watt bulb. WOW! When Ida came on her inspection round (which she did about every ten minutes) she was furious, and started to lecture me on the price of electricity, and how we could not afford to waste it. She grabbed the bulb to change it back and, in doing so, almost burnt her hand! This of course made her even more angry, and made me think that perhaps I didn't want that job after all, and I was left with my myopic problems in the dark hole.

However, she refrained from sacking me, and I soon got promoted to Orchestral Assistant. The job was a breeze so long as you were fit and strong, and didn't get anything wrong! We used to load the van up with percussion instruments, music stands, and the music, but the most onerous job was to carry the three timpani down from the third floor, carefully and without bashing any of the large mirrors that Ida had strategically placed around the building in order to enable her to see round corners (you weren't safe anywhere if you wanted to chat with a girl). After we had loaded the van, it would hurtle off down Oxford Road at full speed with Ida, Griff and myself strap-hanging for dear life in the back. On arrival at the Houldsworth Hall on Deansgate we would unload, and after the concert the whole procedure would be reversed. The real downer here of course was that I had to carry the three timpani back up to the third floor. The three of us would then be taken by Ida to a good restaurant to have a slap-up meal, all paid for by her.

Ida was an extremely generous lady: while I was buying my Bechstein piano from Forsyth's at about the age of 22 she got wind of the fact that I was a bit behind with the payments, and she sat down and wrote a cheque out for £44 (a lot of money for me then) and said 'just pay me back when you can'. She never would let me repay her, and when I mentioned it one day in her house not long before she died, she just smiled and said, 'Money is no use to anyone if you can't help someone with it.' I could write many stories about Ida, as she was such an integral part of my life. There are not many like her. She was a wonderful woman.

John Wilson

MEMORIES OF COLLEGE LIFE are dominated by Miss Carroll and the unflappable Griff, in his little office by the entrance door always ready to offer calming advice and help in any crisis. I remember one partic-

(*Royal Northern College of Music*)

ular lunchtime going for a drink with Duncan Taylor at Auntie's Bar directly opposite the college and the Principal's office. Eventually we staggered out of the double swing doors arm in arm singing and pretending to be drunk and looked up to see Miss Carroll staring right at us from her window with a look of thunder on her face; by the time we walked through the college doors Griff was waiting for us saying,

'Miss Carroll wants a word with you two. Now!' I will never forget going up to her office full of trepidation and receiving a serious dressing down; she made it quite clear that she didn't ever expect to see a repeat performance, and she never did!

In the winter of my first year back at college I was late for one of Miss Carroll's aural classes; she was very keen on punctuality and asked me why I was so late. I explained that I had run out of coal and coke in my flat and had no heating, and had been trying to find a coal merchant to deliver me some, but they had all run out because of the demand. She told me to stay behind after the class and I thought I was going to get a lecture about the virtue of punctuality, but to my amazement she told me to come to her house after college that night and help myself from her coal bunker, and stay for tea as well! I recall I brought a couple of empty buckets and filled them; she came out to check how I was doing and said, 'That's no good! Come here' and swiftly picked up a spade and started shovelling coal into the back of my A35 van, showing me what to do, insisting that I fill the whole of the back of the van, which I did.

She made the Northern a warm and friendly place to be. We her students were her family: she knew everyone by name and found time to speak to you individually, and give you encouragement and guidance.

Peter Thornborrow

ALTHOUGH THE STUDENTS of the old RMCM and NSM were generally unaware of any managerial interaction between the two establishments, there was plenty of gossip among the musicians when we met on the flourishing amateur choral and orchestral circuit in the area at that time. The Lady with the Double Bass figured prominently, but it was some time before I had the pleasure of becoming more closely acquainted with the formidable character that was Ida Carroll.

My work at the BBC included auditions for both solo artists and orchestral players. Recommendations from Ida were short, sharp and straight to the point. I suspect that this quality coloured the discussions that preceded the successful merger we now call the RNCM. It would be difficult to avoid emphasising the importance of her contribution to the high standards we now almost take for granted; if nothing else, her enthusiasm and her dedication to professionalism of the highest standards continue to be the Ida Carroll legacy.

David Ellis (former Head of Music, BBC North)

WYSIWYG: THIS NOW FAMILIAR abbreviation could certainly have been fittingly applied to the late Ida Carroll, who was a remarkable character in every way.

In my early days as student and tutor at the old Royal Manchester College of Music Ida had already earned a formidable reputation as Principal of 'the other place' up the (Oxford) Road, the Northern School of Music. When the two colleges – RMCM and NSM – were to be merged into the new Northern College of Music the Mancunian Way was being constructed. This meant that the NSM would lose the city end of its building. Ida was determined that the demolition would be 'so far and no further', and as the bulldozers moved in she did a 'Canute' by sitting in the room adjacent to the space being created for the new road. Her statement (through gritted teeth) that 'they will have to demolish me as well as this room if they go too far' was typical of her character. It goes without saying that – unlike Canute – Ida won her battle, emerging (after some days) with a glint in her eye.

On the amalgamation of the two colleges Ida became one of the deans in the new Northern College of Music (the royal charter was transferred from the RMCM a year or so later). Typically she immersed herself in her new role, and this is when our paths crossed on a more frequent basis than formerly. Ida had a keen eye for detail, taking a special interest in the teaching facilities in the new building, in particular the construction of the teaching studios. There was some (friendly) rivalry between Dr Wray (ex-Director of Studies at the RMCM) and Ida, which resulted in some rather amusing 'battles'. One such concerned the soundproofing of the teaching studios. Ida was adamant that they were totally soundproof; Dr Wray was equally adamant that they were not. A 'showdown' was arranged: Ida went into one room and closed the door; Dr Wray did the same in the adjacent room. Ida then said: 'I bet you can't hear me.' Back came Dr Wray's reply through the brick wall: 'Oh yes I can!' I cannot remember any other occasion when Ida came out on the losing side!

I could chronicle many more examples of Ida's indomitable spirit, her zest for life, and her amazing capacity for hard work. But – as in Dr Watson's account of the exploits of Sherlock Holmes – such accounts must wait for the future.

From the above very brief pen-portrait Ida may emerge as a rather cold workaholic, but there was a very warm and sympathetic nature below the somewhat forbidding exterior. Her care for 'Manchester things' is legendary. The memorial window to Hilda Collens (Ida's predecessor as Principal of the NSM) in St Ann's Church is one of the results of Ida's vision: she was a founder member of the Friends of St Ann's. She was also influential in facilitating the memorial 'positif' department on the organ at St Ann's. This was installed as a memorial to William Hardwick, a former organist of St Ann's and a member of staff at the NSM.

I crossed swords with Ida on only one occasion. From 1970 to 1973 I was Director of Studies at the RMCM. My job was to 'wrap up' the degrees and diplomas of the College prior to the new academic courses being established in the new College. Dr Wray and I had worked until nearly midnight to clear up some urgent academic paperwork, and I was advised by the good doctor to come in a little later on the morrow. Consequently I arrived at about 9.30 a.m. the following day to be greeted by Ida, who was ostentatiously looking at her watch. IC: 'You are late.' RF: 'No.' IC: 'At NSM we always started earlier than this.' RF: 'Really?' With this Ida stalked off in search of Dr Wray, who explained in no uncertain terms why I was late.

But I remember Ida with great affection and respect. She had a ready and sympathetic listening ear for students, and her practical help in many cases is just one of her numerous legacies. But above all I remember Ida as a no-nonsense Mancunian, expecting and inspiring loyalty and high standards in all who came into contact with her.

Ronald Frost

FOLLOWING AN EXHIBITION of some of my paintings and drawings at the RNCM during the early seventies, it was suggested that I should make a series of drawings depicting the many various activities of the College. To my delight Ida was very kind, encouraging and co-operative, so I enjoyed having access to wonderful tutorials and rehearsals, etc. Happy days! – Allegri String Quartet et al. BUT: when it came to making a drawing of Ida herself, she would contrive to swing her instrument – at the last moment – so that she was quite obscured from my view, no matter how I had positioned myself. I was in despair until I did manage to manoeuvre her so that I could actually glimpse her reflection in the large mirror on the wall behind her, without her seeming to realize it, and get down some note of her and her strong personality and authority onto my paper. I was of course thrilled, too, that she bought some of my work to give to the College in posterity.

Dorothy Bradford

IDA'S CARE for her students went beyond the call of duty. An example of this was that we were chaperoned by her when we went to London to do our diplomas!

I have cause to be very grateful to Ida in many ways. Notably, one day in 1953, Miss Carroll met me in the Northern School lobby. 'Jean,' she said, 'the BBC is advertising for a viola player and I have submitted your name. It will do you good to do an audition.' I later learned that the BBC Northern had decided to enlarge its viola section by the addition of one player. It then became a section of six.

(*Royal Northern College of Music*)

This was the entrée to many happy years playing with the Northern Orchestra, later the BBC Northern Symphony Orchestra, and then, as a freelance, with the BBC Philharmonic as it now is.

Jean Soni

PINE ROAD (where I live) and Lapwing Lane (the Carrolls' home) use the same post office. Ida had lovely handwriting and she wrote a lot of letters. We both had the habit of hurrying to the pillar box, as did other neighbours, to catch the 4 o'clock Sunday clearance – and then

relaxed, exchanging news. When Sunday collections were discontinued for several years, until huge protest restored a limited collection,
it was a real social loss.

In 1958 or thenabouts Ida had invited me to serve on the governing
body of the Northern School of Music on which Charles (later Sir
Charles) Groves also served. This was before amalgamation with the
Royal Manchester College of Music became a serious proposition.
The Northern School was operating in a dreadful office block in
Oxford Road, which was to be demolished to make way for the new
elevated highway. This was great, as the local authority would be
obliged to pay for a replacement building. I was a newish member of
Manchester City Council and Deputy Chairman of the Further Educa-
tion Sub-Committee with thirteen new FE colleges in our post-war
building programme – one of which I hoped might become a dedicated college of music, giving a new home for the Northern School.
But this was not to be.

When the plan for the new road came before the City Council, it
was turned down by the narrowest of margins. In theory the Lord
Mayor has a casting vote, but traditionally having to be above party
politics for the year, the Lord Mayor must never use it, so much so that
a wooden cover is fixed over the voting button to prevent this happen-
ing in a moment of excitement. Equal voting is very rare, but, when
the plan for the road was debated, equal votes For and Against were
recorded. Alderman Quinney, the Lord Mayor that year, who had set
his heart on this plan and worked assiduously for it for several years,
nearly broke down in anguish. There is a ban of six months before a
re-submission. The plan was revised, realigning the road about a
hundred yards further north, and the office block was no longer
threatened. Had the original alignment been agreed, how differently
music in Manchester might have developed.

The rest is history. Ida put the best face that she could on the
prospect of amalgamation with the RMCM; the years flew by and she
continued to make her considerable contributions to music, both in
Manchester and nationally. An abiding memory of mine is a vivid and
heart-rending vision of two elderly, broad-beamed people, Ida and her
stalwart friend and erstwhile Bursar, known to everyone as Griff,
walking together across Booth Street West towards the Business
School car park. Later, when Griff was in an old people's home in
Lapwing Lane, we would watch in fear as Ida intrepidly negotiated the

big Palatine Road crossing on her daily visits to see him. Those of us who knew Ida well will never forget her.

Dame Kathleen Ollerenshaw

MOST OF THE warm tributes to Ida Carroll printed in the programme of the inspiring celebration of her centenary held at the Royal Northern College of Music on 24 September 2005 rightly concentrated on her remarkable qualities as a human being. But I feel something should be said about some of the enterprising and very worthwhile musical events that the Northern School of Music promoted under her leadership and most of which, as a critic, I attended. It was no surprise to me at the 2005 Buxton Festival that Nicolai's *The Merry Wives of Windsor* proved to be such a success and that people were asking 'Why don't we hear this more often?' Its charms were revealed to me in July 1956 when the NSM staged it in the Lesser Free Trade Hall. The NSM had begun its opera productions in 1952 with Smetana's *The Bartered Bride*. The duo of Aylmer Buesst as conductor and Sumner Austin as producer was formed then and continued with *Die Fledermaus*, *The Marriage of Figaro* and *The Magic Flute*. But these were during Hilda Collens's time as Principal. She died in April 1956, leaving Ida Carroll as acting Principal until March 1958. Ida continued the tradition of an annual opera and there followed Donizetti's *Daughter of the Regiment* (1958) and *L'elisir d'amore* (1959), *The Bartered Bride* (1960), and a double bill of Weber's *Abu Hassan* and Puccini's *Suor Angelica* (1961). Flotow's *Martha* followed in 1962, *The Magic Flute* in 1963 and again in 1970, then *Faust* (1964), *La Traviata* (1965), *Figaro* (1966), *Idomeneo* (1967), Vaughan Williams's *Hugh the Drover* (1968), Gluck's *Alcestis* (1969), Verdi *Nabucco* (1971) and Weber's *Der Freischütz* (1972).

The choice of concert works was also anything but routine. In 1958 Ernest Read conducted Dyson's *The Canterbury Pilgrims* and he returned in 1962 for Elgar's *The Music Makers*, then much more of a rarity than it is now. In 1963 we find Maurice Handford (who had just been appointed the Hallé's associate conductor to Barbirolli) conducting the first performance in the north of England of Stravinsky's *Apollo*. Later that year he conducted Bruckner's *Te Deum* with the soprano Alison Hargan among the soloists and on 10 December Elgar's *The Dream of Gerontius* with Alfreda Hodgson as the Angel, for many of us our first encounter with this memorable artist. She and the soprano Pauline Tinsley took part in May 1964 in the first Man-

chester performance of Tippett's *A Child of our Time*. Handford's
work for English music continued in 1965 with performances of
Holst's *Choral Symphony* and Elgar's *The Kingdom*. With *Faust* in
1964 he had taken over the conducting of the NSM operas. Elgar's
The Apostles (Tinsley, Hodgson, Stephen Taylor, Ellis Keeler. Peter
Walker and James Calladine as soloists) was performed in February
1967 (and splendid it was, too), Beethoven's *Missa Solemnis* in 1968
and Walton's *Belshazzar's Feast* in 1969. The last three big choral
events were the superb concert performance of Vaughan Williams's
opera *The Pilgrim's Progress* in 1970, with John Noble as Pilgrim and
Handford conducting, Berlioz's *The Damnation of Faust*, conducted
by Charles Groves in 1971 and Verdi's *Requiem*, conducted by James
Robertson, in 1972.

This measure of achievement – and the emergence of such artists
as Alfreda Hodgson, Alison Hargan, Pauline Tinsley, Maureen Guy,
John Rawnsley, John Wilson and Michael Hancock, and the support
of such teachers as Clifford Curzon, Dorothy Pilling, Irene Wilde,
Maurice Clare and Kendall Taylor to name only a few – was reason
enough for her to fight like a tigress to ensure that in the proposed
amalgamation with the Royal Manchester College of Music the Northern School should not be submerged. The RMCM might have a royal
charter and enjoy greater prestige, but if the two were to become one
it should be on equal terms and there could be no compromise. As a
member of the Joint Committee that brought about the merger into the
new Northern College of Music (no Royal at first), I know how
doughtily, not to say obstinately, Ida fought. Her tactics may have
delayed the advent of the new college by a few years, but she was not
bothered about that. There can be little doubt that she was also
carrying a lance for her late father, who had acrimoniously resigned
from the teaching staff of the RMCM in 1920. One can only admire
and salute her tenacious loyalty. If to some of the Joint Committee she
must sometimes have seemed like an Amazonian battleaxe, this impression soon faded when she turned on her considerable feminine
charm. And it is enormously to her credit that, the battle won, she put
it all behind her in 1972 and gave unswerving loyalty to the Principal
of the new college and brought all the best aspects of her work at the
NSM into the new institution. For that alone, but for much more, she
deserves an honoured place in the history of music in Manchester.

Michael Kennedy

The following is a slightly edited transcript of the speech by Sir John Manduell CBE at the celebrations for Ida Carroll's centenary held at the RNCM on 24 September 2005.

SO MANY OF US knew and loved Ida. You think of what she did at the Northern School of Music in all those years and we forget and over-look it at our peril. All right, it might be thirty years since the last Northern School of Music student graduated (I think I'm right in saying that that was in 1975), but just think of the great artists who came through the School, of singers of the calibre of Alfreda Hodg-son, Pauline Tinsley, and John Rawnsley, of string players like Colin Staveley, of numerous wind players – you delighted in the bassoon playing of Laurence Perkins today, and you can think of any number of others. And John Wilson and Michael Hancock, both here today, strongly represent the pianists produced by the School. The Northern School really did produce some very fine performers who've enriched our field so much.

I thought it was very appropriate that we began with a piece by Walter Carroll because in all this, you know, the influence of Ida's remarkable father is never very far absent and stays with us today in a way which I think is remarkably strong. He had a wonderful gift for writing music that young people, in particular, could respond to. If I may be personal for a moment, I'll take you back to Johannesburg about seventy-two years ago where a small boy of five is perched on a piano stool in the dining room of the headmaster's house in Johan-nesburg. Dorothy Boxall, a lady I shall never forget, had come to give me my first piano lesson. And what did she put in front of me straight away but *Scenes at a Farm*, and number two, *The Jolly Farmer*. That was the first piece I ever learned. Dear Dorothy Boxall, I doubt that she's in a position now to listen to this, because it was a very long time ago, but there've been lots of Dorothy Boxalls throughout the world who have picked up Walter Carroll's pieces and helped young chil-dren to have a first love of music in a way that he was uniquely able to inspire. And of course Ida, then, carried on that mantle, which she inherited too through Hilda Collens.

I think of those first meetings with Ida. She was already a vener-ated lady, a distinguished leader in music education, and I was just starting out, having escaped from the BBC. We met in a very unpropitious place, in a way. Our very first encounter was in the underpass at Lancaster Station. Not exactly a romantic sort of location for such an meeting, but she had, with typical generosity, agreed that she would come up to Lancaster to have a chat about the future and to see how we could get on. That was the point at when the die had been cast. This remarkable building was in the process of beginning to be constructed, and from then on we proceeded to have eighteen months of planning - centred on Lancaster, physically. Percy Welton, here today, will remember all this very clearly as a distinguished member of what we then formed as the steering committee.

I shall always remember lively moments with this steering committee because Ida would not put up with any sort of nonsense (as you know very well and will remember), but she also had very strong convictions. I remember one occasion when we were talking about the new building and she said: 'Well, what are the colours going to be?' And I was lucky in that I'd just been talking to the architect, John Bickerdyke, whose Persian wife was actually the colour mistress of the whole concept, and I said: 'We're going to have purple in the concert hall and bottle green in the theatre.' 'Ah, bottle green', said Ida. 'That's a good colour. Yes let's have bottle green. I think it's my favourite.' And I imagined at that moment that if we hadn't ended up with bottle green in the theatre, there'd have been all hell to pay.

Ida was very kind, you know. It's often said that middle-age is a time when you begin to fall into the trap of giving advice that isn't wanted, or alternatively, that it's the time when you stop giving advice that isn't necessary. And Ida never never did in all that time, though she must have found it quite tiresome to deal with a relatively young person. She had – and this characterised all her life – untold compassion. She had the biggest heart in the business, and she was so kind to everyone whilst at the same time being realistic and purposeful.

We think of Ida too as a double-bass player, and of course that's why the piece of mine you heard this afternoon had just a few notes for the double-bass here and there. She was also a very wide-ranging musician. If you look at John Robert-Blunn's book *Northern Accent*, you will find reproduced in it a most beautiful portrait of Ida at the piano. It's a portrait by Harold Riley, and who more distinguished than Harold Riley to have painted it. And you just look at the poise with which Ida is seated there in this lovely, lovely portrait. She never lost poise, despite the many difficulties she had to contend with, and she never lost her ability to give a measured response to any situation that arose. Things often had to be done in a great hurry, because she never spared herself. We all know how she would hurtle from one engagement or location to another; she was forever boarding a train, forever hopping on a bus somewhere. She knew every timetable by heart for every means of transport that she might wish to have recourse to, and she never ever failed to be where she needed to be, although as far as I know she never drove a car.

One of her great strengths I think was (and I'm sure we can all remember), the remarkable band of people that she gathered around her at All Saints' down the road there. Several are here today; we've mentioned Percy Welton , of course, and it's such a delight too that Pamela Stones is here with us. Thank you Pamela for coming. And we all remember Griff with such affection. Who can forget Griff, or would ever want to? You see they were people who helped Ida to make the whole thing *work*. And that is true of her staff: I single out for mention Dorothy Pilling the teacher of David Dubery whose piece we had the pleasure of hearing this afternoon, as well as a whole phalanx of very gifted instrumental teachers.

The Northern School of Music was a remarkable place and it lives on, I'm sure, in the memory of all who knew it. I shall always remember my introduction, and there were two events happened after I'd been appointed that stick in my memory. On one occasion Ida said: 'We're putting on *Der Freischütz*.' And I thought that's very brave, jolly good. And where were we putting on *Der Freischütz*? In none other but the Lesser Free Trade Hall. And it was a stunning performance, given that it was in that funny little box which was the old Lesser Free Trade Hall. And on another occasion we repaired, and I'm sure Michael Hancock will remember this, to Salford, for an orchestral concert conducted by Maurice Clare, in which Michael played the Grieg concerto. And that gave me an early flavour of how good things could be at the Northern School of Music, with artists of that calibre.

When we started up here, we were extremely fortunate to be able to incorporate the services of so many of Ida's staff, who are well known to all of you: one of them at least who hasn't been mentioned so far is here today and that is Neville Duckworth; and there were many others who alas are not here today with us. I could ramble on that topic for a very long time, but I do want to speak of the genuine affection held for Ida. When we were starting up here, and she was leaving behind her own very substantial and distinguished patch down the road, she never for a moment held back on anything that we were projecting or trying to. She might say, quite laconically, 'Well if you think that's the right way to go about it'; and I would know that probably meant 'Take heed young man and think twice before you go ahead', which was, bless her, very sound advice. We managed to start off with a triumvirate here: John Wray who'd come over from the RMCM and had the post of Dean of Studies; Terence Greaves, who is here today (we were fortunate enough to entice him away from Birmingham) who became Dean of Development – in those days development didn't mean what it does now, which is sort of money-raising – what Terry had to do was to forge the whole damn' shoot for us, and he did it, brilliantly. And then Ida: Dean of Management, and I think (no, I know) that that was a wonderfully successful appointment, because it gave Ida the opportunity to bring everybody together. We would go off at the end of the long vacation and repair to conferences. Once we went to Giggleswick and then again to Lancaster and everybody could meet everyone else, and while we were there I would watch Ida going round, talking to everybody and saying 'Now you don't know him yet but you ought to because you're going to work together' and off she would go; she had this wonderful direct way of working, and you never gainsaid Ida anything in that respect.

So this college started off extremely strongly and was very fortunate to have Ida in that key position for those first years. But Ida's influence went far beyond the RNCM. She was a very distinguished president of the ISM, for instance, and we had a wonderful conference here in 1977. That was typical of Ida's influence: it extended far beyond Manchester, and into fields that you wouldn't have expected, very often, that Ida would have had the time or perhaps even the inclination to explore, but she did.

We all remember her. We all remember what an intrepid fighter she was for everything that she believed in. She fought with magnanimity; she fought with a resolution which embraced people rather than rejected them, and that's why you're all here today in such numbers. You're here because Ida's spirit lives on with us all. We're enormously privileged to have known her, and thank you for letting me try to put what I hope are your thoughts into a few words this afternoon. If you've got glasses, or even if you haven't, to Ida's health and memory, God bless her, Ida Carroll.

CD Reviews

DAVID ELLIS, CHRISTOPHER FIFIELD, PAUL HIND-
MARSH,
MICHAEL KENNEDY, PETER MARCHBANK,
MARK ROWLINSON, STUART SCOTT

Borderlands: Contemporary British Piano Trios
Chagall Trio: Nicoline Kraamwinkel (violin), Tim Gill (cello), Julian Rolton (piano)
Campion Cameo 2053 (British Composer Series). Available from DI Music: dimus@aol.com

THIS CD was recorded in August 2004 in the newly opened Cosmo Rodewald Hall at Manchester University – an excellent venue for this range of musical forces. Among the list of generous patrons and subscribers who made its production possible are the University of Manchester and the Ida Carroll Trust.

Clearly the Chagall Trio feel very much at home with contemporary repertory; their confident style and technical assurance are evident in this not over-generous coupling of four works totalling around 50 minutes. But then, quality is certainly to be preferred to quantity every time.

Of the composers represented, both Camden Reeves and Philip Grange have strong Manchester links, while John Pickard (University of Bristol) and his former pupil Paul Mealor (University of Aberdeen) have had associations not too far away in North Wales. The accompanying booklet is commendably and comprehensibly informative in respect of details concerning the composers and their music.

Reeves must be the only composer whose inspiration combines plainchant with a penchant for squid; the result, *Starlight Squid* (2001), is a fascinating seven minutes of contemporary musical escapism, but wrought in a wholly individual manner. At no time does the means of the work's composition intrude into one's enjoyment of its colourful and virtuosic progress.

A more intense backdrop informs the 2004 trio by Paul Mealor that gives the recording its title. Again, a specific influence, this time the poetry of W. B. Yeats, is cited as the inspiration for the music's structure. It is however not the 'Irishness' of the poet but his philosophy which determines the content of the score and its personality.

Borderlands is music that is strong when quietly reflective, but lyrical at climactic moments.

The orchestral music of John Pickard has impressed sufficiently for listeners to expect more regular hearings of his scores. His Piano Trio (1990) would seem to be the first smaller-scale work of his to have appeared on CD, though despite only three players being involved it feels like music for a larger canvas. Often the piano writing dominates to the extent that both cello and violin are danger of becoming swamped, and some astute balancing on the part of the backroom staff is apparent. Even in the quieter middle section there is tension, which is resolved only when the energy of the final *allegro* is dissipated.

The longest work is the four-movement *Homage to Chagall* (1995) by Philip Grange. The composer cites as his inspiration the general influence of the painter, rather than any specific canvas (plus, of course, the skills of the performers who commissioned the piece). Although the music is both challenging and demanding, it is clearly articulated in its formal structure and a rewarding musical journey even without the Chagall images to help those who might miss the visual connotations.

DAVID ELLIS

Autumn Sequence: The Music of Douglas Steele and his circle
Carlisle Cathedral Youth Choir (director David Gibbs), Carlisle Cathedral Choristers (director Jeremy Suter), Chetham's Lower School Choir (director Peter Hatfield), Dalston Handbell Ringers; Stephen Hough (piano), Richard Baker (speaker), John Turner (recorder), John Powell (baritone), Vanessa Williamson (mezzo-soprano), Michael Hancock (piano), Peter Lawson (piano), Susan Bettaney (piano), Jeremy Suter (organ).
Campion Cameo 2040–2041 (British Composer Series). Available from DI Music: dimus@aol.com

I MUST DECLARE a personal interest here. When I went to Manchester in 1965 to study music on the joint course (Manchester University and the Royal Manchester College of Music, as it then was), I had a room in Woolton Hall, Fallowfield. My principal practical study was the organ, and across the road stood the parish church of Holy Innocents,

Fallowfield. With the recklessness of youth I knocked at the rectory door and asked the vicar, Tom Kennaugh, if I might do my practice on the church organ. He agreed, provided I in turn would assist the Director of Music at the church, a man called Douglas Steele, by playing occasionally for services on Sunday and taking weekly choir practice. For this I was also paid the princely salary of £2 per week. I met Douglas and sat in on some services while he showed me the musical and liturgical ropes before I took up the post. He was ready to retire altogether from playing and so it was only a matter of time before I took over completely (though our roles were reversed when he happily stood in for me during university vacations). Douglas was an eccentric bachelor, with a history of mental breakdowns, but he possessed an impish sense of humour and was hugely gifted as a teacher and musician, a fine organist with an exceptional talent for improvisation – in short, a thoroughly likeable man from whom I learned a great deal, and whose mischievous ways I promptly copied by improvising on themes from Wagner's *Tristan* during Holy Communion, or the *Song of the Volga Boatmen* during funerals (much to the amusement of the musically knowledgeable Tom).

Before the Second World War Douglas Steele studied conducting in Salzburg under Bruno Walter and Nicolai Malko, then spent a considerable period as Beecham's secretary, librarian and general factotum. His post-war career was in teaching, at Chetham's School and (when I knew him) at Stockport Grammar School. This pair of discs has been compiled as a worthy tribute, some of the performers being pupils or friends. John Turner's note conveys the warmth and affection in which he was held in Manchester and the surrounding areas from Carlisle to Stockport, and I wish to add my belated pennyworth, for I lost touch when I moved abroad and then stayed down south – to my great regret, from having listened to these discs.

The music is highly enjoyable: steeped in the English tradition, and usually in miniature pastoral format, it is filled with charm, wistful tunes and clever settings, is never over-sentimental and is occasionally (especially in his organ music and playing) rich in grandeur. Besides piano and organ works and songs spanning Douglas's career, the first disc also includes five Blake settings for baritone, recorder and piano (1987) by Arnold Cooke, and a group of four pieces for recorder and piano (2001), each contributed by a composer – Philip Cowlin, Martin Bussey, Stephen Hough, Emma Hancock – who knew Douglas as a friend, colleague or pupil. The second disc is devoted to *Autumn*

Sequence, an inventive composition written in 1969 for the Stockport Grammar School choir. How they must have enjoyed singing it, and one can only wish and hope that other schools will take it up. The instrumentation is based around the piano but also includes colourful sounds from handbells to organ. *The Three Mariners*, with the recorder expertly played by John Turner, is the catchy scherzo of the work, but what follows in *The Cock-Fight* is pure Gershwin, so enjoyable indeed that both pieces were given an immediate re-hearing by this reviewer. Apparently Douglas would improvise between the movements, and it is easy to imagine this causing chaos and unbridled mirth; these CDs will become an eloquent memorial to the man and his music. All the performers sound as if they are having fun and enjoying themselves, which the composer, in his modest way, would have loved. The last chord, sung beautifully by the children's choir, is 'FAREWELL' – a fitting valediction to Douglas from all those of us who retain the fondest recollections of him.

CHRISTOPHER FIFIELD

British Tuba Concertos
James Gourlay (tuba), Royal Ballet Sinfonia conducted by Gavin Sutherland
Naxos 8.557754 (20th Century British Music series)

JAMES GOURLAY is an exceptional and enterprising artist. Like the great John Fletcher before him, he has raised the profile of the tuba as a solo instrument through commissions and performances of solo and concerto works. This new recording includes the two British concertos that have come closest to standard repertory status: the pioneering concerto by Vaughan Williams and the vibrant early work by Edward Gregson. Gourlay has recorded them before in wind and brass band versions, but this recording brings them together in their orchestral versions for the first time. The coupling is apt, since Gregson pays direct homage to the Vaughan Williams by quoting part of it in his first movement.

Gourlay's approach is admirable. I have rarely heard either piece played with such range. His cantabile is beautifully shaped and sustained in the higher registers of the slow movements of both concertos. The central movement of the Gregson is perhaps the highlight of the whole disc. Gregson's orchestral colouring is subtly atmospheric, the string textures so much more telling than in the brass band original. In all his concertos there is an 'English' lyricism, drawn from the modal tradition of Vaughan Williams, which contrasts with a more pan-European or transatlantic eclecticism. In the first movement there are echoes of Hindemith and Bartók as well as RVW, rhetoric and virtuosity in equal measure; in the second a Shostakovich-like intensity, and in the finale a Waltonian wit and humour. James Gourlay captures the full range of this attractive work in his vibrant performance.

His characterisation, and range of gesture and tone, in the Vaughan Williams are equally authoritative. Once again the haunting lyricism of the Romance is the highlight. Two premiere recordings complete the disc, an intimate and less demonstrative concerto from Roger Steptoe and a brilliant showpiece from the Manchester composer John Golland. Stylistically, Steptoe's short work is the most cerebral of the four. Originally three pieces for tuba and piano, it was scored by Steptoe for tuba and strings at James Gourlay's suggestion. It is lyrical and gentle for much of the time, beginning and ending quietly and a well-chosen contrast to the more vigorous works that surround it.

John Golland was a prolific and popular composer for wind and brass band, whose music combined colourful 'modern' techniques, often based on strong dance rhythms, with a love of neo-romantic melody. He once confessed to me that he cultivated this deliberately accessible idiom because his more serious work was not being performed. What the concerto may lack in refinement of structure it makes up for in its colourful orchestration, rhythmic flair and tunefulness. It is designed to display the full range of the soloist's virtuosity, which James Gourlay achieves as to the manner born.

Some occasional rough edges in orchestral sound do not detract from the experience of hearing one of the world's finest tuba players at the top of his form. This must-have recording for the brass enthusiast is highly recommended as a way in to some of the uncharted but rewarding areas of the concerto repertory.

PAUL HINDMARSH

Points North
Piano duets by Walton, Rawsthorne, Pitfield, Isaacs, Roy Heaton
Smith, Norman Cocker and Percy Young
Keith Swallow and John Wilson (piano)
Campion Cameo 2036 (British Composer Series)

THIS ENTERPRISING DISC brings together some splendid piano duet
works by British composers played with élan and virtuosity by two of
Manchester's finest pianists, although Keith Swallow and John Wilson
are not of course exclusively claimed by Manchester. Of special
interest is Walton's own arrangement of his overture *Portsmouth Point*
(1925). There is no way in which even two pianists on one piano can
evoke the crackle and sparkle of the orchestral version, yet (like
Stravinsky with *Petrushka*) Walton makes a different work of it within
the context of the restricted medium and nothing is lost of its vitality
and rhythmic punch. His arrangement of *Siesta* (1926) does however
lack the languorous Mediterranean charm of the original except perhaps in its coda. The *Duets for Children*, composed for Walton's
nephew and niece, were written for piano solo but recast as duets and
later orchestrated (with one added). These are wholly delightful and
sound thoroughly pianistic. They are played enchantingly, with a wry
humour characteristic of their creator. He would have enjoyed the
misprint in the sleeve-note, by the way, which attributes to him music
for the coronation of George the Fourth – rather apposite, come to
think of it.

Walton's friend, the still-too-neglected Alan Rawsthorne, is represented by his Izaak Walton-inspired suite *The Creel* (1940). This too
was written for children, and its expert writing for the instruments is a
reminder – as if his two concertos were not enough – that Rawsthorne
was a pupil of Egon Petri and a resident pianist at Dartington. He was
certainly more accomplished as a pianist than Walton and it shows in
this amusing suite. Unless I am mistaken, Thomas Pitfield's music is
enjoying a breakthrough, thanks above all to John Turner's advocacy.
Minor composer perhaps, but a very civilized and wide-ranging one.
There is little dross in his output. His dance suite *Minors* (Galliard,
Sarabande, Sinister Dance and Rigaudon) was written in 1963 for his
RMCM colleagues Hedwig Stein and Iso Elinson, whom many Mancunian musicians will remember with affection. The allegretto

(Sinister Dance), which originated as accompaniment to recitation of a Phoebe Hesketh poem called 'Skeleton Bride' (see the review of *Flying Kites*, below), is the most striking of these pieces, typical of Pitfield's quirky style. The Sarabande is in memory of Elinson (who died in 1964) and is a touching elegy.

The duets on folk-tunes and folk-dances by Leonard Isaacs and Percy Young traverse familiar ground with adroitness but I was more impressed and entertained by Norman Cocker's eight duets written between 1913 and 1915, two of them affectionate parodies of Percy Grainger, and another a homage to Leslie Stuart. For ten years from 1943 until his death Cocker was organist of Manchester Cathedral. One of his descendants is Mark Elder.

Perhaps the surprise on this disc is the *Sonatina* by Roy Heaton Smith, the last work he wrote before giving up composition in 1990 at the age of 62. The three short movements show extraordinary inventiveness and a superb grasp of the capabilities of the piano-duet medium. They must be rewarding to play. Heaton Smith was a Richard Hall pupil and won several prestigious prizes. On this evidence we should hear more of his music, so perhaps this performance will spark off some others.

MICHAEL KENNEDY

Flying Kites: A Trafford Miscellany
Richard Baker (reciter), John Turner (recorder), Keith Swallow (piano), Damien Harron (percussion)
Campion Cameo 2044

IT WAS a happy idea to assemble a disc associated with the area of South Manchester now known as the Borough of Trafford. As one who lived there for over 50 years, I found it a nostalgic as well as a rewarding musical journey to listen to David Beck's *Dunham Pastorale*, an evocative piece for recorder and piano preceded by Richard Baker's reading of Tom Pitfield's poem 'Dunham Park (Winter Evening)', another reminder of Pitfield's many-sided talents (the cover of the CD is his drawing of a bridge over the Bollin). Turner's genius for drawing magical sounds from the recorder is explored fully in this quite extensive work.

Pitfield is well represented – by a jaunty and often poetic xylophone sonata; a bagatelle for piano which takes unexpected turns in its brief course; by *Rain*, a recitation with xylophone and piano, and *Bones*, in which the xylophone, as you would expect, accompanies the voice. In *Bones*, as in *Skeleton Bride*, the humour is laced with a macabre streak which gives Pitfield's work an extra and searching dimension. Four of his nursery-rhyme texts are settings for reciter, recorder and piano by Robin Walker, with neat and witty sideways glances at *Façade* that go beyond mere parody.

The disc remembers that John Ireland was born in Bowdon and he is represented by his classic piano piece *The Island Spell*, played with magical nuances of colour and expression by Keith Swallow, and his recitation *Annabel Lee*, which Baker delivers with a characteristic understatement that misses nothing of the sinister emotional power of Poe's verse. A Pitfield pupil, the late Robert Elliott, remembered as Alfred Deller's harpsichordist and Head of Keyboard Studies at the RNCM from 1978 until 1991, presents almost a self-portrait in the precision and whimsical humour of his *Sonatina*.

I enjoyed the *River Dances* for recorders (treble, sopranino and descant) and piano by Martin Ellerby with movements entitled Castle Mill, Dunham Town, Ashley Mill and Swan with Two Nicks. This is music of no pretensions beyond entertainment and nostalgia delivered with a sure touch and played by Turner and Swallow with elegance and grace. Fond memories of the BBC producer James Langley, who died in 1994, are stirred by his *Five Shakespeare Dances* for solo recorder. The Strathspey movement, inspired by 'When the bagpipe sings i'the nose' from *The Merchant of Venice*, demands, and receives, a special kind of virtuosity. The disc takes its title from a pleasing piece for recorder and piano 'depicting the flight of kites on a breezy day' by Sasha Johnson Manning, director of music at St Mary's, Bowdon. Both these discs deserve circulation beyond a local region. The sound quality is good: *Points North* was recorded in Peel Hall, Salford University, and *Flying Kites* in King's School, Macclesfield; both were produced by David Ellis.

MICHAEL KENNEDY

British Recorder Concertos
John Turner (recorder), Camerata Ensemble conducted by Philip McKenzie
Dutton Epoch CDLX7154

THIS IS AN ATTRACTIVE disc made up of six pieces for recorder and small orchestra in which the soloist is John Turner. Despite coming to prominence as a colleague of the late David Munrow, he is perhaps the only recorder player in Britain today who still takes seriously the matter of re-creating and refreshing the repertory for his instrument. Certainly, at least three of these works were written for him and his performances are ably supported by the Camerata Ensemble under Philip McKenzie.

Peter Hope's Concerto, composed in 2003, displays the composer's great facility in the field of light music. The music is essentially melodic and delightfully scored, with the small string orchestra being reinforced by a harp and percussion. The last movement is a relentless Tarantella which lingers in the memory long after the work has ended.

The whimsical title of David Beck's *Flûte-à-Beck: Concerto* disguises a work of quite serious intent. In both of the first two movements, the textures are sparse with the soloist rhapsodizing over string chords or being accompanied by the harp. Following an attractive middle section, the central movement ends with a pastoral in which birdsong can be heard against a lonely and misty landscape. The concerto ends with a scherzo-like Finale which has echoes of Bartók. As one would expect from a composer who has spent much of his life working as a violinist, the string writing is wonderfully idiomatic.

Hans Gál spent much of his life in Edinburgh, though he was born and educated in Vienna. His *Concertino* was composed in 1961 for Carl Dolmetsch, and this is probably the first time that the work has been played with a string orchestra as originally intended. It is cast in the traditional four movements and is intensely lyrical with a sparkling final Rondo.

David Ellis composed his *Divertimento Elegiaco (in memoriam Ida Carroll)* over a period of eight years, originally as a chamber work and more recently in the version for string orchestra, marimba and harp. The first movement, Canticle, is quiet and thinly scored, while the second is much more lively. The final Chaconne is the most substantial of the three movements and ends with the soloist tolling a medieval bell over slowly moving chords. It is clearly a deeply felt work, written from the heart.

Ian Parrott's *Sinfonia Concertante* has important parts for solo violin and xylophone in addition to the recorder. It begins with a hesitant Reverie which almost convinces one that the main theme is a folk-tune. The Ritornello is more athletic while the Rhapsody is a tense and dramatic movement. After much that is imaginative, the work ends with a rather conventional March based on themes from the earlier movements.

The disc ends with *Mrs Harris in Paris*, a charming concert waltz for recorder and string orchestra by David Dubery.

Delightful and well written though much of this music is, I wonder what will become of it. Is it destined to lie on a dusty shelf until some future John Turner comes along? Will any of these composers ever get the chance to hear their work in the concert hall to see how an audience responds to it? It would be pleasing to think so, but I'll not hold my breath ....

PETER MARCHBANK

Anthony Gilbert: On Beholding a Rainbow
... Into the Gyre of a Madder Dance
RNCM Wind Ensemble conducted by Clark Rundell

Certain Lights Reflecting
Susan Bickley (mezzo-soprano), BBC Symphony Orchestra conducted by Andrew Davis

Unrise
RNCM Wind Ensemble conducted by Clark Rundell

On Beholding a Rainbow
Anthony Marwood (violin), RNCM Symphony Orchestra conducted by Garry Walker

NMC D105

GIVEN THAT THE Royal Northern College of Music has had as its two Principals so far the composers Sir John Manduell and Professor

Edward Gregson, it is hardly surprising that the teaching and performance of contemporary music have been fostered and vigorously championed with enthusiasm throughout its 30 years' existence. Responsible for setting up the composition department at the fledgling college was Anthony Gilbert who went on to become Head of the School of Composition and Contemporary Music until his retirement in 1999. Before that Gilbert taught at the University of Lancaster, Morley College and Goldsmiths College. He had been Music Editor and Head of Production of Contemporary Music at Schott's, and before that a Music and Record Library Assistant at the City of Westminster Public Library. Clearly, Gilbert is a man who has given a lifetime's commitment to furthering the music of others. It is fitting, then, that the performances of his own music on this CD should be given by some of the staunchest allies of new music in Britain. This is music making not only of consummate skill and artistry but also of total dedication to and genuine affection for the music. Our reward, as listeners, is to have our emotions stirred as richly as our ears are stimulated by Gilbert's vivid and opulent creative palette.

Beginning with the rich sonorities of what Gilbert describes as 'a long chorus of blurred woodwind harmonies in distinctly unstable rhythm', ... *Into the Gyre of a Madder Dance* is a contrast between two groups of instruments each struggling against the other, with the woodwind eventually succumbing to the more regularly rhythmic and insistent horns and trumpets. This short work was inspired by the poetry of Sarah Day, a Tasmanian born in Lancashire who shares Gilbert's love of Australia and all its natural phenomena. It is given a very persuasive account here by the RNCM Wind Ensemble, on top form under Clark Rundell. The contemporary music scene in Manchester has been enriched for a good many years now by this ensemble under both Timothy Reynish and, latterly, Rundell.

The poetry of Sarah Day is again at the heart of *Certain Lights Reflecting*, a song cycle setting five of her poems. This performance was a live event in the BBC's Maida Vale Studios performed by Susan Bickley with the BBC Symphony Orchestra under Andrew Davis. It is a potent reminder of just how much the BBC has done for contemporary music – and composers in particular – since the advent of the Third Programme in 1946. The producer on this occasion was Stephen Plaistow, for many years the BBC's Chief Producer, Contemporary Music, a true champion and great friend of new music. It is impossible to conceive of a more convincing depiction of this ravishing score.

Interestingly, Gilbert uses traditional forms – variations, a scherzo, a 'hidden' fugue, an arietta and a passacaglia – yet the ear is throughout seduced by the colours, textures and sensuous sonorities he conjures up to portray the sights, sounds and aromas of the ever-changing Australian landscape and, especially, its flora and fauna, described so vibrantly by Day's poems.

For *Unrise* Anthony Gilbert took his inspiration from words by the Hebrew poet Avraham ben Yitzhak and also from a melody and two symmetrical scales taught to him just before the Second World War by a young Viennese refugee who had been given shelter in the Gilberts' family home in London. It is the most recent piece on the CD, written in 2001 as a belated 60th birthday present for Timothy Reynish, 'in gratitude for over a quarter of a century of support, encouragement and fine performances'. The three movements are mostly derived from the music of the young Viennese refugee, but transformed by the fragment of Hebrew poetry describing the cock crowing at dawn, with 'trumpetings', 'echoings' and 'not-rising'. Yet again, this is a multi-coloured score, at times gaudy, at others brooding, and it is captured keenly by Rundell and the RNCM Wind Ensemble.

Finally, *On Beholding a Rainbow* is a full-scale violin concerto and its position on the CD, following *Unrise*, is uncanny. It is as if it emerges organically from the wind piece. It doesn't, of course – it was written between 1992 and 1997 – but the juxtaposition of the two works is a fortunate one. However, there is common ground in that *On Beholding a Rainbow* is a Jewish affirmation of trust which Gilbert describes as 'a private message to its dedicatee, the composer's friend Ian Goldstone, whose tragic death shocked the work into existence in its final form'. In this final form the work received its first performance in 1999 with the BBC Philharmonic under Rumon Gamba. The soloist on that occasion, Anthony Marwood, is also the soloist on this CD, this time with the RNCM Symphony Orchestra conducted by Garry Walker. At just over 32 minutes in length and in the standard three-movement fast–slow–fast form, the work is conceived on a much broader scale than the other pieces heard here. Again, Gilbert turns to conventional forms, but he hides them beneath the surface, the ear noticing more the unrelenting intensity of the struggle in the various conflicts and arguments that give the piece its strength and character. It is a demanding part for the soloist and Marwood breezes through it with ease. While the RNCM Symphony Orchestra is not yet at the level of the BBC Philharmonic, they make a pretty good fist of this exacting score under Garry Walker.

Altogether this CD is a first-rate account of four really stimulating works, and a valuable addition to the catalogue.

MARK ROWLINSON

Thomas Pitfield: Piano Concertos Nos. 1 and 2
Studies on an English Dance-Tune, Arietta and Finale, Toccata, Xylophone Sonata
Anthony Goldstone (piano), Peter Donohoe (piano and xylophone)
Royal Northern College of Music Orchestra conducted by Andrew Penny
Naxos 8.557291 DDD (British Piano Concertos series)

THERE HAS BEEN a notable absence of British piano music in concerts and recordings made over the last 35 years or so, and it is therefore to be applauded that Naxos has started to produce a 'British Piano Concertos' series. Fortunately this has increased the number of works by Thomas Pitfield available to us on CD.

Born in the first years of the twentieth century and belonging to a generation of composers whose works found their way into the concert hall following the Second World War, Thomas Pitfield was a largely self-taught composer who wrote prolifically for all kinds of instruments and for every type of ensemble. Folk music influenced the style and form of his compositions but always remained subservient to self-expression. Of the pieces recorded here, it is most apparent in the second Piano Concerto ('The Oak and the Ash') and the *Studies on an English Dance-Tune* ('Jenny Pluck Pears').

Good craftsmanship is a quality ever present in Pitfield's music and one that readily reveals itself in the Piano Concerto No. 1 in E minor, written in 1946–7 for Stephen Wearing who gave the first performance with the Liverpool Philharmonic Orchestra under the direction of Hugo Rignold in November 1949. This is one of Pitfield's best large-scale works, and it presents the soloist with some technical problems which Anthony Goldstone, well supported by Andrew Penny and the RNCM Orchestra, copes with admirably.

The interplay between piano and orchestra, especially in the canonic treatment of the first theme in the opening movement, is skilfully marked by clarity of line and texture in this performance. The canonic writing here is not only important as a hint of the canonic compression of the final movement's rondo theme at the end of the work, but is also a hallmark of Pitfield's style. The outer two movements of the concerto are brilliant, but the composer's inventive musical charm and beauty show themselves to good effect in the middle movement which has a memorable main theme of some solemnity. Here too is a short, and beautifully written, mysterious scherzo-like section, deftly realized by the soloist. Moments such as this, along with Anthony Goldstone's generally sympathetic interpretation, lift the music to a level of inspiration beyond the simply pleasing and tasteful.

The length and form of the Piano Concerto No. 2 was governed by the restrictions imposed by the commissioner, the publisher Max Hinrichsen, who was looking for a miniature concerto for the use of American piano students in performance auditions. The result is a work of very unusual form but its main characteristics are unmistakably Pitfield. A quotation from Milton at the head of the score sums it up well: '… and bring with thee Jest and youthful Jollity'.

Inventiveness is the keynote of this work. The first movement (Dance-Prologue), using three simple tunes on the white keys treated with ostinati, hymn-like harmonization, various rhythms and decorations, is followed by a scherzo (Interlude on White Keys) built upon running figures and modal melody. The last movement is curious in that it embodies both the slow movement and the finale presented as a set of variations on the English folksong, 'The Oak and the Ash'. Here the performers enjoy themselves in the playful rhythms of the first and third variations, which are separated by a delightfully contemplative variation scored for piano alone.

Both concertos are recorded with good piano presence and endowed with a rhythmic energy so essential to the composer's style.

The works for solo piano should not disappoint, as Pitfield's favoured 5/8 and 7/8 rhythms, pianistic decoration and harmonies of almost French flavour can all be found in his tuneful music. *Studies on an English Dance-Tune*, written for John McCabe who first performed it while still a student at the RMCM in 1961, subjects the folk-tune 'Jenny Pluck Pears' to various rhythmic, modal and playing treatments in seven short movements. Peter Donohoe's technique and artistry are shown to good effect in this and the other two works for solo piano included on the disc.

Although an early piece, *Arietta and Finale* is all one would expect of the composer, but it is the *Toccata*, written for Lucy Pierce and published in 1953, which demands the listener's attention with its exuberance.

Always looking to the needs of performers, Pitfield often found himself writing for unusual instruments or combinations of instruments. His four-movement Xylophone Sonata, composed for the Hallé Orchestra's principal percussionist, Eric Woolliscroft, and superbly executed here by Peter Donohoe, is a work that falls into that category. This lively piece using 7/8 and 10/8 rhythms was published in 1967 and deserves to be heard.

All in all, this collection is truly representative of Thomas Pitfield's output of music for piano. The recording gives much pleasure and, for those who are not already familiar with his works, the budget price makes it particularly attractive and well worth exploring.

STUART SCOTT

First Performances in Greater Manchester and Neighbouring Towns, 2004

Compiled by GEOFFREY KIMPTON

Each entry is a world premiere unless otherwise stated.

Alexander, Colin
String Quartet 'Circassian Rhythms'
10 January
Royal Northern College of Music, Lord Rhodes Room
Adastra Quartet

Basford, Daniel
Solo 1, for vibraphone
28 June
Royal Northern College of Music
Polly McMillan

Basford, Daniel
Solo 3, for English horn
28 June
Royal Northern College of Music
Alexia Pelling

Basford, Daniel
Threads, for instrumental ensemble
3 February
Royal Northern College of Music, Studio Theatre
RNCM New Ensemble, conducted by Clark Rundell

Basford, Daniel
The Temptation of St Anthony, for orchestra (from
Three Dali Paintings)
30 September
Royal Northern College of Music, Concert Hall
RNCM Orchestra, conducted by Mark Heron

Bayliss, Colin
Grumpy Tunes, for recorder and guitar (Stizzoso; Adagio;
Moderato; Andante con moto; Tempo di marcia)
30 November
University of Salford, Peel Hall
John Turner, Neil Smith

Bayliss, Colin
Valentines: romantic interludes for piano
14 October
Flixton House, Urmston
John Williamson

Beck, David
… for a rag man's long at the briny
(Anagrams for Anthony Gilbert)
for soprano, recorder and piano
16 October
Bridgewater Hall, Barbirolli Room
Lesley-Jane Rogers, John Turner, Peter Lawson

Beck, David
Seven Duets for violin and viola (Hurdy-Gurdy; Sadness;
Ostinato; Frantic; Canon; Ballad; Jogging)
14 October
Flixton House, Urmston
David Beck, Geoffrey Kimpton

Beck, David
Sonata for solo treble recorder (Fanfare; Dance;
Interrupted Lullaby; Hornpipe; Incantations)
30 November
University of Salford, Peel Hall
John Turner

Bedford, Luke
Rode with Darkness, for orchestra (BBC commission)
8 January
Bridgewater Hall
Hallé Orchestra, conducted by Mark Elder

Berezan, David
Styal (acousmatic work, using sounds from the historic
Quarry Bank Mill)
15 October
University of Manchester, Cosmo Rodewald Concert Hall
Mantis (24-speaker sound diffusion system)

Blezard, William arr. Stephen Dodgson
Three Gawthorpe Dances for recorder and harpsichord
(Courtly Dance; Lyric Interlude; A Touch of Spanish)
12 August
St Mary's Church, Nantwich
John Turner, Tony Metcalfe

Boondiskulchok, Prach
String Quartet No. 2
11 January
Royal Northern College of Music, Lord Rhodes Room
McCarroll Quartet

Bosch, Oscar Colomina I.
String Quartet No. 1, 'The Labyrinth'
10 January
Royal Northern College of Music, Lord Rhodes Room
Tetrakis Quartet

Bourgeois, Derek
Pet Hen's Odd Song Op. 202, for soprano, recorder
and harpsichord
3 April
Bridgewater Hall, Barbirolli Room
Lesley-Jane Rogers, John Turner, Pamela Nash

Boyd, Anne
Yuya, for tenor recorder and string quartet
16 October
Bridgewater Hall, Barbirolli Room
John Turner, Camerata Ensemble

Bullard, Alan
Turner's Tarantella, for recorder
11 May
St James's Church, Gatley
John Turner

Carpenter, Gary
Distanza, for instrumental ensemble
16 October
Royal Northern College of Music, Concert Hall
Ensemble 10:10, directed by Clark Rundell

Castiglioni, Niccolò (UK premiere)
Sinfonia con giardino
2 April
Bridgewater Hall
BBC Philharmonic, conducted by Gianandrea Noseda

Cheng, Chin Man
Insane Colour, for trombone and percussion
18 March
University of Manchester, Cosmo Rodewald Concert Hall
Psappha: Phil Goodwin, Tim Williams

Chilcott, Bob
Simple Pictures of Tomorrow, for double choir
(Manchester Chorale commission), poem by Paul Eluard,
translated by Gilbert Bowen
5 December
Royal Northern College of Music, Concert Hall
The Manchester Chorale, directed by Laura Jellicoe

Daugherty (UK premiere)
String Quartet 'Sing Sing: J. Edgar Hoover'
11 January
Royal Northern College of Music, Lord Rhodes Room
Ozarka Quartet

Daverson, Steve
Gold by Bronze Heard Iron Steel, for trumpet and percussion
28 June
Royal Northern College of Music, Lord Rhodes Room
RNCM soloists

Davies, Max Charles
String Quartet 'Iridescence'
11 January
Royal Northern College of Music, Lord Rhodes Room
Sacconi Quartet

Dawson, Ben
Resolve, for orchestra
30 September
Royal Northern College of Music, Concert Hall
RNCM Orchestra, conducted by Chris Houlding

Debussy, orch. Colin Matthews
Four Preludes: La puerta del vino; Des pas sur la neige;
Les fées sont d'exquises danseuses; La Sérénade interrompue
19 February
Bridgewater Hall
Hallé Orchestra, conducted by Kristjan Järvi

Del Tredici, David (UK premiere)
In Wartime, for wind orchestra
26 March
Royal Northern College of Music, Concert Hall
RNCM Wind Orchestra, conducted by Clark Rundell

Earl, Brian
Sinfonia Concertante, for horn and wind orchestra
26 March
Royal Northern College of Music, Concert Hall
Frank Lloyd, RNCM Wind Orchestra, conducted by
Clark Rundell

Ellis, David
Seventeen or Eighteen Inaudible Canons, for piano
16 October
Bridgewater Hall, Barbirolli Room
Peter Lawson

Ellis, David
String Quartet No. 3
7 April
Royal Northern College of Music, Concert Hall
Camerata Ensemble

Emmerson, Simon
Arenas, concerto for piano, brass quintet and electronics)
29 April
University of Manchester, Cosmo Rodewald Concert Hall
Philip Mead, RNCM Brass Ensemble conducted by
James Gourlay, Simon Emmerson (sound projection)

Feng, Si-si
When Fire Taste Snow, fantasy for piano
28 June
Royal Northern College of Music, Studio Theatre
Si-si Feng

Fitkin, Graham
Hurl, for saxophone quartet
11 February
Royal Northern College of Music, Concert Hall
Apollo Saxophone Quartet

Fitkin, Graham (World Premiere Tour)
Plan B, for saxophone quartet and strings
27 February
Royal Northern College of Music, Concert Hall
Apollo Saxophone Quartet, Goldberg Ensemble
directed by Malcolm Layfield

Fitzhugh, Richard
These Are the Little Things, for orchestra
18 December
BBC Studio 7 Concert Hall
BBC Philharmonic, conducted by James MacMillan

Forshaw, David
Into the Light, for string orchestra
6 November
United Reform Church, St Helens
St Helens Sinfonietta, conducted by Alan Free

Franks, Paul-Isaac
Anima Sola, for cor anglais
1 December
Royal Northern College of Music, Lord Rhodes Room
Alexia Pelling

Franks, Paul-Isaac
Divertimento, for alphorn and French horn
28 June
Royal Northern College of Music, Studio Theatre
Reto Stadelmann, Marcia Wallace

Franks, Paul-Isaac
Music for Film, for flute, cor anglais, clarinet / bass clarinet,
piano, percussion, viola and cello
2 June
Royal Northern College of Music, Theatre
RNCM instrumentalists

Fraser, Luke
Quartet 'for strings'
9 January
Royal Northern College of Music, Lord Rhodes Room
Bergonzi Quartet

Garbett, Andrew
'Air', from Symphony No. 1 'The Elements'
30 September
Royal Northern College of Music, Concert Hall
RNCM Orchestra, conducted by Mark Heron

Garbett, Andrew
'No thoughts to think, no tears to cry …', based on Bach's
Prelude BWV 939, for double wind quintet
30 January
Royal Northern College of Music, Concert Hall
Northerly Winds and Pelling Quintet, conducted by
Lancelot Fuhry

Garbett, Andrew
Monologue 3, for clarinet
22 June
Royal Northern College of Music, Lord Rhodes Room
Paul Vowles

Garbett, Andrew
Piece, for clarinet solo
28 June
Royal Northern College of Music, Studio Theatre
Juliet Davies

Garbett, Andrew
Piece for Ensemble
28 June
Royal Northern College of Music, Studio Theatre
Juliet Davies

Gardiner, Ian
Toccata; Canzona; Ricercare (Ensemble 10:10 commission)
16 October
Royal Northern College of Music
Ensemble 10:10, conducted by Clark Rundell

Gardner, John
Minuet for Stephen, for recorder and piano
3 April
Bridgewater Hall, Barbirolli Room
John Turner, Bernard Roberts

Gaunt, Benjamin
Fingers, based on Bach's Prelude BWV 939, for double
wind quintet
30 January
Royal Northern College of Music, Concert Hall
Northerly Winds and Pelling Quintet, conducted by
Lancelot Fuhry

Gilbert, Anthony
Ondine, song cycle for soprano, recorder, cello and harpsichord,
poems by Aloysius Bertrand: Le Clair, Le Chant, Le Récit,
… de Lune
16 October
Bridgewater Hall, Barbirolli Room
Lesley-Jane Rogers, John Turner, Jonathan Price, Janet Simpson

Gilbert, Anthony (world premiere tour)
Palace of the Winds (Goldberg Ensemble commission)
20 February
Royal Northern College of Music, Concert Hall
Goldberg Ensemble, directed by Malcolm Layfield

Glasser, Stanley
Wood, for harpsichord, treble recorder and acoustic guitar
(Root; Seed and Leaf; Tree)
3 April
Bridgewater Hall, Barbirolli Room
Pamela Nash, John Turner, Craig Ogden

Gorb, Adam
Magnification X, for soprano, recorder, cello and harpsichord
Poem by Sarah Day
16 October
Bridgewater Hall, Barbirolli Room
Lesley-Jane Rogers, John Turner, Jonathan Price, Janet Simpson

Gordon, Michael Zev
Three Basho Haiku for Tony, for soprano, recorder and piano
16 October
Bridgewater Hall, Barbirolli Room
Lesley-Jane Rogers, John Turner, Peter Lawson

Gregory, Will
Scintillation and High Life, for saxophone quartet
11 February
Royal Northern College of Music, Concert Hall
Apollo Saxophone Quartet

Gregson, Edward
Serenata Notturno, for cello and piano (world premiere of this version)
6 May
Royal Northern College of Music, Concert Hall
Victoria Simonsen, Benjamin Frith

Griffin, Peter
The Lesson, for solo harpsichord and tape
28 March
University of Manchester, Cosmo Rodewald Concert Hall
Jane Chapman

Griffiths, Andrew
Into My Heart, five songs from A. E. Housman's
'A Shropshire Lad'
28 June
Royal Northern College of Music, Studio Theatre
Robert Meinardi, Andrew Griffiths

Grossner, Sonja
Sonata in One Movement, for viola and piano
14 October
Flixton House, Urmston
Geoffrey and Rita Kimpton

Guneratne, Alexis
Boundary of Presence, for violin and cimbalom
12 March
University of Manchester, Cosmo Rodewald Concert Hall
Psappha: David Routledge, Tim Williams

Harper, Philip
The Legend of Sangeet, for brass band
18 January
Royal Northern College of Music, Concert Hall
Black Dyke Band, conducted by Nicholas Childs

Harris, Richard Leigh
Karumi, for solo recorder
16 October
Bridgewater Hall, Barbirolli Room
John Turner

Heaton, Wilfred (UK premiere)
Variations, for brass band
17 January
Royal Northern College of Music, Concert Hall
The Fairey FP (Music) Band, conducted by Howard Snell

Higgins, Gavin
Coogee Funk, for wind orchestra
19 October
Royal Northern College of Music, Concert Hall
RNCM Wind Orchestra, conducted by James Gourlay

Hope, Peter
A Herrick Garland, for voice, recorder, cello and harpsichord
10 June
St Bartholomew's Church, Church Minshull
James Bowman, John Turner, Jonathan Price, David Francis

Hopson, Graeme
Dance Fragments, for instrumental ensemble
3 February
Royal Northern College of Music, Studio Theatre
RNCM New Ensemble, conducted by Clark Rundell

Hopson, Graeme
Introit, for alphorn
28 June
Royal Northern College of Music, Studio Theatre
Reto Stadelman

Howard, Emily
Alchemical Fire, for instrumental ensemble
12 March
Royal Northern College of Music, Studio Theatre
RNCM New Ensemble, conducted by Lancelot Fuhry

Howard, Emily
Hiding (poem by Neil Cadwallader) for soprano and piano
28 June
Royal Northern College of Music, Studio Theatre
Janet Fischer, Ben Dawson

Howard, Emily
Lhotse, for string quartet
8 January
Royal Northern College of Music, Lord Rhodes Room
Gilks Quartet

Hunt, Jordan
Four Etudes, for piano (Accidental Jazz; Interior; Exterior;
Moto perpetuo)
22 June
Royal Northern College of Music, Lord Rhodes Room
Isabel Chaplais

Hunt, Jordan
Gossamer, for brass ensemble
17 December
Bridgewater Hall
Groves Brass Ensemble

Hunt, Jordan
The Esoteric Marriage, for narrator and string quartet
(poem by John Hayward)
2 June
Royal Northern College of Music, Theatre
David Butt-Philip, Maraini Quartet

Hunt, Jordan
The Voice of the Garden, chamber opera in one act (libretto by
Alastair Lord), for soprano, baritone and instrumental ensemble
2 June
Royal Northern College of Music, Theatre
Katherine Broderick, Marcus Farnsworth with ensemble
conducted by Jordan Hunt

Jackson, Francis
Sonata for Trumpet and Organ Op. 145
(Allegro moderato; Aria; Allegro giocoso)
All Saints and Martyrs Church, Langley, Middleton, Manchester
Malcolm Tyner, Philip Lowe

Jackson, Tim
Hush the Frightful, for violin and cimbalom
12 March
University of Manchester, Cosmo Rodewald Concert Hall
Psappha: David Routledge, Tim Williams

James, Daniel
Lamentation and Lampoon, for trombone and percussion
18 March
University of Manchester, Cosmo Rodewald Concert Hall
Psappha: Phil Goodwin, Tim Williams

Kim, Earl
Three Poems in French, for soprano and string quartet
6 May
Royal Northern College of Music, Concert Hall
Rachael Russell, International Sejong Soloists,
director Hyo Kang

Kim, Hee-Jung
Remembrance, for trombone and percussion
18 March
University of Manchester, Cosmo Rodewald Concert Hall
Psappha: Phil Goodwin, Tim Williams

Kimpton, Geoffrey
Owdham Footbo', music theatre piece based on a poem by
Ammon Wrigley, for two actor musicians
1 May
St Matthew's Church Hall, Stretford
Geoffrey and Rita Kimpton

King, Alastair
Concerto for Youth Orchestra
25 November
Bridgewater Hall
Stockport Youth Orchestra, conducted by Philip Mackenzie

Lawson, David
Variations on Bach's Prelude BWV 939, for double wind quintet
30 January
Royal Northern College of Music, Concert Hall
Northerly Winds and Pelling Quintet, conducted by Lancelot Fuhry

Lawson, David
Zoetrope, for wind ensemble
24 June
Royal Northern College of Music, Concert Hall
RNCM Wind Ensemble, conducted by James Gourlay

LeFanu, Nicola (world premiere tour)
Amores, for horn and strings (Goldberg Ensemble commission)
20 February
Royal Northern College of Music, Concert Hall
Richard Watkins, Goldberg Ensemble directed by Malcolm Layfield

Lewis, Anwen
remembering AGe: quintet for recorder, cello, soprano,
pendulum metronome and piano
16 October
Bridgewater Hall, Barbirolli Room
John Turner, Jonathan Price, Lesley-Jane Rogers, Janet Simpson

Lewis, Jeffrey
Litania, for two piccolos, harp, celeste and percussion
5 April
Royal Northern College of Music, Concert Hall
Fiona Slominska, Benjamin Griffiths, Amy Liptrott, Ian Tate,
Mark Concar, directed by David Jones

Lord, Alastair
Clamant, for flute
20 October
Royal Northern College of Music, Lord Rhodes Room
Sarah Robinson

Lord, Alastair
Quartet for clarinet, saxophone, viola and piano
28 June
Royal Northern College of Music, Studio Theatre
The Fortune Quartet

Lumsdaine, David
Soundscape: Hunting a Crested Bell-Bird for Dr Gilbert
at Palm Creek
16 October
Bridgewater Hall, Barbirolli Room

McClelland, Chris
String Quartet 'Components of Mu'
9 January
Royal Northern College of Music, Lord Rhodes Room
Nero Quartet

MacMillan, James (European premiere)
A Scotch Bestiary, for organ and orchestra
11 December
Bridgewater Hall
Wayne Marshall, BBC Philharmonic, conducted by
James MacMillan

Malone, Kevin (UK premiere)
Count Me In (acousmatic)
30 January
University of Manchester, Cosmo Rodewald Concert Hall
Mantis (Manchester Theatre in Sound)

Manduell, John
Bell Birds from Nelson, for solo recorder (treble and descant)
16 October
Brigewater Hall, Barbirolli Room
John Turner

Manning, Sasha Johnson
Flying Kites, for treble recorder and piano
12 August
St Mary's Church, Nantwich
John Turner, Tony Metcalfe

Manning, Sasha Johnson
Two settings of poems by Christina Rossetti, for soprano and piano
'Beneath Thy Cross' and 'For the Least of all the Saints'
14 October
Flixton House
Holly Marland, David Forshaw

Manning, Sasha Johnson
The Shepherd's Carol, for children's choir
13 December
Manchester Cathedral
Choir of Bowdon Church School

Manning, Sasha Johnson
Carols: Sweet was the Song; I Sing of a Maiden;
When Christ was born of Mary free;
The World's Desire; Dark the Night Lay
15 December
Sale Music Society
Sasha Johnson Manning (soprano), Holly Marland (mezzo-soprano)

Manning, Sasha Johnson
Winds at the Manger, a play with five songs
16 December
Withington Girls' School
The Junior School, with Andrew Dean (piano)

Manning, Sasha Johnson
A Wonder of Angels, for choir (SATB) and organ
19 December
Bowdon Parish Church
Bowdon Parish Church Choir, with Robin Coulthard

Manning, Sasha Johnson
'Balulalow' and 'Mary and Jesus'
22 December
Manchester Cathedral
Cathedral Choristers conducted by Christopher Stokes

Marshall, Nicholas (first performance of this version)
The Garden of Eden, for recorder and piano
Adam; Eve; Siesta; The Serpent; A Little Temptation
12 August
St Mary's Church, Nantwich
John Turner, Tony Metcalfe

Matheson, Iain
Every Moment Alters, for orchestra
18 December
BBC Studio 7 Concert Hall
BBC Philharmonic, conducted by James MacMillan

Moseley, Ivan
Changes 11 (2), for string quartet
28 June
Royal Northern College of Music
Fields Quartet

Moseley, Ivan
Duets and Refrains, for instrumental ensemble
23 June
Royal Northern College of Music, Concert Hall
RNCM New Ensemble

Moseley, Ivan
A Game of Two Halves, for orchestra
30 September
Royal Northern College of Music, Concert Hall
RNCM Orchestra, conducted by Chris Houlding

Moseley, Ivan
Variation on Bach's Prelude BWV 939, for double wind quintet
30 January
Royal Northern College of Music, Concert Hall
Northerly Winds and Pelling Quintet, conducted by
Lancelot Fuhry

Muldowney, Dominic
'Scarlatti', for wind ensemble (woodwind and horns)
30 January
Royal Northern College of Music, Concert Hall
Wind Ensemble (14 players), conducted by Dominic Muldowney

Murray, Simon
Pierre Musicale, for saxophone quartet
2 November
Royal Northern College of Music, Concert Hall
Veya Saxophone Quartet

Musgrave, Thea (European premiere)
Turbulent Lancscapes, for orchestra
13 November
Bridgewater Hall
BBC Symphony Orchestra, conducted by David Zinman

Newton, Rodney
The King of Elfland's Daughter, for brass band
18 January
Royal Northern College of Music, Concert Hall
Buy As You View Cory Band, conducted by Robert Childs

Nichol, Peter
Tears and Dancing, for orchestra
23 October
University of Manchester, Cosmo Rodewald Concert Hall
University of Manchester Sinfonietta, conducted by Oliver-John Ruthven

Nielson, Emma
Four-eye Gin German, for marimba
28 June
Royal Northern College of Music, Studio Theatre

Nielson, Emma
Sleep, Fleshly Birth, for mezzo-soprano, two oboes & cor anglais
2 June
Royal Northern College of Music, Theatre
Rachel Gilmore, Alexia Pelling, Xian Bi Liu, Lindsey Dixon

Norris Richard
Further Musing, for orchestra
18 December
BBC Studio 7
BBC Philharmonic, conducted by James MacMillan

Osborn, Gavin
Winter Music, for trombone, percussion & audio CD
18 March
University of Manchester, Cosmo Rodewald Concert Hall
Psappha: Phil Goodwin and Tim Williams

Osborn, Gavin
Two Pieces for harpsichord
29 March
Cosmo Rodewald Concert Hall
Gavin Wayte

Penderecki, Krzysztof (UK premiere)
Concerto Grosso, for three cellos and orchestra
8 May
Bridgewater Hall
Frans Helmerson, Lluis Claret, Claudio Bohorquez,
BBC Philharmonic, conducted by the composer

Percy, Ian
The Pictures on your Wall (Florence 1), for trombone and percussion
18 March
Cosmo Rodewald Concert Hall
Psappha: Phil Goodwin, Tim Williams

Pitkin, Jonathan
Soundlessly Down, Purpled Steel, for brass band
4 March
Royal Northern College of Music, Concert Hall
RNCM Brass Band, directed by John Miller

Poole, Geoffrey
Snow Mountain Piper, for recorder
11 May
St. James's Church, Gatley
John Turner

Rathbone, Arthur
New Year's Revolutions, for solo harpsichord and tape
28 March
Cosmo Rodewald Concert Hall
Jane Chapman

Riain, Ailis Ni
'Silently in Space …', for string quartet
10 January
Royal Northern College of Music, Lord Rhodes Room
Dibley Quartet

Russell, Barry
Three Improvisations, for saxophone quartet
11 February
Royal Northern College of Music, Concert Hall
Apollo Saxophone Quartet

Sergeant, Matthew
Sift, cadenzas and duos for clarinet and percussion
28 June
Royal Northern College of Music, Studio Theatre
Rebecca Thorn, Polly McMillan

Sergeant, Matthew
Variation on Bach's Prelude BVW 939, for wind ensemble
30 January
Royal Northern College of Music, Concert Hall
Northerly Winds and Pelling Quartet, conducted by
Lancelot Fuhry

Shardlow, Nicholas
String Quartet
8 January
Royal Northern College of Music, Lord Rhodes Room
Wu Quartet

Simonsen, Victoria
Parallel Spheres, for orchestra
30 September
Royal Northern College of Music, Concert Hall
RNCM Orchestra, conducted by Philippe Bach

Simpson, Mark (world premiere tour)
Space, for violin and cimbalom
28 March
University of Manchester, Cosmo Rodewald Concert Hall
Psappha: David Routledge, Tim Williams

Solomons, David
Orientations, for violin and piano
14 October
Flixton House
David Beck and Rita Kimpton

Sotelo, Mauricio
String Quartet No. 2 'Artemis'
24 September
Bridgewater Hall
Artemis Quartet

Stadelmann, Reto
Serenade, for two string quartets and double bass
28 June
Royal Northern College of Music, Studio Theatre

Stamatakis-Brown, Andrew
Miniatures, for organ
23 June
Royal Northern College of Music, Concert Hall
Darren Hargan

Stamatakis-Brown, Andrew
Slow-motion rollercoaster, for orchestra
30 September
Royal Northern College of Music, Concert Hall
RNCM Orchestra, conducted by Sadu Muramatsu

Strachan, Duncan
String Quartet, 'Realpolitik'
9 January
Royal Northern College of Music, Lord Rhodes Room
Howarth Quartet

Talbot, Joby
Blue Cell, for saxophone quartet
11 February
Royal Northern College of Music, Concert Hall
Apollo Saxophone Quartet

Thomas, Augusta Read (European premiere)
Murmurs in the Mist of Memory, for string ensemble
6 May
Royal Northern College of Music, Concert Hall
International Sejong Soloists, director Hyo Kang

Thomas, Augusta Read
Whispers of Summer, for three cellos
(RNCM International Cello Festival commission)
6 May
Royal Northern College of Music, Concert Hall
Patrick Demenga, Thomas Demenga, Tomas Djupsjobacka

Thompson, Barbara (world premiere tour)
Concerto for saxophone quartet and strings (Apollo commission)
22 February
Royal Northern College of Music, Concert Hall
Apollo Saxophone Quartet, Goldberg Ensemble, directed by
Malcolm Layfield

Thornecroft, John
Piano Sonata No. 2 (2003)
14 October
Flixton House
John Thornecroft

Thornecroft, John
Sonatina for horn and piano
14 October
Flixton House
Joanna Treasure, John Thornecroft

Tovey, Bramwell (UK premiere)
Requiem for a Charred Skull, for brass band and choir
17 January
Royal Northern College of Music, Concert Hall
Fodens Richardson Band, RNCM Chorus, conducted by
Bramwell Tovey

Vadillo, Eneko
Mutara, for orchestra
18 December
BBC Studio 7, Concert Hall
BBC Philharmonic, conducted by James MacMillan

Venables, Philip
String Quartet
10 January
Royal Northern College of Music, Lord Rhodes Room
Artea Quartet

Walker, Robin
His Spirit over the Waters, for solo cello
10 June
St Bartholomew's Church, Church Minshull
Jonathan Price

Waterhouse, Graham
Blind Cupid (Prior), for soprano, recorder and harpsichord
3 April
Bridgewater Hall, Barbirolli Room
Lesley-Jane Rogers, John Turner, Pamela Nash

Wendler, Edwin
Consolatio, for chorus and orchestra (European premiere)
25 November
Bridgewater Hall
Stockport Youth Orchestra, Burnley Municipal Choir,
Manchester Bach Choir, Stockport Grammar School
Choir, conducted by Philip Mackenzie

Whiteman, Nina
Twango, for harpsichord
28 March
University of Manchester, Cosmo Rodewald Concert Hall
Gavin Wayte

Williams, Alan
Jazz Disasters, for euphonium and piano
25 November
Bridgewater Hall
David Childs, John Wilson

Williams, Gareth
String Quartet
9 January
Royal Northern College of Music, Lord Rhodes Room
Ceoil Quartet

Williamson, John
Sonata for viola and piano
14 October
Flixton House
Geoffrey Kimpton, John Williamson

Willson, Flora Natalie
Oscillations across a Spark-gap, for harpsichord
28 March
University of Manchester, Cosmo Rodewald Concert Hall
Gavin Wayte

Wood, Philip
Aria, Recitative and Rondo, for counter-tenor and cello
10 June
St Bartholomew's Church, Church Minshull
James Bowman, Jonathan Price

SUBSCRIBERS

Eric Adshead
Grace M. Allen
Michael Almond
Jonathan Alwyn
Sir James Anderton
Bob Ashworth
H. Valerie Bailey
Michael and Miriam Ball
William Ball
Roderick Barrand, Mus.B, ARNCM, GRNCM
Dr Robert Beale
David Beck
Dr Colin Beeson
Richard Beith
John M. Belcher
David Benger
John Bethell MBE
Birmingham Central Library
Keith Bisatt
Leon Bosch
John P. Boydell
Dorothy Bradford
Gerald A. Brinnen
Dr Terry Broadbent
Christine Brown
C. Susan Buchan
Alan Bullard
Ruth Burbidge
Joan Burns MBE
Professor Donald Burrows
Bury Grammar School
Arthur Butterworth MBE
Gary Carpenter
Roger Carpenter

Douglas R. Carrington
Michael and Hazel Carter
Andrew Challinger
Margaret Challinger
Malcolm Chapman
Tim Chapman
Bettie Cohen
Mr and Mrs J. Coloff
Barry A. R. Cooper
Cornell University
Christopher Cotton
Gordon Crosse
Dr Nicole Crossley-Holland
Sarah Crouch
Graham and Jennifer Curtis
Harvey Davies
Peter S. Davison
Dr James Dickenson
Paul Driver
Dorothy Duarte†
David Dubery
Gail Dudson and Martin Roscoe
Dunelm Records
John East
John Eckersley
Betty Edwards
Patricia Elcombe
J. F. Ellis
Patricia and David Ellis
Mary Evans
William Everett
Richard Fallas
David Fallows
Polly Fallows
Trevor Farrington

Jean Fielden
Roger and Rosemary Firman
James Flett
Dr Peter Flinn
Valerie Floyd
Lewis Foreman
Helen Foster
Paul Fowles
Mavis Fox
Maggie Gibb
Tony Gibb
Dr Rachel C. Gick
Anthony Goldstone
Rosalind and Raphael Gonley
Adam Gorb
James Gourlay
Prof. Philip Grange
Terence Greaves
David Green
John Greenhalgh
Prof. Edward Gregson
Don Hargreaves
Sir Martin and Lady Harris
Michael A. Harris
Peter Henry
Nicholas Henshall
Elisabeth Hessey
Dr Peter Hick
Derek Hodgkiss
Christopher Hogwood
Clive and Hilda Holland
Peter Hope
Michael Horwood
Anthony Hose
Stephen Hough
Alan R. Howarth

Crawford Howie
Garry Humphreys
Patricia Hurst
Gillian Hush
Vernon G. Hyde
Ishbel Isaacs
Geoffrey and Josephine Jackson
David Jones
David Ll. Jones
Eira Lynn Jones
Fae J. Jones
Philip Jones
Anne Jubb
Renna Kellaway
David Kent
Doreen and Harry Knipe
Andrew Lamb
Valerie Langfield
Beryl Langley
Peter Lawson
John Leach
Raymond Leppard
Colin Lomas
Alistair Lomax
Philip Lowe
John McCabe CBE
Mr and Mrs Patrick McGuigan
Philip Mackenzie
Manchester City Council –
    Henry Watson Music Library
Manchester Music Service
Sir John Manduell
Derrick Margerson
George A. Marshall
John Myerscough
Dr Roy Newsome

New York Public Library
Northwestern University Library, Evanston, Illinois
G. Michael Nuttall
Prof. and Mrs P. Ormerod
Daphne Oxenford (Marshall)
Joyce Lindley Parker
Prof. Emeritus Ian Parrott
Valerie Pocklington
David Powell
John Powell and Martin Lessons
Michael and Judith Redhead
Timothy Reynish
Maurice E. Ridge
Sheila W. Ridgway
J. Edward Rigg
Angela Louise Roberts
Christopher Robins
Roger Rostron
Alec Roth
Mark Rowlinson
Royal College of Music
Royal Northern College of Music Library
Clark Rundell
John Rylands University Library of Manchester
Chinchinha Sainter
Salford University
Graham and Yi Xin Salvage
Rev. Roger Scoones
Jonathan Scott
Stuart Scott
Charles H. Sellers MBE
Graham Shrubsole
Mrs Elizabeth Siddall

Nicholas Simpson
Antony Sluce
Alan and Mary Smith
Helen I. L. Smith
Miss J. M. Smith
Michael Smith FCSD
Michael A. Smith
Neil Smith
Roy Heaton Smith
Jean Soni (Blundell)
Peter E. Spaull
Dr Ronald Stevenson FRMCM
Stockport Grammar School
Stockport Metropolitan Borough Council – Libraries
David Sumbler
Frank Summerfield
Peter Syrus
Tameside Local Studies
John Tasker-Brophy
Martin Thacker
Sheila Thacker
Kay Thomas
Callum L. Thomson
Brian N. Thorpe
Stephen and Kathleen Threlfall
Pamela Thurlow (nee Green)
Ernest Tomlinson
Colin Touchin
John and Margaret Turner
Roger Turner
F. C. Valéry
Dr R. O. Vasey
Peter Waddington
Peter Wainwright
Raymond J. Walker

Robin Walker
David S. Walton
Dr. Robin Walton
John Ward
Irving Wardle
David H. Watt
Joan Watt
Percy and Anne Welton
Alison Wilkinson
Stephen Wilkinson
Enid M. Williams
Gladys Williams
Roger Williams
John R. Williamson
Peter Willis
Edith Wilson
Dr Susan Wollenberg
Ros Wood
Christopher Yates
Keith Yearsley
Renée Morris (Mrs Percy) Young
T. M. Young

Names in italics are those of founder subscribers.

.